CARBOHYDRATES

OF

LIVING TISSUES

CARBOHYDRATES

OF

LIVING TISSUES

M. STACEY, F.R.S.

Mason Professor and Head of the
Department of Chemistry
University of Birmingham

S. A. BARKER, D.Sc.

Lecturer in Organic Chemistry
University of Birmingham

D. VAN NOSTRAND COMPANY LTD

LONDON

TORONTO   NEW YORK

PRINCETON, NEW JERSEY

D. VAN NOSTRAND COMPANY LTD
358 Kensington High Street, London, W.14

D. Van Nostrand Company Inc.
120 Alexander Street, Princeton, New Jersey
24 West 40 Street, New York 18, New York

D. Van Nostrand Company (Canada) Ltd
25 Hollinger Road, Toronto 16

PRINTED IN GREAT BRITAIN BY
J. W. ARROWSMITH LTD., BRISTOL

CONTENTS

INTRODUCTION

THE human organism, the cells of which at one time were thought to consist largely of protein, creates within its cells a whole series of carbohydrates ranging from the simple disaccharide lactose (milk sugar) to the most complex mucoproteins (polysaccharide-protein complexes) and mucolipids (polysaccharide-lipid complexes) which are present in large amounts. In this book we are concerned with those carbohydrates which occur in some polymeric union with other large molecules rather than with the wonderful series of sugars and sugar phosphates constituting one of the body's metabolic chain of reactions. Such polysaccharide complexes termed mucosubstances (e.g. mucoproteins and mucolipids) fulfil such diverse functions as a blood anticoagulant, blood components, an energy reserve, and many are structural materials.

The mucosubstances have been known under many names in the past, e.g. mucins, mucoids, glycoproteins, glycolipids, mucoproteins, etc. and at present in these early days of investigating them it is almost impossible to get a good agreed nomenclature system. In this book mucopolysaccharide denotes a complex of carbohydrate and protein whose reaction is predominantly polysaccharide, mucoprotein is a similar complex whose reaction is predominantly protein while mucolipid is a carbohydrate fat complex.

It is agreed, however, that all mucosubstances possess among their simple sugar components a proportion of nitrogen containing monosaccharides. These are termed 'amino sugars' or more correctly amino deoxy sugars of which the commonest examples are glucosamine ('chitosamine') 2-amino-2-deoxy-D-glucose and galactosamine ('chondrosamine') 2-amino-2-deoxy-D-galactose which are important constituents of the chitin of insect cuticle and the chondroitin sulphate of cartilage respectively. Sulphate and acetyl groups are prominent constituents also.

The animal body may be regarded as a highly complex machine built mainly of plastic materials with some constituent parts composed of rubber-like products, with others containing fibres of high tensile strength and with all moving parts lubricated by fluids of remarkable efficiency.

The structural materials, thanks to great advances in modern techniques for purifying and characterizing natural macromolecules, are now slowly yielding up the secrets of their molecular structures and shape. In addition to the method of their continuous formation and breakdown by the body's catalysts—the enzymes—their biological functions and importance are gradually being elucidated. The mucosubstances form the membranes of cells, they form cement to hold the cells together, they form biologically

ix

active cell surface components and they form the liquid in which the cells move and by which they and other moving parts are lubricated. Altogether, it is quite striking to note how closely they are associated with movement of all parts of the body, listed as follows:

Movement	*Mucosubstance*
Blood	Serum mucoids and surface substances of corpuscles
Water and ions	Urinary mucoids
Anatomical and muscular movement	Joint fluids
	Ocular fluids
Digestive movement	Salivary mucin
	Gastric mucin
	Intestinal mucin
Fertilization	Seminal fluids
Parturition	Cervical mucin

The soluble muco-lubricants can form solutions in physiological saline of high viscosity and some form thick gels even at low concentration. The physical state of these is important in rheumatism and in inflammatory conditions. The gels have a remarkable capacity of combining with proteins and sometimes fats (lipids). Many of the body's defences are comprised of mucoproteins with varying contents of carbohydrates ranging from less than 1% to as much as 45%. Only when the complete structures of such materials are fully known will the exact details of their functioning be made clear. The wonderful function of the gangliosides, the most important mucolipid present in our grey matter, is only now being guessed at. Recently these substances have been shown to restore the metabolic response to electrical pulses of cerebral cortex slices that have been inhibited by keeping in cold media or by incubation with protamines and histones. It is sad but true that much more is known about the carbohydrates present in animal cells than in human cells. Post-mortem material often gives misleading information about the original constituents present in normal human tissues. An obvious case in point is the fate of glycogen following death. Material obtained at operation first becomes the concern of the surgeon and thereafter the pathologist. In many cases the latter can only tell that an abnormality is present, and it should be the task of a competent chemist to say just what is the exact nature of the abnormality. Such a task is at present outside the scope of the biochemists normally found doing such valuable routine work in our hospitals. There are exceptions, and excellent work is done by the Medical Research Council units attached to hospitals in overcoming this problem. However, such units are concerned more with long range research; the era of the clinical chemist has yet to come. Now that antibiotics and the great advances in surgery promise to leave us with only those syndromes which are hereditary (e.g. certain mental diseases, etc.) or constitutional (chronic bronchitis, asthma, cancer?) it is of urgent necessity to know precisely the normal constituents of human tissues. This book is dedicated to helping to fulfil that purpose. The authors dream of the day when the chemist has earned the same privilege as the pathologist in aiding diagnosis. However, the chemist has yet to develop many micromethods which will permit the separation and identification of components of human tissues. This book will give many clues as to how this could be achieved with the carbohydrate macromolecules. It is quite true to say that the pathologist has been greatly hampered by the lack of such precise knowledge of tissue components.

The isolation of pure entities from tissues must be our first concern. The delicacy of our methods will determine whether we isolate a true component such as a hyaluronic acid–protein complex or just hyaluronic acid. Another important factor is the continuing action of enzymes during the actual isolation—a particularly robust enzyme in this respect is ribonuclease. The introduction of enzyme inhibitors or dialysis to remove activating metal ions is often advisable.

The four main macromolecular constituents of human tissues are polysaccharides, nucleic acids, proteins and certain lipids all of which are retained inside the normal dialysis tubing. However, small constituents that are water-insoluble will dialyse only slowly, if at all, and hence it is sometimes preferable to dialyse against buffers of varying ionic strength or even non-aqueous solvents.

In separating the four main macromolecules it is advisable to remove lipids and other fats first by solvent extraction particularly where these are present in large amount. A series of solvents (acetone, ether and methanol-chloroform) is available to effect such extraction. Such a step can be omitted with many of the body fluids such as synovial fluid, bronchial mucus or human tears.

The major recent discovery in separating the remaining macromolecules has been the effective use of detergents such as cetylpyridinium chloride and cetyltrimethylammonium bromide. These large positively charged ions complex readily with negatively charged groups such as phosphate groups in the nucleic acids or sulphate and carboxylic acid groups in mucopolysaccharides and mucoproteins. Such complexes are insoluble in water but show a gradation of solubilities in aqueous solutions of varying ionic strength. The complexes may be also sometimes soluble in organic solvents such as ethanol in contrast with the original polysaccharide or mucoprotein. Selective precipitation can be accomplished of sulphated polysaccharides when acid conditions are such as to suppress the ionization of carboxylic acid groups. The use of detergents under neutral conditions has enabled the intact polysaccharide–protein complex to be isolated in many cases. An extension of such separations can be achieved by selective formation of borate complexes at various alkaline pH's, the negative charge thus created on what could have been originally a neutral polysaccharide will enable it to be precipitated with cetyltrimethylammonium bromide. Commercially available detergents are rarely pure and are generally mixtures of a range of homologues. It has been our experience that superior separations can be achieved with the pure ionic detergent.

Two more most valuable methods of separating macromolecules are the use of conventional ion exchange resins and the new ion exchangers such as diethylaminoethyl cellulose. The latter, if used intelligently, are vastly superior. Columns of starch, cellulose etc. can also be used. Where the mixture is a highly viscous gel recourse may be had to ionophoresis on glass bead columns.

The separation of macromolecules on the basis of molecular size is becoming of increasing importance and particular interest is being paid to the use of the ultracentrifuge and novel molecular 'sieves' such as 'Sephadex', which is made from a cross-linked polysaccharide dextran.

Micromethods available for the assessment of purity of polysaccharides and mucoproteins include electrophoresis on paper or even better still on cellulose acetate. Where the macromolecule or impurity is antigenic then diffusion against antiserum in an agar gel is one of the most valuable recent techniques. An extension of this is immuno-electrophoresis which involves initially electrophoretic separation in an agar gel and later diffusion in the same medium. Indications of homogeneity by such techniques together with passage through an analytical ultracentrifuge are generally considered reliable proof of the presence of a single entity. Where one of these techniques cannot be applied it could be replaced with supplementary information obtained from infrared and ultraviolet spectroscopy. Constancy of optical rotation and refractive index may also offer some support for the claim to purity. More than one test of homogeneity should be applied to the macromolecule isolated before one can claim a molecular entity.

Three major techniques are utilized in the structural determination of polysaccharides. Complete acidic hydrolysis to component monosaccharides and partial hydrolysis to di- and oligosaccharides is the first of these. The sequence of monosaccharides in a disaccharide A–B is obtained by some modification to the reducing group present either through reduction to the alcohol A–B' with sodium borohydride or oxidation to the aldobionic acid A–B'' with alkaline hypoiodite. Subsequent hydrolysis and examination of the fragments determines whether the monosaccharide A or B has been modified and so originally must have occupied the reducing position. The same kind of procedure is adopted with a trisaccharide

A–B–C which is partially hydrolysed to disaccharides A–B and B–C and the sequence determined by modification to the alcohol A–B–C' or acid A–B–C''. The point of attachment of the glycosidic linkage in the disaccharide can be ascertained by methylation and periodate oxidation studies. The anomeric character of the linkage (α or β) can usually be determined from the optical rotation and infrared spectrum of the disaccharide.

Periodate oxidation studies of the polysaccharide should include an assessment of the amount of periodate consumed per anhydrohexose or other monosaccharide unit together with determination of products such as formic acid, formaldehyde, ammonia and carbon dioxide. Reduction of the periodate oxidized polysaccharide to the polyalcohol can be accomplished with sodium borohydride. Acidic hydrolysis of the polyalcohol and subsequent analysis of the mixture produced will reveal the periodate-resistant sugar units while the nature and amounts of the polyhydric alcohols obtained give valuable evidence as to the point of attachment of the glycosidic linkages. Alternatively the periodate oxidized polysaccharide can be degraded with phenylhydrazine.

The third major technique utilized in structural elucidation is methylation, by which all the free hydroxyl groups are replaced by —OCH$_3$ groups. Hydrolysis of the methyl ether will release partly methylated sugars and so identify those hydroxyl groups engaged in glycosidic linkage and which have remained unmethylated.

The functional groups present in polysaccharides can be readily detected from the infrared spectrum of the polysaccharide. Information as to the character (α or β) and even sometimes the point of attachment of glycosidic linkages can also be obtained. The stereochemistry of certain substituent groups (e.g. sulphate groups) may also be forthcoming.

The application of the above techniques to specific polysaccharides is dealt with fully in the ensuing chapters. It was felt however, that brief mention of them should be made by way of introduction.

The structures of mucoproteins pose new problems. The use of acidic conditions for hydrolysis inevitably gives rise to the suspicion that some of the products will be artefacts resulting from a facile reaction of the Maillard or browning type between amino acids and sugars. The initial reaction is a condensation between the amino group of the amino acid and the aldehydic reducing group of the sugar. Thereafter a series of reactions ensues under the acidic conditions causing destruction of the sugar moiety and formation of furfuraldehyde derivatives. One way of avoiding these complications would be to submit the mucoprotein first to periodate oxidation. The polyalcohol resulting from the reduction of the periodate oxidized mucoprotein will then be much more acid labile than the original mucoprotein. Luckily one of the important components of mucoproteins, namely neuraminic acid, which we discuss later, is attached by a glycosidic linkage that is much more acid labile than those linking the other monosaccharide constituents. Hence this can be preferentially hydrolysed with little damage to the remaining structure. Alternatively a specific enzyme neuraminidase, can be used to accomplish the scission.

The use of alkaline conditions of hydrolysis gives rise to other complications. One possibility, which as yet has no experimental support, is that peptides attached through their carboxylic groups to the hydroxyl groups of carbohydrates to form alkali-labile ester linkages will undergo alkaline migration. Such a migration is already a well-established feature of acyl groups (e.g. acetyl, benzoyl) and phosphate groups attached to carbohydrates. Certain glycosidic linkages, such as those of the $1 \rightarrow 3$ type, are particularly susceptible to alkali. While this can in the case of mucoproteins yield disaccharides useful for structural elucidation, a complicated series of other products are also formed from the action of alkali on reducing sugars leading to the saccharinic acids and anhydro hexosamines. Probably because of the formation of an intermediate complex, limewater and baryta are sometimes more effective in alkaline scission than sodium and potassium hydroxide. Nothing definite is yet known of the linkages binding proteins, amino acids, or fatty complexes, to sugars.

To the unwary the use of enzymes for structural elucidation is the obvious way to degrade a mucoprotein. Now that the structures of at least four proteins are known completely the action patterns of trypsin, chymotrypsin, pepsin, papain and other crystalline proteinases can be determined. The story of enzyme chemistry has, however, been a continual series of reports of impurities being detected in crystalline enzymes which have given misleading information as to action patterns. Readers familiar with the study of the literature on the use of enzymes in starch and glycogen chemistry realize the pitfalls that face the unwary. With proteinases the most difficult thing to prove will be the amount of transpeptidization accompanying pure enzymic scission of peptide bonds. If pure enzymes can be obtained and their action patterns determined then we will indeed have the most beautiful way of unravelling mucoprotein structure.

It is obvious from the foregoing discussion that many of our troubles would disappear if the mucoprotein could be split specifically into its component carbohydrate and protein moieties. The provision of model synthetic carbohydrate–peptide compounds on which various chemical reagents can be used is therefore of urgent necessity. New solvents for these entities are also required since dimethylformamide, dimethylsulphoxide, tetrahydrofuran and tetrahydropyran will find only limited use. The main linkages between carbohydrate and amino acids which can be envisaged are those formed by condensation between:

(1) the reducing (generally C_1) hydroxyl group and the —COOH group, —NH$_2$ group or —SH group of a peptide.

(2) a secondary hydroxyl group and —COOH, —NH$_2$ or —SH groups of a peptide and

(3) a primary hydroxyl group and —COOH, —NH$_2$ or —SH group of a peptide.

Other possibilities include more remotely the condensation between the carboxylic acid group of neuraminic acid and the hydroxyl groups of amino acids such as serine and threonine as well as the —SH and amino groups of others. Ether linkages between the hydroxyl groups of carbohydrates and those of threonine or serine should also be considered as distinct possibilities. When it is remembered that all these groups can occur in different monosaccharides and different amino acids the need for model substances becomes essential to investigate selective reductive scission.

Methylation should be preceded by conversion of all carboxylic acid groups in the carbohydrate (e.g. neuraminic acid) and the peptide to methyl esters and this could be accomplished using diazomethane. Thereafter the introduction of methyl ether groups by the conventional methods of methylation can be considered. There is a distinct possibility that certain carbohydrate–peptide linkages will suffer alkaline or reductive scission with the Haworth (NaOH/Me$_2$SO$_4$) method or the Freudenberg (Na/MeI/liq. NH$_3$) technique. Prolonged use of diazomethane may be rewarding since it is known that N-acetyl hexosamine residues can be to some extent O-methylated with this reagent. The enhancement of O-methylation by diazomethane has been accomplished in the case of ascorbic acid by the use of fluoroboric acid. The partially methylated mucoprotein may then be suitable for methylation by the Kuhn (Ag$_2$O/MeI/dimethyl formamide) method. Further information will doubtless be obtained by 'labelling' ester groups produced using diazomethane. This may be accomplished by reduction to the —CD$_2$OH groups using sodium borodeuteride and subsequent exchange with water. Ester type carbohydrate–peptide linkages could also be tracked by the same reagent.

Infrared spectroscopy is now from our own studies expected to afford valuable information as to the structures of mucoproteins. Exchange of the various hydroxyl groups in the mucoprotein for —OD groups may help considerably the interpretation of the spectra. Such techniques are the most valuable of those available since no degradation of the mucoprotein is involved with its attendant production of artefacts. Functional groups such as those liable to be present in mucoproteins (—COOH, N-acetyl, O-acetyl, N-glycollyl, etc.) could be detected if both the infrared spectra of the sodium salt of the mucoprotein and the zwitterion form of the mucoprotein were studied. Information about hydrogen bonding would also be expected.

Finally the conventional methods of stepwise degradation of peptide chains must not be neglected. Suitable controls to determine the effect of the various reagents on the carbohydrate portion will be needed but it is virtually certain that the mucoprotein must first be freed from neuraminic acid.

By analogy with the valuable information obtained already from the cross-reactivity of anti-pneumococcus sera with various polysaccharides, antisera produced against synthetic antigens containing the different types of neuraminic acid and other monosaccharide constituents of mucoprotein would be expected to cross-react with mucoproteins. A spectrum of such antisera would be extremely useful in tracking the types of carbohydrate 'end' groups uncovered during stepwise degradation of mucoproteins.

Many, if not all, of the inherited diseases discussed in the following chapters are caused by some enzyme lesion. When assayed in the normal manner it is found that one of the enzymes is either sadly deficient or even completely absent. In the latter case death in early childhood generally occurs since although the human organism sometimes has two pathways for making the same product (e.g. glycogen) the balance of metabolism is upset and accumulation of certain harmful metabolites results. Until quite recently no hope of curing such syndromes could be envisaged since dieting gives only partial relief. The pioneering work of Monod, Cohn, Klein and others on the induction of enzymes in bacterial cells now gives cause for cautious optimism. A growing selection of enzymes have been induced such as the β-galactosidase of *E. coli*, depolymerases in *B. palustris*, α-amylase in *P. saccharophila*, and penicillinase in *B. cereus*.

It is generally agreed that the linkages required for induction of hydrolytic enzymes are the same as those which are attacked by them. Some molecules in this class are both inducers and substrates for the enzyme, but in the case of β-galactosidase, phenyl β-D-thiogalactoside is an inducer but not a substrate. Both maltose and starch cause the formation of an extracellular α-amylase in resting cell suspensions of *P. saccharophila*. Will the day come when the same enzyme induction can be accomplished in animals and man? We hope so.

We present this book as an interim report only; we realize there are many omissions, and that information on many interesting topics is tantalizingly lacking. We hope, however, that it will be of some help, particularly to those entering the field. We believe that many medical and biological developments of the future will come from the study of mucoproteins. We know that such enormous macromolecules possess all the complexities of polysaccharide and protein chemistry—indeed sometimes with those of fats, nucleic acids and pigments thrown in. Their chemistry presents us with a great challenge and we can go forward in our work with high hope for success in the future.

We thank Miss Triste M. Z. Gasking for typing the manuscript and are grateful to Mr. E. Horwood and other members of the Van Nostrand publishing staff for their help in the preparation of this book.

MAURICE STACEY
SIDNEY ALAN BARKER

Chapter 1

GLYCOGEN

Introduction

THE polysaccharide glycogen is the major energy and carbohydrate reserve of the human body, and is stored widely in the liver, muscles, heart and other tissues. In many ways glycogen serves the same function in animals as starch does in plants, although it is found also in many microorganisms. Unlike starch which consists of two components, amylose (the linear polymer of α-1:4-D-glucopyranose units) and amylopectin (the branched polymer in which chains of α-1:4-D-glucopyranose units are joined by α-1:6-linkages), glycogen is generally accepted to be constituted of a single molecular species although it is highly polymolecular. Most glycogens have a highly branched structure comprising several hundred unit chains of *ca.* twelve α-1:4-linked D-glucopyranose residues with inter-chain links of the α-1:6-type. It thus resembles amylopectin to some extent, the major difference being that in the latter the average chain length is about twenty glucose residues. From the evidence presented below the structure of glycogen and its molecular size can be seen to vary somewhat from one animal to another and even in the various tissues of the same animal. Despite this, however, the overall structural details of the various glycogens are quite similar except during the onset of certain diseases. Since both the molecular size and structure of glycogen may be to some extent governed by the method of isolation employed this will be dealt with first.

Methods of Isolation

The two major methods of isolation of glycogen from tissues involve the use of either 5%–10% aqueous trichloracetic acid in the cold (0°) or the more conventional Pflüger (1905) extraction with 30% potassium hydroxide at 100°. In each method this extraction is followed by precipitation of the glycogen from solution by addition of ethanol. The products obtained by these methods and the effects of variation of these conditions have been the subject of extensive studies by Stetten, Katzen and Stetten (1956, 1958). These workers showed that the weight-average molecular weight of glycogen declined when dissolved in hot aqueous potassium hydroxide and that this decline was more rapid in 1N-KOH than in 10N-KOH and faster under oxygen than under an atmosphere of nitrogen. Less extensive degradation occurred using the trichloracetic acid method although even with this reagent some degradation does occur. Thus the molecular weight of a sample of liver glycogen dissolved in 5% aqueous trichloracetic acid fell from 71×10^6 to 44×10^6 at $0°$ in 2 hours and to 14×10^6 at $23°$ in the same time. Using the trichloracetic acid method glycogens were obtained from rabbit liver, rabbit muscle, and rat leg muscle having molecular weights of $45\cdot2 \times 10^6$, $11\cdot9 \times 10^6$ and $43\cdot8 \times 10^6$ respectively. From the same sources values of $2\cdot7 \times 10^6$, $3\cdot1 \times 10^6$ and $6\cdot1 \times 10^6$ were obtained for glycogens isolated by the potassium hydroxide method. These results are not in agreement with those obtained much earlier by Staudinger (1942) and Bridgman (1942) who reported that glycogen extracted with cold trichloracetic acid and hot alkali from two halves of a rabbit liver had a similar molecular weight.

Bryce, Greenwood, Jones and Manners (1958) have studied the effect of isolation procedure on the sedimentation constant of the isolated glycogen. Glycogens isolated from two halves of the same rabbit liver using (a) boiling water and (b) 30% aqueous potassium hydroxide had almost the same sedimentation constants (relative values 85:86 respectively). Subsequent reprecipitation of a potassium hydroxide extracted glycogen with 80% acetic acid (Bell and Manners, 1952; Manners and Archibald, 1957) similarly had a negligible effect on the value of the sedimentation constant S_{20}. By contrast further digestion of a rabbit liver glycogen in 8% aqueous sodium hydroxide at $100°$ for $1\cdot5$ hr reduced S_{20} from 86 to 57×10^{-13} c.g.s. units and increased the polymolecularity showing that hot dilute alkali degrades glycogen rapidly. These results were in agreement with those of two earlier workers (Oakley and Young, 1936) who claimed that glycogens obtained by alkaline extraction or by water extraction followed by precipitation with acetic acid in each case had the same molecular size when determined by osmotic pressure.

Determination of Glycogen

In general, methods used for the determination of glycogen in tissues are preceded by an extraction process either with boiling 30% potassium hydroxide or cold aqueous trichloracetic acid as discussed above. The glycogen precipitated from the extract by means of alcohol can then be assayed by determination of the reducing sugars produced by acid hydrolysis (Good, Kramer and Somogyi, 1933; Cori, 1932) or by direct treatment of the precipitated glycogen with anthrone reagent (Morris, 1948; Seifter, Dayton, Novic and Muntwyler, 1950). The major controversies over which method to choose centre round (a) the completeness of the extraction procedure and (b) whether the sole carbohydrate present in the precipitate is glycogen. Bloom, Lewis, Schumpert and Shen (1951) found that in the livers of unfasted rats the concentration of the glycogen determined by trichloracetic acid extraction was consistently 85% of that found after alkali digestion. The trichloracetic acid extractable glycogen of muscle in normal fed rats was 55% of that obtained by alkali extraction. In an alternative procedure Kemp and van Heijningen (1954) claimed that all the glycogen could be brought into solution by grinding the tissue with trichloracetic acid solution and then heating the resulting suspension for 15 min at 100°. In a critical appraisal of the various methods, Carroll, Longley and Roe (1956) found that a boiling 30% potassium hydroxide extract of liver contained material that was not glycogen. This material was dialyzable, anthrone-sensitive, reduced alkaline copper solutions and was therefore a source of error in glycogen methods based upon alkali extraction of tissues. These workers contended that a series of five extractions with 5% trichloracetic acid in a Servall omnimixer at 14,000 r.p.m. sufficed to extract all the glycogen even from livers of fasted rats. Precipitation of the glycogen with 5 volumes of 95% alcohol and direct determination of the glycogen with anthrone was claimed to give a sound reliable method.

Electrophoresis of Glycogen and Related Polysaccharides

Foster, Newton-Hearn and Stacey (1956) have studied a wide range of amylosaccharides by paper ionophoresis in alkaline borate and other buffers. These amylosaccharides were located by immersion of the paper in water–ethanol–conc. hydrochloric acid (10:1:1), and thereafter spraying the dried paper with ethanolic iodine (0·4%). The M_G values obtained (mobility with respect to glucose) in borate buffer pH 10 were D-glucose, 1·00; maltose, 0·36; amylose, 0·18; amylopectin, 0·25; glycogen (rabbit liver), 0·31.

Besides paper, two other supports, glass paper and silk were investigated for use in the separation of polysaccharides (Fuller and Northcote, 1956). A modified p-anisidine spray was used to detect the polysaccharides on glass paper. Taking the movement of yeast mannan as 1·0, yeast glycogen had a mobility of 0·45, amylose, 0·38 and amylopectin 0·45 on glass paper in 0·1M-borate buffer, pH 9·3. Other electrophoretic studies of glycogen have been carried out by Bertrand and Laszt (1956) and Geldmacher-Mallinckrodt and Wienland (1953).

Northcote (1954) used a Tiselius electrophoresis apparatus to separate glycogen and other related polysaccharides. In 0·1M-glycine buffer at 0° their mobilities (cm^2V^{-1} $sec^{-1} \times 10^{-5}$) were as follows: yeast glycogen, 0·7, 0·0; rabbit liver glycogen, 1·0; potato starch, 2·2, 0·0; potato amylopectin 1·7, 0·0. As will be seen some of the polysaccharides moved as two components. The mobilities of the polysaccharides in 0·05M-borate buffer, pH 9·2° at 0° were also studied.

A preparative method for the column electrophoresis of polysaccharides including glycogen was described by Hocevar and Northcote (1957). Separation of a mixture of inulin, glycogen, mannan and galactan (each

10 mg) could be accomplished on a column of glass wool (*l*, 80 cm; diam, 2·5 cm) using 0·05M borate buffer, pH 9·2 as the electrolyte and applying 3V/cm for 9 hr. The fractions were then eluted from the column with more borate buffer and the polysaccharides detected using the anthrone reagent (Seifter, Dayton, Novic and Muntwyler, 1950).

Detection of Glycogen in Tissues

The general basis of histochemical techniques for the detection of glycogen in tissues is (1) the strong reaction it gives in the periodic acid-Schiff (PAS) reaction and (2) the fact that it can be distinguished from other PAS-positive substances by its easy removal with α-amylase. In the application of the periodic acid-Schiff reaction the tissues should be as fresh as possible preferably obtained within one hour of death. Preservation of the tissue can be effected by freeze-drying (Mancini, 1948) followed by a suitable fixative, freeze-substitution (Lisbon, 1949) or acetic-form alin-alcohol (Gendre's fluid). Prior to staining many investigators cover the section with a thin film of celloidin (collodion, nitrocellulose) to keep the glycogen in position. The PAS reaction was introduced into histology by McManus (1946) who recommended exposure for 2 minutes in a 0·5% solution of periodic acid in distilled water. Other variations introduced by Lillie (1947) included periodate acidified by the addition of 0·5% *v*/*v* conc. nitric acid, 10 minutes in a solution of 1 gm sodium periodate in 100 ml of 70% nitric acid, 0·69% KIO_4 in 0·3% nitric acid at pH 1·9 for 10 min (Lillie, 1950), and finally a 1% aqueous solution of paraperiodic acid (H_5IO_6) at 20° for 10 min (Lillie, 1954). Hale (1957) in an excellent review of this subject recommends the use of the Hotchkiss alcoholic periodic acid method (Hotchkiss, 1948). This procedure involves 5 minutes' treatment with a solution containing periodic acid (400 mg) dissolved in distilled water, to which is added 5 ml of 0·2M sodium acetate and 35 ml. ethyl alcohol. After exposure to the oxidant the section is washed to remove excess oxidant, exposed to Schiff's solution (leucofuchsin) for 15 to 30 minutes and then further washed in a sulphite solution to remove excess leucofuchsin. A 5-minute wash with water between the oxidant and the Schiff's solution is generally adequate (Hale, 1955). The aldehydic structure of periodate-oxidized glycogen gives a bright magenta colour with Schiff's solution which is basic fuchsin (rosaniline, pararosaniline and magenta II) reduced by the action of sulphite. The subsequent rinse with sulphite prevents false positive reactions resulting from the recolorization of the Schiff's solution by atmospheric oxidation.

Since many other carbohydrate containing components of tissue give a positive PAS reaction it is highly desirable that the identification of glycogen should be checked by prior digestion with α-amylase. In this procedure the tissue is not covered by a celloidin film but incubated directly with centrifuged saliva at room temperature for one hour. It would perhaps be preferable to use crystalline salivary α-amylase itself since Lillie, Greco and Laskey (1949) report that saliva contains a ribonuclease-like activity.

Sulkin (1960) reports that some mucopolysaccharides which cannot be revealed by the PAS technique can in fact be detected using the technique of Kramer and Windrum (1953; 1954). This is based on the sulphation of neutral mucopolysaccharides in tissue sections which are then visualized by their metrochromatic staining properties following toluidine blue staining.

Molecular Weights and Polydispersity

Molecular weight determinations of glycogens were carried out as early as 1936 by determination of osmotic pressure (Oakley and Young, 1936). The values obtained (rabbit liver glycogen, $1\cdot2$–$2\cdot2 \times 10^6$; rabbit muscle glycogen, $0\cdot7$–$1\cdot8 \times 10^6$) were the number average molecular weights. Values of the same order were obtained by Bell, Gutfreund, Cecil and Ogston (1948) using sedimentation and osmotic pressure measurements; horse muscle glycogen, $2\cdot9 \times 10^6$; rabbit muscle glycogen, $2\cdot6 \times 10^6$; human muscle glycogen, $2\cdot4 \times 10^6$; rabbit liver glycogen $4\cdot4 \times 10^6$. The glycogen was isolated from each source under alkaline conditions.

Examination of a glycogen in an ultracentrifuge is particularly useful since it reveals any inhomogeneity; it indicates also that the glycogen molecules behave in solution as spheres. Bridgman (1942) found that rabbit liver glycogen exhibited a spread of values from 20 to 120S with the maximum component having a sedimentation constant of 70S. Polglase, Brown and Smith (1952) found that normal human liver glycogen contained two polydisperse components with sedimentation constants in the ranges 60–100S and 150–300S. A glycogen isolated from a liver biopsy specimen obtained from one patient with von Gierke's disease contained only the lighter material. Examination of human muscle glycogens from two normal patients revealed a major heavy component and a minor light component, but from a third normal patient a glycogen with only the heavy component was obtained. Glycogen obtained from a patient having glycogen storage disease of muscle had a much greater proportion (30–40% instead of 10–15%) of the lighter component present irrespective of whether it was obtained at autopsy or biopsy or from skeletal or heart muscle.

Although determination of molecular weights of glycogen by light scattering gives weight-average molecular weights, and thus attributes relatively more significance to the large than to the small molecules in a polydisperse population, this method has found favour with many recent workers particularly in combination with ultracentrifugation studies. The molecular weights determined by Stetten, Katzen and Stetten (1956) using the light scattering technique have already been mentioned. The method tends to indicate larger particle sizes; values of $1\text{--}20 \times 10^6$ being obtained by Putzeys and Verthoeven (1949) and Staudinger (1948).

The method of Isbell (1951) in which the combining weight of a polysaccharide is calculated from the radioactivity of the product of addition of $Na^{14}CN$ with the unique reducing end of each polysaccharide molecule is unsuitable for native glycogen. Meyer's colorimetric method (Meyer, Noelting and Bernfeld, 1947) is only suitable for degraded liver glycogens in the range M.W. < 300,000.

Structural Studies of Glycogen

Products from methylated glycogen

Treatment of glycogen triacetate in acetone solution with a mixture of methyl sulphate and potassium hydroxide afforded a partially methylated glycogen (OMe, 40%). Repeated treatments gave a trimethyl glycogen

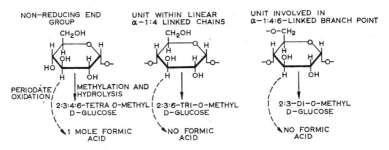

Fig. 1.1a   *Glucose units in glycogen*

(OMe, 43·7%; $[\alpha]_D^{20} + 208°$ in $CHCl_3$) in 90% yield (Haworth, Hirst and Webb, 1929). When heated with boiling 2% methanolic hydrogen chloride for 24 hr, this trimethyl glycogen afforded a mixture of products from which methyl 2:3:6-tri-O-methyl glucoside could be recovered by distillation *in vacuo*. Subsequent aqueous hydrolysis of the latter gave crystalline 2:3:6-tri-O-methyl α-D-glucopyranose (see Fig. 1.1a). Haworth and Percival (1931) later degraded trimethyl glycogen with acetyl bromide and oxidized the products with bromine in the presence of barium benzoate. After remethylation and esterification they obtained methyl octamethyl maltobionate which itself yielded crystalline 2:3:4:6-tetra-O-methyl D-glucopyranose and 2:3:5:6-tetra-O-methyl γ-gluconolactone on aqueous acid hydrolysis. Haworth and Percival (1932) succeeded subsequently in isolating crystalline 2:3:4:6-tetra-O-methyl D-glucopyranose from methylated rabbit liver glycogen in a yield (9%) indicative of the presence of one non-reducing end group for every twelve residues. Glycogens were later investigated in which this ratio was found to be one in every eighteen glucose residues (Bell, 1936; Haworth, Hirst and Isherwood, 1937). The latter workers also isolated an amount of dimethyl glucose equivalent to that of the tetramethyl glucose and suggested a laminated formula for glycogen in which the adjacent chains of α-1:4-linked glucopyranose residues were joined as in Fig. 1.2a. Haworth, Hirst and Smith (1939) found that three specimens of glycogen from dogfish, haddock, and hake liver and one from dogfish muscle contained a repeating unit of 12 α-1:4-linked glucopyranose residues. The introduction of a small scale method for the analysis of mixtures of tetra-, tri- and di-O-methyl sugars on silica columns greatly simplified and rendered more reliable the end group assay of methylated polysaccharides (Bell, 1944). Methylated horse muscle glycogen assayed in this way had an average chain length of 12 glucose residues.

The nature of the linkage uniting the chains in glycogen still remained a problem. Although Bell (1948) succeeded in analysing the mixture of dimethyl glucoses (obtained from methylated glycogens) by periodate oxidation the difficulty of ensuring full methylation of the glycogen rendered only approximate his findings that the major dimethyl glucoses were 2:6 and 2:3.

Acid hydrolysis products

From the knowledge that maltose hydrolyses four times faster than *iso*maltose (see Fig. 1.1b) in 2% concentration in 0·050 N-sulphuric acid at 99·5°, Wolfrom, Lassettre and O'Neill (1951) calculated that the maximum yield of *iso*maltose obtainable from the hydrolysis of glycogen was 6·8% and that this maximum occurred when 89% of the glycogen had been destroyed. Rabbit liver glycogen was hydrolysed with 0·05 $N-H_2SO_4$ at 100° for 8 hr (degree of hydrolysis, 66%) and the hydrolysis products acetylated with sodium acetate/acetic anhydride. Separation of the acetylated hydrolysate on a column of Magnesol-Celite (5:1) afforded crystalline β-D-glucopyranose pentaacetate, β-maltose octaacetate, β-*iso*maltose octaacetate and β-maltotriose hendecaacetate. In later work, Wolfrom and Thompson (1957) fractionated the acid hydrolysate of a beef liver glycogen (69% hydrolysis; 92 g) on a carbon column into disaccharide and trisaccharide fractions. Separation of the acetylated disaccharide mixture on Magnesol-Celite gave crystalline β-maltose octaacetate, β-*iso*maltose octaacetate and β-nigerose (3-O-α-D-glucopyranosyl-D-glucopyranose) octaacetate in amounts of 5·2 g; 4·6 g and 2 mg respectively. Separation of the trisaccharide mixture by paper chromatography afforded crystalline panose [O-α-D-glucopyranosyl-(1 → 6)-O-α-D-glucopyranosyl-(1 → 4)-D-glucopyranose] and amorphous *iso*maltotriose (see Fig. 1.1b).

The structure of the latter was rigidly established by the nature of the partial acid hydrolysis products of the *iso*maltotriose and its reduction product, *iso*maltotriitol. The yields of panose and *iso*maltotriose obtained were 1·05 g and 0·67 g respectively. Maltotriose, isolated as its crystalline hendecaacetate (0·12 g), was also obtained. The above work firmly established that the major branch points in glycogen were constituted by

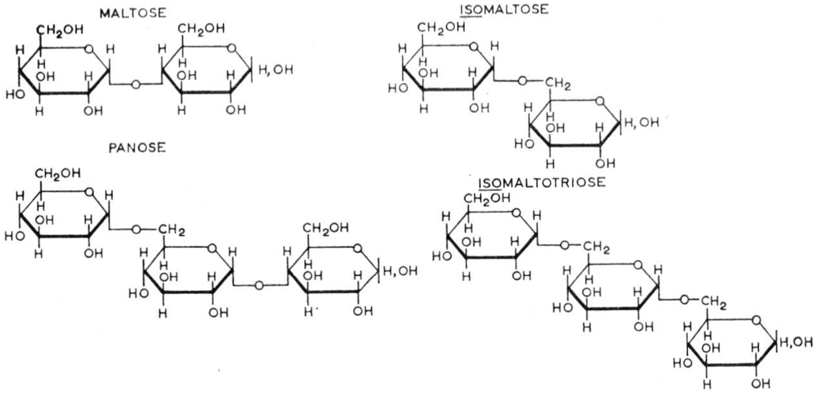

Fig. 1.1b   *Acid hydrolysis products of glycogen*

joining the adjacent chains of α-1:4-linked glucopyranose residues with α-1:6-glucosidic linkages and to a very minor extent with α-1:3-glucosidic linkages. The significance of the finding of *iso*maltotriose, which implies that some of the α-1:6-linkages are adjacent, has been neglected by many subsequent workers. The finding of nigerose in such small quantities may be due to its formation via acid reversion of glucose.

Evidence from periodate oxidation

Halsall, Hirst and Jones (1947) applied the technique of periodate oxidation to various glycogens and from the amount of formic acid produced, calculated the number of glucose residues/non-reducing end group since only the latter groups would afford formic acid (see Fig. 1.1a). Oxidation of various glycogens with sodium periodate in the presence of potassium chloride at 20° in dim light gave the following average chain lengths: human muscle, 11; rabbit muscle, 13; horse muscle, 14; guinea-pig liver, 13 and various glycogens from rabbit liver, 14–18. These results were in good agreement with those obtained by the methylation method. Abdel-Akher and Smith (1951) using sodium periodate alone at 5–6° in the dark studied some thirty-seven samples of glycogens from all sources and obtained values from 10–14 including human liver glycogen, 11; rabbit liver, 11–13; horse liver, 11; ox liver, 13; dog liver, 12; and guinea-pig liver, 10. All the glycogens were highly purified and had $[\alpha]_D$ from $+185$ to $+198°$ in water. Fifteen samples of glycogen were assayed by Manners and Archibald (1957) using potassium periodate oxidation and twelve of these had average chain lengths of 10–14 glucose residues. However, some exceptions found by Manners and Archibald (1957) and Bell and Manners (1952) include samples of glycogen from human liver, 6 *Helix pomatia*, 7 and from *Mytilus edulis c.* 5, 9, 13 and 17.

Further valuable information as to glycogen structure can be obtained using a method developed by Hirst, Jones and Roudier (1948). The principle involved postulates that in glycogen each glucose unit except those linked at the branch points through either the 1:2:4 or 1:3:4-positions will be oxidized by periodate and on hydrolysis will yield a dialdehyde; if periodate oxidation is complete the presence of glucose in the hydrolysate will indicate interchain linkages of the 1:2 or 1:3-type. Gibbons and Boissonnas (1950) found that with one glycogen the ratio of the number of interchain linkages at C_2 or C_3 to those at C_6 was not greater than 1:42. Bell and Manners (1954) found that a hydrolysate of periodate-oxidized cat glycogen contained no glucose. Abdel-Akher, Hamilton, Montgomery and Smith (1952) applied a variation of this technique which involved acid hydrolysis of the hydrogenated periodate-oxidized glycogen. One sample of glycogen so treated yielded 1% glucose, suggesting that not all the branch points were of the 1:4:6-type. The value of this last variation of the application of periodate oxidation is that determination of the nature and amount of the other products of hydrolysis (glycerol, erythritol, glycollic aldehyde) provide a method of end-group assay and confirm the 1:4 linkages within the chains.

Action of β-amylase

The enzyme β-amylase can be obtained from wheat (Meyer, Spohr and Fischer, 1953), barley (Meyer, Fischer and Piquet, 1951), soya beans (Peat, Pirt and Whelan, 1952) sweet potatoes (Balls, Walden and Thompson, 1948) and other sources. The action of all types of β-amylase involves attack from the non-reducing ends on the exterior chains of the α-1:4-linked glucose residues in amylopectin or glycogen until the enzyme action is obstructed by the interchain α-1:6-linkages. This process, termed β-amylolysis, results in the liberation of maltose from these exterior chains and leaves a 'β-limit' dextrin of high molecular weight with only two or three glucose residues projecting beyond each branch point. Some of the branching end-group arrangements which have proved resistant to β-amylase are shown in Fig. 1.1c (French, 1960). The determination of the percentage of maltose liberated affords a measure of the exterior chain length in glycogens and amylopectins. The results obtained with certain glycogens are quoted in Table 1.I.

Table 1.I.   *Reactions of glycogens with β-amylase*

Glycogen from:	Average chain length	Conversion (%) into maltose	Source of β-amylase
Beef liver[1]	—	45	Wheat
Rabbit liver[2]	—	45	Wheat
Rabbit liver[3]	12	43	Barley
Rabbit liver[4]	13	43	Sweet potato
Rabbit liver I[5]	13	25	Barley
Rabbit liver III[5]	13	51	Barley
Rabbit liver V[5]	14	51	Barley
Rabbit muscle[4]	13	45	Sweet potato
Rabbit muscle II[5]	11	39	Barley
Foetal-sheep liver[4]	13	49	Sweet potato
Cat liver[4]	13	48	Sweet potato
Cat liver IV[5]	·13	53	Barley
Cat liver VI[5]	12	52	Barley
Human muscle[4]	12	41	Sweet potato
Human muscle II[5]	11	40	Barley

[1] Meyer and Press (1941); [2] Morris (1944); [3] Northcote (1952); [4] Bell and Manners (1952); [5] Liddle and Manners (1957).

Most glycogens therefore have exterior chain lengths of *ca.* 8 glucose residues and interior chain length of *ca.* 4 glucose residues although quite a large degree of variation exists even in glycogens from the same type of animal tissue.

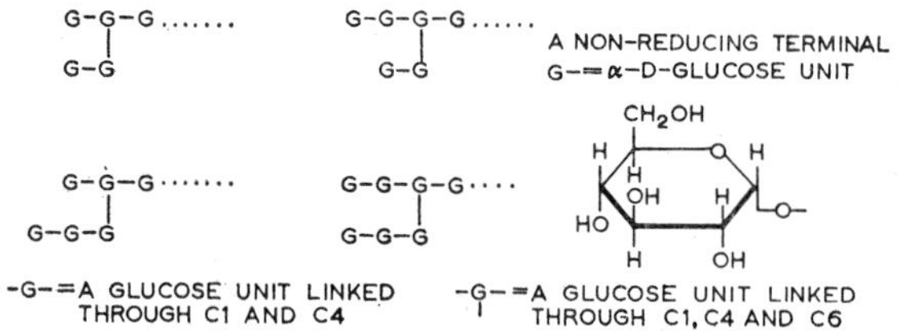

Fig. 1.1c

Action of α-amylase

Human saliva is a rich source of α-amylase (Meyer, Fischer, Staub and Bernfeld, 1948). Whereas the sole products of the action of salivary α-amylase on amylose are maltose and maltotriose (Whelan and Roberts, 1953) those resulting from the incubation of glycogen with the enzyme include in addition a series of branched α-dextrins (Whelan and Roberts, 1952). The α-1:6 linkages present in these α-dextrins are susceptible to attack by R-enzyme, a 'debranching' enzyme obtained from potatoes and broad-beans (Hobson, Whelan and Peat, 1951). The number of reducing groups liberated during the scission of the α-1:6-linkages in the α-dextrins can be determined and gives yet another method of assessing the average chain length of glycogen.

Roberts and Whelan (1960) have shown that treatment of glycogen with α-amylase yields maltose, maltotriose (ratio 2·03:1) together with α-limit dextrins the smallest of which is a pentasaccharide. No splitting of α-1:6 linkages was detected. A small amount of maltulose (4-*O*-α-D-glucopyranosyl D-fructose) was detected among the products of α-amylolysis of rabbit liver glycogen. High concentrations of salivary α-amylase will hydrolyse maltotriose further to glucose and maltose and a tetrasaccharide can then be detected among the products from the α-amylolysis of glycogen (Walker and Whelan, 1960).

The nature of the α-dextrins obtained from glycogen also provides further evidence as to the fine structure of this polysaccharide. Various

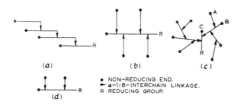

Fig. 1.2

types of branched structures are possible for glycogen among which are a singly branched 'laminated' structure Fig. 1.2a (Haworth, Hirst and Isherwood, 1937), a 'comb-like' structure (Fig. 1.2b) proposed by Freudenberg and the multiply branched 'tree' structure (Fig. 1.2c) of Meyer and Bernfeld (1940). Examination of the α-dextrins (Whelan and Roberts, 1952) revealed that some were doubly branched (Fig. 1.2d) showing that multiple branching occurs in glycogen and favouring a structure of the type shown in Fig. 1.2c. Three types of chains of α-1:4-linked D-glucopyranose residues exist in Fig. 1.2c.

A—is a chain joined to the rest of the molecule only by one α-1:6-linkage.

B—is a chain to which one or more A-chains are attached and which is itself linked to an adjacent chain by an α-1:6-linkage.

C—is the chain terminated by the sole reducing group.

Other evidence for a multiply branched structure in glycogen has been obtained by the stepwise degradation of glycogen with phosphorylase and amylo-1:6-glucosidase (Larner, Illingworth, Cori and Cori, 1952).

Glycogen—Iodine Complexes

When stained with iodine/potassium iodide under the standard conditions used for the determination of blue value (Bourne, Haworth, Macey, and Peat, 1948), glycogens stain only weakly compared with potato amylose (B.V. 1·25), amylopectin (B.V. 0·19) and starch (B.V. 0·41). If, however, the concentrations are altered so that the light absorption is 2·5 times that used in blue value determinations (Peat, Whelan, Hobson and Thomas, 1954) the iodine complex of oyster glycogen is found to exhibit a λ_{max} at ca. 480 mμ. Eight samples of glycogen from various sources examined in this way were found to give glycogen–iodine complexes with maximum absorption at 420–470 mμ (Liddle and Manners, 1957). Potato amylose and potato amylopectin give iodine complexes with λ_{max} at 640 mμ and 560 mμ respectively. Absorption at these longer wavelengths thus seems characteristic of the much longer α-1:4 D-glucopyranose chains present in amylose and amylopectin although the exact correlation still remains to be established.

Reaction between Concanavalin-A and Glycogen

Many years ago, Sumner and Howell (1936) discovered that concanavalin-A, a globulin extracted from Jack Bean meal, precipitated glycogen from aqueous solution. This protein–carbohydrate reaction can be measured turbidimetrically and has been used for the determination of glycogen (Cifonelli and Smith, 1955) in the range 0·1 to 1·0 mg/ml. Neither periodate-oxidized glycogen nor the polyalcohol derived therefrom by reduction show any reaction with concanavalin-A. Methylated glycogen likewise shows no precipitating ability (Cifonelli, Montgomery and Smith, 1956). However, removal of the outer chains of glycogen by β-amylolysis actually renders it more readily precipitable by an amount approximately proportional to the degree of hydrolysis. The glycogen value (G.V.), which is the precipitating capacity with respect to a standard rabbit liver glycogen (G.V. = 1·00), varies for glycogens isolated from different sources: ox liver, 0·95; horse liver, 1·05; rat liver, 1·40; human liver (von Gierke's disease), 1·30; human liver (normal), 1·00. Concanavalin-A does not react with amylopectins, waxy corn starch, potato starch, *Leuconostoc mesenteroides* NRRL 512B dextran or laminarin. Concanavalin-A does, however, form an insoluble complex with yeast mannan (Sumner and O'Kane, 1948) while with it heparin (Cifonelli, Montgomery and Smith, 1956) has 50% more precipitating power than normal human liver glycogen. However, chondroitin sulphate, hyaluronic acid and beef lung galactogen give no precipitation reaction with concanavalin-A.

Reaction of Glycogens with Antipneumococcal Horse Sera

Type II *Pneumococcus* polysaccharide contains D-glucose units involved in 1:4:6-branch points together with L-rhamnose and D-glucuronic acid residues (Butler, Lloyd and Stacey, 1955; Butler and Stacey, 1955). Type II antipneumococcus sera cross-reacts with glycogens from human liver, dog liver and oysters (Heidelberger, Aisenberg and Hassid, 1954), tamarind seed polysaccharide (Heidelberger and Adams, 1956), dextrans (Heidelberger and Aisenberg, 1953) and other polysaccharides (e.g. amylopectin) containing α-1:4:6-linked D-glucose units. Similar cross reactions are shown by Types VII, IX, XI, XVIII, XX and XXII antipneumococcal horse sera.

Enzymic Synthesis of Glycogen

Phosphorylases

The first evidence concerning the mechanism of synthesis of glycogen was found by Cori, Colowick and Cori (1937; 1938a) and Cori, Schmidt and Cori (1939) using a dialyzed muscle extract. These workers established the reversibility of the reaction whereby a salt of α-D-glucopyranose 1

$$n. \ C_6H_{11}O_5 \ . \ O \ . \ PO_3K_2 \rightleftharpoons (C_6H_{10}O_5)_n + nK_2HPO_4 \qquad (1)$$

(dihydrogen phosphate) was converted by muscle phosphorylase *in vitro* to a polysaccharide giving an intense blue stain and resembling amylose the unbranched α-1:4-glucosan. Later Hassid, Cori and McCready (1943) demonstrated that muscle phosphorylase required the presence of a primer such as glycogen before it would exhibit any synthetic activity. Rabbit skeletal muscle phosphorylase was isolated in the crystalline form by Green and Cori (1943) and found to have a molecular weight of 340,000–400,000. This enzyme was designated phosphorylase *a* and showed 60–70% of its full activity without addition of adenylic acid. The solubility of the enzyme was greatly increased in weak salt solutions by the addition of cysteine. A more soluble protein, phosphorylase *b* was also present in rabbit muscle but was inactive without added adenylic acid (Cori and Green, 1943). In the presence of adenylic acid both forms of the enzyme had the same activity per mg of protein. The American workers also isolated another enzyme (PR) from muscle or spleen which when incubated with phosphorylase *a* converted it to phosphorylase *b*. The same conversion could be achieved by incubation with crystalline trypsin at pH 6 (Cori and Cori, 1945). The PR enzyme had very low activity in the absence of cysteine and its activity in the presence of cysteine was accelerated two to three times by 5×10^{-4}M-Mn^{++} ions. The PR enzyme was inhibited by glucose 1-phosphate in 0·03M-concentration. On the basis of its function PR enzyme has been called phosphorylase phosphatase. Investigation of the conversion of phosphorylase a to b by this enzyme has been studied using P^{32}-labelled phosphorylase a and has enabled the equation for this reaction to be written.

$$\text{phosphorylase } a \rightarrow 4 \text{ inorganic P} + 2 \text{ phosphorylase } b \qquad (2a)$$

Phosphorylase phosphatase attacks those phosphopeptides derived from phosphorylase a which contain a carboxyl-terminal arginyl residue. No activity was detected on casein, phosvitin, glycylserylphosphate, serylphosphate glycine, glycylserylphosphate glycine, phosphoserine and other low molecular weight phosphate esters (Graves, Fischer and Krebs, 1960).

Cori (1945) showed that during muscle contraction phosphorylase a was converted to phosphorylase b and suggested that the temporary inactivation of phosphorylase a might represent a regulatory mechanism which would prevent the exhaustion of glycogen stores in fatigue. Krebs and Fischer (1955) found that resting muscle contained predominantly phosphorylase b and later (Fischer and Krebs, 1958) achieved its crystallization. The same workers (Fischer and Krebs, 1955) accomplished the conversion of phosphorylase b to phosphorylase a using a cell-free muscle extract, divalent metal ions and adenosine triphosphate. The enzyme responsible, muscle phosphorylase b kinase, catalyses the overall reaction shown in (2b) which does not appear to be reversible (Krebs, Kent and Fischer, 1958).

$$2 \text{ phosphorylase } b + 4\text{ATP} \xrightarrow{\text{Kinase}} \text{phosphorylase } a + 4\text{ADP} \qquad (2b)$$

In the conversion phosphorylase $b \rightarrow$ phosphorylase a a doubling in molecular weight of the enzyme occurs. This dimer–monomer relationship existing between phosphorylases a and b was noted originally by Keller and Cori (1956).

To explain the relationship between phosphorylase a and b, Korkes (1956) has suggested that phosphorylase a consists of two protein moieties (En and En^1) linked to each other through two molecules of uridine monophosphate (UMP) and that the transfer of glucosyl units from glucose 1-phosphate (G–I–P) proceeds via a uridine diphosphate glucose-enzyme complex (En–UDPG) thus:

$$\text{En—UMP—PMU—}En^1 + \text{G-I-P} \rightleftharpoons \text{En—UDPG} + En^1\text{—UMP} \qquad (3)$$

$$\text{En—UDPG} + \text{Primer} \rightleftharpoons \text{En—UDP} + \text{G—Primer} \qquad (4)$$

$$\text{En—UDP} + En^1\text{—UMP} \rightleftharpoons \text{En—UMP—PMU—}En^1 + \text{P} \qquad (5)$$

In these equations phosphorylase a is En—UMP—PMU—En^1 and phosphorylase b is En—UDP. The activation of phosphorylase b by adenylic acid was then explained by the reactions

$$En—UDP + AMP \rightleftharpoons En—UMP + PMA + P \qquad (6)$$

$$En—UMP—PMA + G\text{-}I\text{-}P \rightleftharpoons En—UDPG + AMP \qquad (7)$$

$$En—UDPG + SG—Primer \rightleftharpoons EnUDP + G—Primer \qquad (8)$$

and the conversion of phosphorylase a to phosphorylase b by the reaction

$$En—UMP—PMU—En^1 + H_2O \rightarrow En—UDP + En^1UR \qquad (9)$$

The conversion of phosphorylase b to phosphorylase a could then be explained by

$$EnUDP + En^1UR + ATP \xrightarrow{Me^{++}} En—UDP + En^1—UMP + ADP \qquad (10)$$

$$EnUDP + En^1—UMP \xrightarrow{Me^{++}} En—UMP—PMU—En^1 + pyrophosphate \qquad (11)$$

Uridylic acid may be obtained after acid hydrolysis of crystalline phosphorylase (Buell, 1952).

Yet a third type of phosphorylase has been reported (Cowgill and Cori, 1955) in lobster muscle. This was an inactive form which could be converted successively to phosphorylase b and then to phosphorylase a. In a study of the phosphorylase system of dog liver, Sutherland and Wosilait (1956) obtained a phosphorylase whose enzymatic activity was increased 15–40% by the addition of adenosine 5-phosphate or inosine 5-phosphate (10^{-3}M). Cysteine and glutathione did not stimulate purified liver phosphorylase. The pH optimum for activity was near 6·4. The enzyme required glycogen in the reaction mixture and catalyzed the formation of a polysaccharide which gave a blue colour with iodine. This liver phosphorylase could be converted to an inactive form and inorganic phosphate by another enzyme in liver. The activity of this inactive form was not restored by adenosine 5-phosphate (Wosilait and Sutherland, 1956). The inactive form (dephosphophosphorylase) could however, be converted to active phosphorylase by liver dephosphophosphorylase kinase in the presence of adenosine-triphosphate and magnesium ions (Rall, Sutherland and Wosilait, 1956).

3

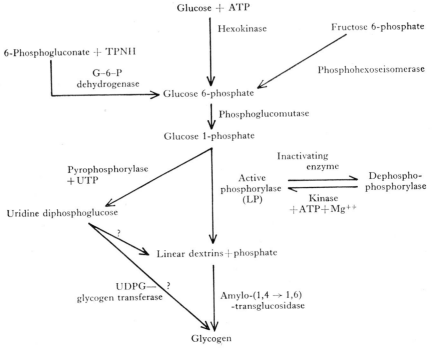

Fig. 1.3   *Enzymic Synthesis of Glycogen in Liver*

Nature of the polysaccharide synthesized by phosphorylase

Bear and Cori (1941) found that *in vitro* muscle phosphorylase converted glucose 1-phosphate into an unbranched polysaccharide of the amylose type and not into glycogen the polysaccharide usually found in animal tissues. This finding was subsequently confirmed by methylation and end-group assay (Hassid and McCready, 1941; Hassid, Cori and McCready, 1943) and by the extent of β-amylolysis. The polysaccharide ($[\alpha]_D + 150°$ in N-NaOH) synthesized using crystalline muscle phosphorylase, was sparingly soluble in water and rapidly retrograded from solution. Like amylose it was completely hydrolysed to maltose by β-amylase and produced a more intense blue stain with iodine than did most natural starches. Hydrolysis of the methylated synthetic polysaccharide ($[\alpha]_D + 210°$ in CHCl$_3$) yielded 2:3:6-tri-O-methyl D-glucose as the major product together with 0·6% of 2:3:4:6-tetra-O-methyl D-glucose and less than 1% of dimethyl glucose. This proportion of 'tetra' corresponded to a chain length of nearly 200 glucose units, while the isolation of 2:3:6-tri-O-methyl D-glucose confirmed that the polysaccharide consisted of 1:4-linked glucopyranose units.

Primer requirement of phosphorylase

Hassid, Cori and McCready (1943) found that a potato amylose which had 0.3% non-reducing end groups showed less than 10% of the capacity of glycogen to function as a primer for muscle phosphorylase *a*. Cori, Cori and Green (1943) in a study of the kinetics of crystalline muscle phosphorylase *a* found that without addition of glycogen no synthesis occurred, while with low concentrations the reaction failed to reach equilibrium. Using intermediate concentrations the rate of reaction was kinetically of the second order and became of the first order at high glycogen concentrations. The American workers believed that polysaccharide synthesis was achieved by a lengthening of the side chains of glycogen and that when the concentration of terminal chains was much smaller than that of the glucose 1-phosphate relatively few long chains would be expected to form. Later workers (Cori, Swanson and Cori, 1945; Swanson and Cori, 1948) established that muscle phosphorylase requires its non-reducing end groups to be supplied as part of a polysaccharide since it was not primed by amylosaccharides containing less than eight glucose units nor by the mild acid hydrolysis products of glycogen. Enzymatic hydrolysis of glycogen with α-amylase likewise caused a rapid loss of priming power.

Composition of phosphorylases

Baranowski, Illingworth, Brown and Cori (1957) have examined highly purified crystalline muscle phosphorylase *a* and found that on precipitation of the enzyme with trichloroacetic acid four of the eight gram atoms of phosphorus present/mole of enzyme (mol. wt. 500,000) were liberated. The phosphorus containing compound split off was identified as pyridoxal 5-phosphate on the basis of its absorption spectrum, behaviour on paper electrophoresis and column chromatography, activation of an apoenzyme preparation of aspartic–glutamic transaminase and of various colour reactions based on the phenolic group and on diazotization. No other phosphorus compounds were detected in the trichloroacetic acid extract and pyridoxal, pyridoxamine and pyridoxine were all absent. The identification of pyridoxal 5-phosphate elucidates earlier work of Velick and Wicks (1951) who, using a microbiological assay for the determination of members of the vitamin B_6 group in samples of phosphorylase hydrolysed in 0.1 N-HCl—10 N-formic acid, reported 0.5 to 1 mole of pyridoxine per mole of enzyme.

Cori and Illingworth (1957) found that the firmly bound pyridoxal 5-phosphate (4 moles/mole of muscle phosphorylase *a* and 2 moles/mole of muscle phosphorylase *b*) can also be split off by treatment with acid in the presence of ammonium sulphate followed by washing of the precipitated protein with alkaline ammonium sulphate solution. The enzymes so treated are inactive but can be reactivated by incubation for 30 min at 30° with amounts of pyridoxal 5-phosphate slightly greater than those removed from the protein. It is of interest that previous work by Madsen and Cori (1956; 1957) had shown that phosphorylase a and phosphorylase b have 4 and 2 binding sites for adenosine monophosphate respectively, and that phosphorylase a (M. Wt. 500,000) is split into four subunits (M. Wt. 125,000) by the action of p-chloromercuribenzoate.

Kent, Krebs and Fischer (1958) independently showed the presence of firmly bound pyridoxal 5′-phosphate in both rabbit skeletal muscle phosphorylase b and in cat muscle phosphorylase. These workers believed that the pyridoxal 5′-phosphate was bound to phosphorylase as follows:

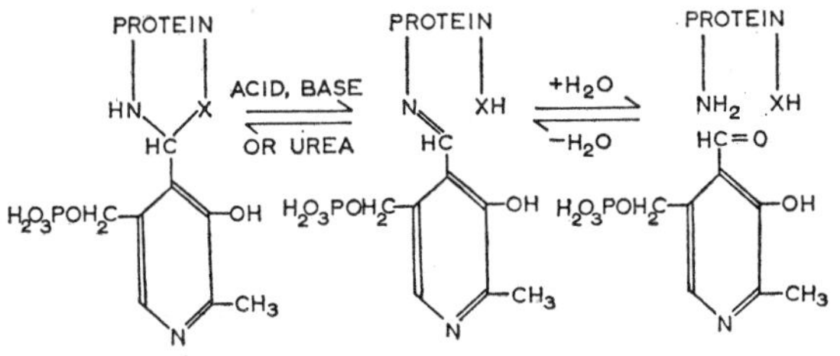

Fig. 1.4

The lower portions of the formulae represent a pyridoxal phosphate residue. Analysis of crystalline phosphorylase b has shown that the determining factor in the crystallization is a 'dimerization' of 2 phosphorylase b molecules each with 2 moles of bound adenosine 5′-monophosphate. This is in accord with the findings of Madsen and Cori (1956; 1957) that phosphorylase b binds 2 moles of AMP.

The total phosphorylase $(a+b)$ activity of the skeletal muscle of rats maintained on a pyridoxine deficient diet has been found to fall to 35% of the normal value (Illingworth, Kornfeld and Brown, 1960). By contrast the phosphorylase a activity of the tissue of these rats has the normal value and the glycogen content of the muscles of such deficient rats is not different from that of control animals. The apparent activity of uridine diphosphoglucose–glycogen transferase (see later) was not changed from the normal level in pyridoxine deficiency.

The crystallization of human muscle phosphorylases a and b has been achieved by Yunis, Fischer and Krebs (1960). The phosphorylase b crystallization was achieved in the presence of Mg^{++} ions and adenylic acid. This phosphorylase b was then converted to phosphorylase a with purified phosphorylase kinase. The sedimentation constant of phosphorylase b was 8·67 and that of phosphorylase a was 13·95. Phosphorylase b contained 2 moles of pyridoxal 5-phosphate/mole of enzyme while phosphorylase *a* contained 4 moles of this coenzyme/mole of enzyme. A striking similarity was observed between the human and rabbit phosphorylases—indeed they were immunologically identical as demonstrated on agar-diffusion plates.

Amylo-(1:4 → 1:6)-transglucosidase

Cori and Cori (1943) demonstrated that whereas muscle phosphorylase alone converted glucose 1-phosphate into linear amylose chains, in the presence of a supplementary enzyme, obtained from heart and liver, it synthesized a polysaccharide which closely resembled glycogen. The liver or heart extract which contained the supplementary enzyme was itself devoid of phosphorylase activity. A similar enzyme was found in the brown adipose tissue of the rat (Creasey and Gray, 1951).

The mechanism of the action of the supplementary or amylo-(1:4 → 1:6)-transglucosidase has been investigated by Larner (1953) using a glycogen in which the outer chains only were labelled with C^{14}-glucose units. The enzymes used for this purpose were obtained from rat liver and rat muscle and shown not to require phosphate. To demonstrate the formation of branch points the labelled glycogen was incubated with the transglucosidase and then degraded by a mixture of phosphorylase and amylo-1,6-glucosidase. Before branching the labelled glucose units were located in the outer chains and were only linked by α-1:4 linkages. After branching if a break occurred within the labelled part of the chain and the segment broken off was reattached in α-1:6-linkage some of the glucose units released by the amylo-1,6-glucosidase would be radioactive. This indeed was found to be the case with the liver enzyme where the average outer chain length of the substrate C^{14}-glycogen was about 11 glucose units but not where the average outer chain length was 6 glucose units. A critical length of outer chain was therefore obviously necessary for the branching enzyme to operate upon.

Barker, Bebbington and Bourne (1953) have demonstrated that the action of the branching enzyme of *Polytomella coeca* is accelerated by the addition of various oligosaccharides and that when C^{14}-maltose was used this was incorporated into the polysaccharide. Studies by Larner and Uwah (1956) have shown that with liver amylo-(1:4 → 1:6)-transglucosidase the rate of reaction is not affected by the presence of maltose, *iso*maltose or panose. These workers believed that this was due to a difference in chain length specificity of the acceptor.

Uridine diphosphoglucose glycogen transferase

Leloir and Cardini (1957) have discovered a new route of glycogen synthesis in rat liver. An enzyme (uridine diphosphoglucose–glycogen transferase) was isolated which transferred glucose units from its substrate uridine diphosphoglucose to a primer molecule which could be a small amount of glycogen or soluble starch but not mono-, di- and oligo-saccharides or hexose phosphates. Thus like animal phosphorylase the enzyme required a primer of high molecular weight.

Robbins, Traut and Lipmann (1959) working with pigeon breast muscle found that glycogen synthesis from UDPG was highly concentrated in particles which had microsomal sedimentation characteristics. When UDPG was incubated with the particles precipitating between 20,000 g and 100,000 g a polysaccharide was formed which gave a purple colour with iodine. This reaction was stimulated by the addition of a non-dialyzable supernatant factor, Mg^{++} and phosphate.

Uridinediphosphoglucose–glycogen transferase has been detected in human muscle by following the disappearance of UDPG via the UDPG dehydrogenase reaction (Hauk, Illingworth, Brown and Cori, 1959). Similar studies on rat muscle uridine–diphosphoglucose–glycogen trans-ferase (Hauk and Brown, 1959) confirmed the necessity of glycogen as a primer for the enzyme and showed that the glucose units transferred were added to the outer chains of the receptor glycogen in α-1:4 linkage. Amylo-heptaose would not serve as a primer for the reaction. The transferase was also inactive in the absence of cysteine and was stimulated 2-fold by 6×10^{-3} M-$MgCl_2$. The reaction was competitively inhibited by uridine 5'-phosphate, inosine 5'-phosphate, cytidine 5'-phosphate and guanosine 5'-phosphate but not by α-glucose 1-phosphate. The enzyme specificity can be judged by the finding that it could not utilize uridinediphospho-galactose, or uridinediphospho N-acetylglucosamine.

Leloir and Goldemberg (1960) have shown that on centrifugation of rat liver extract the enzyme responsible for the synthesis of glycogen from UDPG (glycogen synthetase) sediments with the 'particulate' glycogen. The enzyme appears to form an enzyme–substrate complex with the 'particulate' glycogen—it shows no such behaviour with potassium hy-droxide extracted glycogen. An interesting observation was that glucose 6-phosphate activates the glycogen synthetase—for half maximal activa-tion it requires 6×10^{-4} M G-6-P. The concentration of G-6-P in liver ranges from 0.5×10^{-4} to 6×10^{-4} moles per kg of wet liver (Steiner and Williams, 1959). Hence it seems likely that G-6-P concentration *in vivo* may be important in the regulation of glycogen synthetase activity.

Breckenridge and Crawford (1960) have demonstrated that glycogen synthesis in rat brain utilizes uridinediphosphoglucose as substrate. Enzymic activity was associated with particles and was maximal at *ca.* pH 8.0. Activation of the enzyme system was achieved by glucose 6-phos-phate; moderate activation was observed in the presence of cysteine. The brain does not have appreciable reserves of glycogen but the concentra-tion differs markedly between structures within the nervous system and accumulations of glycogen within nerve cells may be the predominant cause of morbidity in generalized glycogen storage disease.

UDPG Pyrophosphorylase

Munch-Peterson, Kalckar, Cutolo, and Smith (1953) have shown that synthesis of UDPG occurs by a reversible reaction thus:

Uridine triphosphate + α-glucose 1-phosphate ⇌ Uridinediphospho-glucose + pyrophosphate

Villar-Palasi and Larner (1960) have described the purification and properties of the UDPG pyrophosphorylase from rabbit skeletal muscle.

Glucokinase

Enzymes which phosphorylate hexoses are widely distributed and have varying degrees of specificity for different hexoses. Thus crystalline yeast hexokinase converts D-glucose, D-glucosamine, D-mannose, 2-deoxy D-glucose and D-fructose to their 6-phosphates (Kunitz and McDonald, 1946) in the presence of adenosine triphosphate. More specific kinases occur in liver and muscle and it was found possible to obtain enzyme preparations from liver and muscle which acted on fructose but not on glucose and *vice versa* (Slein, Cori & Cori, 1950). Vestling, Mylroif, Irish and Grant (1950) found that in rat liver, fructose phosphorylation occurred ten times more readily than glucose phosphorylation.

Amylomaltase (Trans α-1,4-glucosylase)

An amylomaltase—like enzyme using maltose as a substrate and synthesizing maltotriose and maltotetraose has been reported in liver by Giri, Nagabhushanam, Nigam and Belavadi (1955). Other workers (Beloff-chain, Catanzooro, Chain, Masi, Pocchiari and Rossi, 1955) have observed the presence of maltose, maltotriose and maltotetraose in rat diaphragm exposed to C[14]-glucose and reported that the synthesis of oligosaccharides and glycogen from glucose but not glucose 1-phosphate was stimulated by insulin. The maltose, maltotriose, maltotetraose and a number of higher glucosyl homologues present in fresh rat liver were isolated by Fishman and Sie (1958) who also investigated the effects of starvation, glucose feeding and insulin. On starvation the rat liver glycogen decreased markedly; the oligosaccharides also decreased but not to the same extent. On administration of glucose to starved rats the oligosaccharides increased but again not at the same rate as the glycogen. Insulin administration resulted in the characteristic marked decrease in liver glycogen paralleled by a diminution in the oligosaccharides. It thus appears that the oligo-saccharides detected were not artefacts and it was unlikely that they resulted from amylase action on the glycogen. This enzyme may play the same role in glycogen synthesis as the D-enzyme found in potatoes does in starch synthesis (Peat, Whelan and Jones, 1957; Walker and Whelan, 1957). D-enzyme, however, utilizes maltotriose as its smallest substrate in the synthesis of higher maltodextrins; glucose being the other product of the reaction. The amylomaltase of E. coli does use maltose as its substrate and can, in the presence of glucose oxidase, be induced to synthesize amylose because of the continuous removal of the glucose produced in the reaction (Monod and Torriani, 1950).

Olavarria (1960) has concluded that the oligosaccharides detected by various workers were produced by degradation of glycogen. A partially purified liver extract which formed glycogen from UDP-glucose was found to form oligosaccharides from glycogen. Addition of UDP-glucose-C^{14} to the system led to labelling of both the glycogen and of the oligo-saccharides. For up to 2·5 min incubation the specific activity of the glycogen was higher than that of the oligosaccharides and the inverse was true for longer incubations. The exterior chains of the glycogen in all cases had a higher activity than the total molecule.

A bovine serum trans (α-1,4-) glucosylase has been crystallized and found to be an α_1-globulin (Miller, 1958; Miller and Copeland, 1956, 1958). This enzyme seemed to restrict itself to α-1:4-linked substrates such as maltose, amylose, amylodextrins and glycogen. It has no effect on isomaltose, cellobiose, gentobiose, trehalose, G-1-P, α- and β-methyl-glucosides and cyclic Schardinger dextrins.

Enzymic Degradation of Glycogen

Whereas in the liver four pathways of glucose 6-phosphate metabolism exist, muscle contains no glucose 6-phosphatase and little glucose 6-phosphate dehydrogenase. For completeness the degradation of glycogen in the liver is therefore discussed.

(i) Phosphorylase

This enzyme is responsible for the initial degradation of glycogen by a process of phosphorolysis in which some of the α-1:4-linked glucopyranose residues in the outer or exterior chains of glycogen are released in the presence of excess phosphate as molecules of glucose 1-phosphate, i.e. by a reversion of the process of synthesis of the linear chains of glycogen. Phosphorolysis proceeds along an A-type chain until there is only a single glucose residue remaining attached to a B-type chain at the branch point. Phosphorolysis of a B-type chain ceases at about the sixth residue from the branch point (Cori and Larner, 1951). The action of phosphorylase does not therefore break or by-pass the 1:6 linkages of the branch point (Hestrin, 1949). After scission of some of the 1:6-linkages in the phosphorylase limit dextrin by amylo-1:6-glucosidase (see below), phosphorolysis can again proceed (Larner, Illingworth, Cori and Cori, 1952).

(ii) Amylo-1:6-glucosidase

The combined action of phosphorylase and amylo-1:6-glucosidase results in the complete degradation of glycogen to a mixture of glucose 1-phosphate and glucose. The glucose arises directly from the action of amylo-1:6-glucosidase on those branch points where there is a single glucose residue left attached to a B chain. The ratio of glucose:glucose 1-phosphate liberated by the combined action of the two enzymes has been used as a method for determining the average chain lengths of glycogens (Cori and Larner, 1951; Illingworth, Larner and Cori, 1952) to give results in agreement with those obtained by chemical methods.

Walker and Whelan (1960) have further investigated the structure of the limit dextrin resulting from the action of rabbit muscle phosphorylase on glycogen. They concluded that the formula previously assigned by Cori and Larner (1951) was incorrect. The side chains were not single glucose units but were probably four units long. Correspondingly the outer portions of the main chains are shorter than was supposed. The previous results of Cori and Larner (1951) might have been due to the presence in amylo-1:6-glucosidase of a transglycosylase acting on maltodextrins. Such an enzyme would account for the formation of glucose when the amylo-1:6-glucosidase acted on phosphorylase limit dextrin.

Amylo-1:6-glucosidase is a persistent impurity in phosphorylase preparations and seven to eight recrystallizations of the phosphorylase are required to free it from the last traces. Treatment of phosphorylase solutions with Norite will also achieve the same result. The preparation of amylo-1:6-glucosidase from rabbit muscle was first described by Cori and Larner (1951). Modifications involving a tenfold increase in purity based on activity per mg protein were later reported by Larner (1955). Such preparations contained no detectable phosphoglucomutase activity and only traces of amylase. Further improvements noticeably increasing the stability of the amylo-1:6-glucosidase were devised by Larner and Schliselfeld (1956) although such preparations still contained phosphorylase and traces of α-amylase. Amylo-1:6-glucosidase action is inhibited by 5×10^{-5} M-p-chloromercuribenzoate and to a lesser extent by o-iodosobenzoate. Both these inhibitions were reversed by the addition of glutathione. No inhibition was noted with 10^{-3} M-iodoacetate, $0 \cdot 0012$ M-isomaltose, $0 \cdot 002$ M-panose, $0 \cdot 003$ M-glucose 1-phosphate or glucose. The 'debranched' phosphorylase limit dextrin was however a competitive inhibitor. The optimum pH range for amylo-1:6-glucosidase action is $7 \cdot 2$–$7 \cdot 6$.

No evidence for the reversibility of amylo-1:6-glucosidase action has been found.

Phosphoglucomutase

The glucose 1-phosphate liberated by phosphorolysis becomes the substrate for phosphoglucomutase which converts it into glucose 6-phosphate. This enzyme has been found in tissue extracts of various animals as well as in yeast extracts (Cori, Colowick and Cori, 1938 a, b). The enzyme, which is activated by Mg^{++} and cysteine, has an optimum pH of 7·5. At equilibrium at 30° there is only 5·5% of glucose 1-phosphate in the equilibrium mixture (Colowick and Sutherland, 1942). The reversibility of the reaction was demonstrated by Sutherland, Colowick and Cori (1941) who showed that when coupled to the phosphorylase enzyme system as much as 33% of the glucose 6-phosphate could be converted to glycogen after a 3 hr incubation at 25°.

The crystallization of rabbit muscle phosphoglucomutase was achieved by Najjar (1948). The enzyme was electrophoretically homogeneous, was most stable at pH 5·0 in 0·1M-acetate buffer and exhibited maximum activity at pH 7·5 in the presence of $0·005$–$0·0025$M-Mg^{++} and cysteine. The enzyme was inhibited by fluoride in the absence of inorganic phosphate. Glucose-1,6-diphosphate has been shown to be an essential coenzyme of phosphoglucomutase (Cardini, Paladini, Caputto, Leloir and Trucco, 1949) and the reaction to proceed by transfer of a phosphate group from the diphosphate to the 6-position of a glucose 1-phosphate acceptor molecule. The diphosphate is thus regenerated continuously and only small quantities are needed to produce full activation.

Glucose 6-phosphatase

The phosphatase that converts glucose 6-phosphate to glucose and phosphate exhibits a high degree of specificity for its substrate (Deduve, Berthet, Hers and Dupret, 1949). The optimum pH for this action is within the physiological range 6·2–6·8. In this pH range the non-specific alkaline and acid phosphatases have very little activity. Conversely glucose 6-phosphatase exerts little activity under alkaline or acid conditions (Cori and Cori, 1952). Glucose 6-phosphatase has the vital function of providing the blood sugar in the liver.

Glucose 6-phosphate dehydrogenase

The action of this enzyme on glucose 6-phosphate provides an alternative pathway for degradation. Triphosphopyridine nucleotide is required as a hydrogen acceptor in this reaction in which the glucose 6-phosphate is converted to 6-phosphogluconate. The reaction can be followed spectrophotometrically using the change in ultraviolet absorption, as TPN^+ is converted to TPNH (Horecker and Smyrniotis, 1951). Cori and Lipmann 1952) have shown that the glucose 6-phosphate reacts in the pyranose form and that phospho-6-glucono-δ-lactone is the immediate product of dehydrogenation. This eventually decomposes to the 6-phosphogluconic acid.

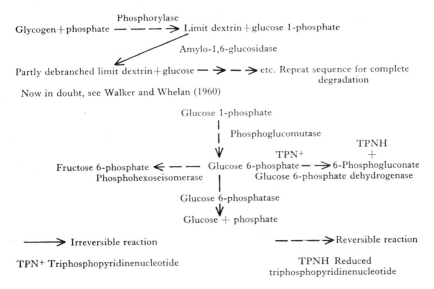

Fig. 1.5   *Enzymic Degradation of Glycogen in the Liver*

Phosphohexoseisomerase

Phosphohexoseisomerase was the first of many enzymes to be discovered (Lohmann, 1933) which catalyse the interconversion of the groupings R—CHOH—CHO into R—CO—CH$_2$OH. In the interconversion of glucose 6-phosphate and fructose 6-phosphate the equilibrium is in favour of the aldose phosphate.

Hormones and Glycogen

Glucagon is a polypeptide (Staub, Sinn and Behrens, 1955; Bromer, Sinn and Behrens, 1957) with hormone-like properties which is capable of stimulating liver glycogenolysis and hence of raising the level of blood sugar. It is believed to be secreted in the alpha-cells of the islets of Langerhans in response to hypoglycemia. Since its action is to produce hyperglycemia this in turn stimulates the release of insulin (Foà, Galansino and Pozza, 1957). The glycogenolytic action of glucagon is believed to be due to increased formation of liver phosphorylase from dephosphophosphorylase (Rall, Sutherland and Berthet, 1957). In this it resembles epinephrine another hormone promoting glycogenolysis. Both hormones produce a similar response in liver homogenates (1) the formation of an active factor in particulate fractions in the presence of the hormones and (2) the stimulation by the factor of liver phosphorylase formation in supernatant fractions of homogenates in which the hormones themselves had no effect. The active factor has been identified as adenosine -3'5' (cyclic) phosphate (Sutherland and Rall, 1957). It will be recalled that the reactivation of dephosphophosphorylase required magnesium ions and ATP and proceeds with the transfer of phosphate to the enzyme protein (Rall, Sutherland and Wosilait, 1956). The two hormones differ in that whereas glucagon is secreted into the portal system and reaches the liver directly, epinephrine reaches the liver only after having been diluted in the general circulation and in great part oxidized (Foà, Galansino and D'Amico, 1959).

There is abundant evidence that insulin enhances glycogen formation in muscles and that part of the immediate hypoglycemic action of insulin is in opening a pathway for glycogen synthesis in skeletal muscle. By contrast the glucose which leaves the blood under insulin hypoglycemia is probably not converted appreciably to liver glycogen (Levin and Weinhouse, 1958). The exact site of insulin action in metabolism has still to be determined but there is no doubt that it promotes the utilization of glucose either by increasing cellular permeability or by increasing the speed of a rate-limiting intracellular reaction.

From a study of the effects of phlorizin on monosaccharide transport, amino acid transport and amino acid incorporation into protein in isolated rat diaphragm, Battaglia, Manchester and Randle (1960) concluded that phlorizin inhibited the uptake of glucose and membrane transport of D-xylose and D-galactose, and the effect of insulin on these processes without affecting incorporation of [14C]-glycine into protein and the stimulation of this process by insulin. Hence the effect of insulin *in vitro* in increasing the incorporation of [14C] amino acids into protein is not necessarily dependent on an effect of the hormone on carbohydrate metabolism. This does not imply that insulin has two separate and distinct effects on muscle metabolism. Randle and Smith (1958) have suggested that insulin accelerates transport of glucose in diaphragm by restricting the access of energy-rich phosphate to a process concerned with the regulation of glucose transport, the energy-rich phosphate thus made more freely available may stimulate protein synthesis.

Haynes (1958) has studied the effect of adrenocorticotropic hormone on the level of active phosphorylase in adrenal tissue. In this tissue cyclic adenosine-3',5'-monophosphoric acid, the production of which is accelerated by adrenocorticotropic hormone, increases the concentration of active phosphorylase.

Glycogen Storage Diseases

Glycogen storage disease was first described by von Gierke (1929). Cori (1958) distinguished four different types of glycogen storage disease. Since then two further types have been discovered.

Type 1 or von Gierke disease is typified by abnormally high glycogen storage in the liver and kidney cortex only. Cori and Cori (1952) found that the glycogen obtained from such cases was normal and that the main cause of abnormal glycogen storage was deficiency of the enzyme glucose 6-phosphatase.

Type 2 is a general glycogenosis with an excessively high deposition of normal glycogen in heart, tongue, diaphragm and skeletal muscles. No enzymic lesion has so far been detected in this form of glycogen storage disease (Hauk, Illingworth, Brown and Cori, 1959). Death generally results within the first year from heart failure.

Type 3 is frequently mistaken for Type 1. Here the storage product in the liver, heart and muscle is not true glycogen but its limit dextrin or a polysaccharide intermediate between these two. It has been shown that the enzyme deficiency involved here is the amylo-1,6-glucosidase or the debranching enzyme. Type 3 is sometimes known as limit dextrinosis. Although Type 3 is a less severe disease than Type 1, involvement of the heart muscle requires special care.

Type 4 appears to be rather rare. Again the structure of the glycogen in the liver and probably other organs is abnormal in that it has long inner and outer branches. Deducing from the structure of this glycogen the enzyme deficiency is probably the $1,4 \rightarrow 1,6$ transglucosidase or branching enzyme.

Type 1 or von Gierke's Disease

The glycogen isolated by Schoenheimer (1929) from the liver of von Gierke's original case was found to contain only glucose, showed the same specific rotation as normal glycogen, and was degraded by minced normal liver. This suggested that one of the enzymes concerned with the degradation of glycogen to glucose was absent in the liver in von Gierke's disease.

Illingworth and Cori (1952) and Cori and Cori (1952) studied some eight cases of this type.

Case 1 was a one-year-old child. An autopsy performed four hours after death showed that the liver weighed 1020 gm compared with a normal 290 gm. The glycogen (11·0%) present in the liver had an average chain length of 12·5 glucose units (enzymatic assay) and was degraded to the extent of 36·4% by phosphorylase. Neither the skeletal nor the heart muscles were involved and the glycogen (0·1%) in the muscle was normal. Only 23 γ of phosphorus (as phosphate) were liberated from glucose

6-phosphate by 100 mg of the liver compared with 429 γ in a normal 1·5 month old child and more than 700 γ in a 4 month old infant. Case 2 involved a 15 month old girl, the daughter of parents who were second cousins. A sibling of these parents had also died of glycogen storage disease. The fat content of the liver (weight, 1300 gm) was 23%. There was excessive storage (3·8%) of normal glycogen (average chain length, 10·5; degradation by phosphorylase, 32·8%) in the kidneys, but the muscles (0·29% glycogen) were not involved. The liver contained 2·8% of normal glycogen. Again the glucose 6-phosphatase activity of the liver was abnormally low (22 γ by biopsy; 15 γ by autopsy).

Cases 3–8 were all examined by biopsy assay which showed normal glycogens (average chain length 13·5–11·2; degradation by phosphorylase, 32·8–42%) stored in the liver in abnormal amounts (10·2–14·2%). Glucose 6-phosphatase assays were performed on cases 5 (155 γ), 7 (402 γ) and 8 (282 γ). Whereas case 3 involved a 3 month old male child who had very low fasting blood sugar and whose disease was probably of a severe type those of cases 4–8 were all older children (3½–19 years old) with a long history of the disease which at no time had been very severe.

In reviewing the fifteen cases of Type 1 studied by her and those reported by Harris and Olmo (1954), Cori (1958) concluded that clinically this Type 1 is characterized by hepatomegaly, low fasting blood sugar and lack of response of the blood sugar to epinephrine injection. In severe or fatal cases the fat content of the liver was usually very high and the glucose 6-phosphatase extremely low. The lack of glucose 6-phosphatase can be demonstrated histochemically in the liver and kidney cortex by the method of Chiquoine (1953). The confinement of Type 1 disease to the liver and cortex is explicable because these (and perhaps the mucosa of the ileum) are the only tissues where glucose 6-phosphatase has been found to occur normally in significant amounts and where glycogen is converted to glucose which enters the blood stream.

Type 2 or General Glycogenosis

Cori (1958) suggested that because of the increased glycogen deposition in all tissues, any enzyme implicated must be one which occurs everywhere. In contrast to Type 1 the fat content of the liver was not significantly elevated. Both glucose 6-phosphatase and hexokinase activity fell within the normal range.

Hauk, Illingworth, Brown and Cori (1959) have reported the results of autopsy studies of five cases of general glycogenosis. Analysis revealed glycogen contents from 6·6–13% in the muscles and from 5·5–11·2% in the heart compared with values of 0·43–0·85% glycogen in muscles and 0·77% glycogen in heart from two infants who were not suffering from any glycogen deposition disease. Neither the specific phosphatase which converts phosphorylase *a* to *b* (PR-enzyme) nor the specific kinase which converts phosphorylase *b* and *a* could be implicated with general glycogenosis. Four of the five cases of Type 2 were examined for uridine diphosphoglucose–glycogen transferase activity. One of these had some activity in the skeletal muscle but no detectable activity in the heart muscle, although both these tissues had glycogen contents of 11%. In another case transferase activity was demonstrated in the heart. No activity could be detected in the muscles of the other two cases or in the heart of one of them. Hauk, Illingworth, Brown and Cori (1959) concluded that the activity of this enzyme, since it was not associated with low phosphorylase activity, did not account for the generalized deposition of glycogen.

Type 3 or Limit Dextrinosis

Polglase, Smith and Tyler (1952) reported a case of glycogen storage disease (liver glycogen, 9·1%; muscle glycogen, 8·9%) in which the average chain length of the liver glycogen was about 25 per cent shorter than normal. The muscle glycogen from this parient was not definitely different in chain length from the glycogen of normal individuals. The subject was an 18 month old girl who had suffered from muscular weakness since the age of 6 months. Her epinephrine and glucose tolerance tests were normal. Several weeks after admission to hospital she expired with pneumonia.

Illingworth and Cori (1952) reported the first full chemical investigation of a case of Type 3 which involved a 12½ year old girl who had had hepatomegaly since 1½ years of age. This child exhibited a delayed blood sugar curve after oral administration of glucose and showed some rise in blood sugar after epinephrine. Biopsy assay showed that the liver contained 8·7% of a 'glycogen' which had a shorter average chain length (9·3 glucose residues) than normal and which was only degraded to the extent of 12·2% by phosphorylase. These results indicated a shorter than normal average outer chain (5·1 glucose units) and a normal average inner chain (4·2 glucose units). The average chain length of the 'glycogen' in the muscle was even shorter (7·6 glucose residues) and constituted 4·6% of the muscle. Again the inner chains were of normal length (3·6 glucose residues) but the outer chains (4 glucose units) were abnormally short. Glucose 6-phosphatase assay of the liver showed that the amount of phosphate liberated (180 γ) was much smaller than usual but did not fall in the range of the fatal cases of von Gierke's disease. However, the lack of glucose 6-phosphatase would not explain the abnormal storage of 'glycogen' in the muscle since this enzyme is normally absent from this tissue. It was suspected that since these 'glycogens' resembled more the phosphorylase limit dextrin the enzyme lesion was amylo-1,6-glucosidase (the debranching enzyme).

Manners (1954) investigated a case of Type 3 (a 12 year old girl) in which the substance stored in the liver was similar but not identical with a phosphorylase limit dextrin. This 'glycogen' had an average chain length of only six glucose residues and was attacked by phosphorylase to only a negligible extent (1%). The β-amylolysis limit (14%) of this 'glycogen' differed, however, from that of phosphorylase limit dextrin (24%). The average chain length of the exterior chains is thus only two glucose residues, while the interior chains are comprised of an average of three glucose residues. The 'glycogen' showed a much lower iodine-binding power than that of normal glycogen and was not stained brown with iodine. Acid hydrolysis gave glucose and no other sugar. Ultracentrifugal examination of the glycogen showed that it was polydisperse and that it contained two components having molecular weights of approximately 2×10^6 and 9×10^6 respectively. Again it was suspected that there was a deficiency in the liver of the debranching enzyme, amylo-1:6-glucosidase, thereby preventing a complete phosphorolysis of the glycogen.

Other cases of limit dextrinosis (Cori, 1958) reported include two who died of the disease and in which it was shown that the storage of a limit dextrin-like glycogen had occurred in the liver, muscle and in the heart. In another surviving case (16 month old baby) biopsy assays revealed that a similar 'glycogen' having short outer chains was stored to the extent of 11% in the liver and 7·5 and 4·5% respectively in two different muscles. A second child in this family had limit dextrinosis. A cousin of the mother of these children had had hepatomegaly since infancy. When a muscle biopsy was taken at the age of 32 a limit dextrin-like glycogen (13·4% end groups) was found to the extent of 4·3%. These findings emphasize the genetic aspect of the disease.

Illingworth, Cori and Cori (1956) finally established that lack of amylo-1,6-glucosidase was the cause of limit dextrinosis. No glucosidase activity could be detected in the heart, psoas and diaphragm muscles of a 13 month old female. A limit dextrin-like glycogen was found in the heart (4·7%), psoas (3·5%) and diaphragm (5·1%) which had from 12·0–12·6% of 1,6 linkages (branch points) and which was degraded only to the extent of 3–6% by phosphorylase. The liver ('glycogen' content 14·2%) was also involved in this case. No glucosidase activity was detected in heart and psoas muscles and only small activity in the diaphragm muscle of a 2 year old girl who had limit dextrinosis. In this case the limit dextrin-like glycogen in the heart (4·5%) and diaphragm muscles (8·9%) was attacked by phosphorylase to the extent of 11% and 26% respectively. Again the liver (8·0% 'glycogen'; degradation by phosphorylase, 10%) was also involved. In both these cases the glucose 6-phosphatase activity (350 γ; 570 γ) of the liver was quite high and the fat content of the liver (2·6%; 11·3%) much lower than in Type 1.

Type 4

Only one case of this type has so far been reported (Illingworth and Cori, 1952) and this involved a 17 month old boy who died of storage disease associated with cirrhosis of the liver. Analysis of the liver at autopsy revealed a remarkable type of glycogen (2·9%) which had a much greater average chain length (21·2 glucose residues) than normal. In particular the outer chains were comprised of on average 14·7 glucose residues leaving inner chains of 6·5 glucose residues. The 'glycogen' was degraded to the extent of 50·5% by phosphorylase. It thus resembled more closely corn amylopectin. Whereas normal baby glycogen has an iodine absorption peak at 470 mμ, this abnormal glycogen showed a maxima at 530 mμ near that of corn amylopectin at 550 mμ. Another striking property of this abnormal glycogen was its sparing solubility in cold water although it was soluble in hot water. It also exhibited the phenomena of retrogradation. Neither of these properties is exhibited by normal glycogen. An X-ray pattern of the abnormal glycogen revealed definite evidence of crystallinity.

The change in structure of the glycogen was attributed to a decreased activity of the branching enzyme in the liver. Cori (1958) suggested that the cirrhosis might have been due to the precipitation of the polysaccharide, the poorly soluble material acting like a foreign body.

Type 5

This type of glycogen storage disease has recently been described by Pearson, Rimer and Mommaerts (1959) in a 19 year old male whose strength was normal at onset of exercise but who, with exercise, became increasingly weak and developed severe cramps. The subject had no muscle wasting. Biochemical and histochemical analysis of thigh muscle revealed a four-fold increase in stored glycogen and no detectable phosphorylase. Glycolysis in tissue homogenate, as indicated by lactic acid production was markedly reduced but was raised to near normal by the addition of glucose 1-phosphate. This type of glycogen storage disease is therefore caused by phosphorylase deficiency in skeletal muscle.

The virtual absence of phosphorylase in this case was specific since other enzymes such as phosphorylase kinase and PR enzyme were present in normal amount. The 4% glycogen therefore found in the muscles must have arisen via uridine-diphosphoglucose and indeed UDPG–glycogen transferase was detected. This pathway of glycogen synthesis is not influenced by inorganic phosphate and has an equilibrium far to the side of glycogen synthesis (Mommaerts, Illingworth, Pearson, Guillory and Seraydarian, 1959).

Type 6

A type of glycogen storage disease arising from reduced phosphorylase activity in liver has been described by Hers (1959).

4

It is characterized by hepatomegaly and clinically simulates the disorder found in patients with a glucose 6-phosphatase deficiency.

No specific treatment is as yet available for glycogenosis but Yim, MacLaughlin and Bessman (1958) state that prolonged treatment with glucagon is beneficial.

REFERENCES

Abdel-Akher, M., Hamilton, J. K., Montgomery, R., and Smith, F. *J. Amer. Chem. Soc.* **74,** 4970 (1952).
Abdel-Akher, M., and Smith, F. *J. Amer. Chem. Soc.* **73,** 994 (1951).
Balls, K., Walden, M. K., and Thompson, R. R. *J. Biol. Chem.* **173,** 9 (1948).
Baranowski, T., Illingworth, B., Brown, D. H., and Cori, C. F. *Biochim. Biophys. Acta* **25,** 16 (1957).
Barker, S. A., Bebbington, A., and Bourne, E. J. *J. Chem. Soc.* 4051 (1953)
Battaglia, F. C., Manchester, K. L. and Randle, P. J. *Biochim. Biophys. Acta* **43,** 50 (1960).
Bear, R. S. and Cori, C. F. *J. Biol. Chem.* **140,** 111 (1941).
Bell, D. J. *Biochem. J.* **30,** 1612 (1936).
Bell, D. J. *J. Chem. Soc.* 473 (1944).
Bell, D. J. *J. Chem. Soc.* 992 (1948).
Bell, D. J., Gutfreund, H., Cecil, R., and Ogston, A. G. *Biochem. J.* **42,** 405 (1948).
Bell, D. J. and Manners, D. J. *J. Chem. Soc.* 3641 (1952).
Bell, D. J. and Manners, D. J. *J. Chem. Soc.* 1891 (1954).
Beloff-Chain, A., Catanzaro, R., Chain, E. B., Masi, I., Pocchiari, F. and Rossi, C. *Proc. Roy. Soc.* B143 (1955).
Bertrand, F. and Laszt, L. *Biochem. Z.* **327,** 354 (1956).
Bloom, W. L., Lewis, G. T., Schumpert, M. Z. and Shen, T. M. *J. Biol. Chem.* **188,** 631 (1951).
Bourne, E. J., Haworth, W. N., Macey, A. and Peat, S. *J. Chem. Soc.* 924 (1948).
Breckenridge, B. M. and Crawford, E. J. *J. Biol. Chem.* **235,** 3054 (1960).
Bridgman, W. B. *J. Amer. Chem. Soc.* **64,** 2349 (1942).
Bromer, W. W., Sinn, L. G., and Behrens, O. K. *J. Amer. Chem. Soc.* **79,** 2807 (1957).
Bryce, W. A. J., Greenwood, C. T., Jones, I. G., and Manners, D. J. *J. Chem. Soc.* 711 (1958).
Buell, M. V. *Fed. Proc.* **11,** 192 (1952).
Butler, K., Lloyd, P. F. and Stacey, M. *J. Chem. Soc.* 1531 (1955).
Butler, K. and Stacey, M. *J. Chem. Soc.* 1537 (1955).
Cardini, C. E., Paladini, A. C., Caputto, R., Leloir, L. F. and Trucco, R. E. *Arch. Biochem.* **22,** 87 (1949).
Carroll, N. V., Longley, R. W. and Roe, J. H. *J. Biol. Chem.* **220,** 583 (1956).
Chiquoine, A. D. *J. Histochem. Cytochem.* **1,** 429 (1953).
Cifonelli, J. A., Montgomery, R., and Smith, P. *J. Amer. Chem. Soc.* **78,** 2485 (1956).
Cifonelli, J. A., Montgomery, R., and Smith, F. *J. Amer. Chem. Soc.* **78,** 2488 (1956).
Cifonelli, J. A. and Smith, F. *Anal. Chem.* **27,** 1639 (1955).
Colowick, S. P. and Sutherland, E. W. *J. Biol. Chem.* **144,** 423 (1942).

Cori, G. T. *J. Biol. Chem.* **96**, 259 (1932).

Cori, G. T. *J. Biol. Chem.* **158**, 333 (1945).

Cori, G. T. *Modern Problems in Pediatrics* III, 344 (1958).

Cori, G. T., Colowick, S. P. and Cori, C. F. *J. Biol. Chem.* **121**, 465 (1937).

Cori, G. T., Colowick, S. P. and Cori, C. F. *J. Biol. Chem.* **123**, 375, 381 (1938a).

Cori, G. T., Colowick, S. P. and Cori, C. F. *J. Biol. Chem.* **124**, 543 (1938b).

Cori, G. T., and Cori, C. F. *J. Biol. Chem.* **151**, 57 (1943).

Cori, G. T., and Cori, C. F. *J. Biol. Chem.* **158**, 321 (1945).

Cori, G. T., and Cori, C. F. *J. Biol. Chem.* **199**, 661 (1952).

Cori, C. F., Cori, G. T. and Green, A. A. *J. Biol. Chem.* **151**, 39 (1943).

Cori, G. T. and Green, A. A. *J. Biol. Chem.* **151**, 31 (1943).

Cori, C. F. and Illingworth, B. *Proc. Natl. Acad. Sciences* **43**, 547 (1957).

Cori, G. T. and Larner, J. *J. Biol. Chem.* **188**, 17 (1951).

Cori, O. and Lipmann, F. *J. Biol. Chem.* **194**, 417 (1952).

Cori, G. T., Schmidt, G. and Cori, C. F. *Science* **89**, 464 (1939).

Cori, G. T., Swanson, M. A. and Cori, C. F. *Fed. Proc.* **4**, 234 (1945).

Cowgill, R. W. and Cori, C. F. *J. Biol. Chem.* **216**, 133 (1955).

Creasey, N. H. and Gray, C. H. *Biochem. J.* **50**, 74 (1951).

Deduve, C., Berthet, J., Hers, H. G. and Dupret, L. *Bull. soc. chim. biol.* **31**, 1242 (1949).

Fischer, E. H. and Krebs, E. G. *J. Biol. Chem.* **216**, 121 (1955).

Fischer, E. H. and Krebs, E. G. *J. Biol. Chem.* **231**, 65 (1958).

Fishman, W. H. and Sie, H. G. *J. Amer. Chem. Soc.* **80**, 121 (1958). *Nature* **182**, 240 (1958).

Foà, P. O., Galansino, G. and Pozza, G. *Recent Progress in Hormone Research* **13**, 473 (1957).

Foà, P. O., Galansino, G. and D'Amico, G. *Modern Problems in Pediatrics* **4**, 237 (1959).

Foster, A. B., Newton-Hearn, P. A. and Stacey, M. *J. Chem. Soc.* 30 (1956).

French, D. *Bull. soc. chim. biol.* in the press (1960).

Fuller, K. W. and Northcote, D. H. *Biochem. J.* **64**, 657 (1956).

Geldmacher-Mallinckrodt, M. and Weinland, H. *Hoppe-Seyl. Z.* **292**, 65 (1953).

Gibbons, G. C. and Boissonnas, R. A. *Helv. Chim. Acta* **33**, 1477 (1950).

von Gierke, *Beitr. z. path. Anat. u.z. allg. Path.* **82**, 497 (1929).

Giri, K. V., Nagabhushanam, A., Nigam, V. N. and Belavadi, B. *Science* **121**, 989 (1955).

Good, C. A., Kramer, H. and Somogyi, M. *J. Biol. Chem.* **100**, 485 (1933).

Graves, D. J., Fischer, E. H. and Krebs, E. G. *J. Biol. Chem.* **235**, 805 (1960).

Green, A. A. and Cori, G. T. *J. Biol. Chem.* **151**, 21 (1943).

Hale, A. J. *J. Histochem. Cytochem.* **3**, 421 (1955).

Hale, A. J. *Int. Rev. of Cytology* VI. 193 (1957).

Halsall, T. G., Hirst, E. L. and Jones, J. K. N. *J. Chem. Soc.* 1399 (1947).

Harris, R. C. and Olmo, C. J. *J. Clin. Invest.* **33**, 1204 (1954).

Hassid, W. Z., Cori, G. T. and McCready, R. M. *J. Biol. Chem.* **148**, 89 (1943).

Hassid, W. Z. and McCready, R. M. *J. Amer. Chem. Soc.* **63**, 2171 (1941).

Hauk, R. and Brown, D. H. *Biochim. Biophys. Acta* **33**, 556 (1959).

Hauk, R., Illingworth, B., Brown, D. H. and Cori, C. F. *Biochim. Biophys. Acta* **33**, 554 (1959).

Haworth, W. N., Hirst, E. L. and Isherwood, F. A. *J. Chem. Soc.* 577 (1937).

Haworth, W. N., Hirst, E. L. and Smith, F. *J. Chem. Soc.* 1914 (1939).

Haworth, W. N., Hirst, E. L., and Webb, J. I. *J. Chem. Soc.* 2479 (1929).

Haworth, W. N. and Percival, E. G. V. *J. Chem. Soc.* 1342 (1931).

Haworth, W. N. and Percival, E. G. V. *J. Chem. Soc.* 2277 (1932).
Haynes, R. C. *J. Biol. Chem.* **233,** 1220 (1958).
Heidelberger, M. and Adams, J. *J. Exp. Med.* **103,** 189 (1956).
Heidelberger, M. and Aisenberg, A. C. *Proc. Nat. Acad. Science* **39,** 453 (1953).
Heidelberger, M., Aisenberg, A. C. and Hassid, W. Z. *J. Exp. Med.* **99,** 343 (1954).
Hers, H. G., *Proc. Int. Cong. Pediat.* 9th Congress Montreal (1959).
Hestrin, S. *J. Biol. Chem.* **179,** 943 (1949).
Hirst, E. L., Jones, J. K. N. and Roudier, A. J. *J. Chem. Soc.* 1779 (1948).
Hobson, P. N., Whelan, W. J. and Peat, S. *J Chem. Soc.* 1451 (1951).
Hocevar, B. J. and Northcote, D. H. *Nature,* **179,** 488 (1957).
Horecker, B. L. and Smyrniotis, P. Z. *J. Biol. Chem.* **193,** 371 (1951).
Hotchkiss, R. D. *Arch. Biochem.* **16,** 131 (1948).
Illingworth, B. and Cori, G. T. *J. Biol. Chem.* **199,** 653 (1952).
Illingworth, B., Cori, G. T. and Cori, C. F. *J. Biol. Chem.* **199,** 641 (1952).
Illingworth, B., Cori, G. T. and Cori, C. F. *J. Biol. Chem.* **218,** 123 (1956).
Illingworth, B., Larner, J. and Cori, G. T. *J. Biol. Chem.* **199,** 631 (1952).
Illingworth, B., Kornfeld, R. and Brown, D. H. *Biochim. Biophys. Acta* **42,** 381 (1960).
Isbell, H. S. *Science* **113,** 532 (1951).
Keller, P. J. and Cori, G. T. *Biochim. Biophys. Acta* **20,** 150 (1956).
Kemp, A. and van Heijningen, A. J. M. K. *Biochem. J.* **56,** 646 (1954).
Kent, A. B., Krebs, H. E. G. and Fischer, E. H. *J. Biol. Chem.* **232,** 549 (1958).
Korkes, S. *Ann. Rev. Biochem.* **25,** 685 (1956).
Kramer, H. and Windrum, G. H. *J. Clin. Path.* **6,** 239 (1953). *J. Histochem. Cytochem.* **2,** 196 (1954).
Krebs, E. G. and Fischer, E. H. *J. Biol. Chem.* **216,** 113 (1955).
Krebs, E. G., Kent, A. B. and Fischer, E. H. *J. Biol. Chem.* **231,** 73 (1958).
Kunitz, M. and McDonald, R. *J. Gen. Physiol.* **29,** 393 (1946).
Larner, J. *J. Biol. Chem.* **202,** 491 (1953).
Larner, J. *J. Biol. Chem.* **212,** 9 (1955).
Larner, J., Illingworth, B., Cori, G. T. and Cori, C. F. *J. Biol. Chem.* **199,** 641 (1952).
Larner, J. and Schiselfeld, L. H. *Biochim. Biophys. Acta* **20,** 53 (1956).
Larner, J. and Uwah, D. N., *J. Amer. Chem. Soc.* **78,** 3647 (1956).
Leloir, L. F. and Cardini, G. E. *J. Amer. Chem. Soc.* **79,** 6340 (1957).
Leloir, L. F. and Goldemberg, S. H. *J. Biol. Chem.* **235,** 919 (1960).
Levin, H. W. and Weinhouse, S. *J. Biol. Chem.* **232,** 749 (1958).
Liddle, A. M. and Manners, D. J. *J. Chem. Soc.* 3432 (1957a).
Liddle, A. M. and Manners, D. J. *J. Chem. Soc.* 4708 (1957b).
Lillie, R. D. *Bull. Intern. Ass. Med. Museums* **27,** 23 (1947); *J. Lab. Clin. Med.* **32,** 910 (1947).
Lillie, R. D. *Anat. Record* **108,** 239 (1950).
Lillie, R. D. *J. Histochem. Cytochem.* **2,** 127 (1954).
Lillie, R. D., Greco, J. and Laskey, A. *Anat. Record* **103,** 635 (1949).
Lison, P. L. *Compt. rend. soc. biol.* **143,** 117 (1949).
Lohmann, K. *Biochem. Z.* **262,** 137 (1933).
MacLaughlin, J., and Bessman, S. P. *Amer. J. Diseases Children* **96,** 549 (1958).
Madsen, N. B. and Cori, C. F. *J. Biol. Chem.* **223,** 1055 (1956).
Madsen, N. B. and Cori, C. F. *J. Biol. Chem.* **224,** 899 (1957).
Mancini, R. E. *Anat. Record* **101,** 149 (1948).
Manners, D. J. *J. Chem. Soc.* 3527 (1954).
Manners, D. J. and Archibald, A. R. *J. Chem. Soc.* 2205 (1957).

McManus, J. F. A. *Nature* **158**, 202 (1946).
Meyer, K. H. and Bernfeld, P. *Helv. Chim. Acta* **23**, 875 (1940).
Meyer, K. H., Fischer, E. H. and Piquet, A. *Helv. Chim. Acta* **34**, 316 (1951).
Meyer, K. H., Fischer, E. H., Staub, A. and Bernfeld, P. *Helv. Chim. Acta* **31**, 2158 (1948).
Meyer, K. H., Noelting, G. and Bernfeld, P. *Experientia* **3**, 370 (1947).
Meyer, K. H. and Press, J. *Helv. Chim. Acta* **24**, 58 (1941).
Meyer, K. H., Spohr, P. F. and Fischer, E. H. *Helv. Chim. Acta* **36**, 1924 (1953).
Miller, K. D. *J. Biol. Chem.* **231**, 987 (1958).
Miller, K. D. and Copeland, W. H. *Biochim. Biophys. Acta* **22**, 193 (1956).
Miller, K. D. and Copeland, W. H. *J. Biol. Chem.* **231**, 997 (1958).
Mommaerts, W. F. H. M., Illingworth, B., Pearson, C. M., Guillory, R. J. and Seraydarian, K. *Proc. Nat. Acad. Sci.* **45**, 791 (1959).
Monod, J. and Torriani, Anne-Marie. *Ann. Inst. Pasteur* **78**, 65 (1950).
Morris, D. L. *J. Biol. Chem.* **154**, 503 (1944).
Morris, D. L. *Science* **107**, 254 (1948).
Munch-Petersen, A., Kalckar, H. M., Cutolo, E. and Smith, E. E. B. *Nature* **172**, 1036 (1953).
Najjar, V. A. *J. Biol. Chem.* **175**, 281 (1948).
Northcote, D. H. *Biochem. J.* **51**, 232 (1952).
Northcote, D. H. *Biochem. J.* **58**, 353 (1954).
Oakley, H. B. and Young, F. G. *Biochem. J.* **30**, 868 (1936).
Olavarria, J. M. *J. Biol. Chem.* **235**, 3055 (1960).
Pearson, C. M., Rimer, D. G. and Mommaerts, W. F. H. M., *Clin. Res.* **7**, 298 (1959).
Peat, S., Pirt, S. J. and Whelan, W. J. *J. Chem. Soc.* **705**, 714 (1952).
Peat, S., Whelan, W. J., Hobson, P. N. and Thomas, G. J. *J. Chem. Soc.* 4440 (1954).
Peat, S., Whelan, W. J. and Jones, G. J. *Chem. Soc.* 2490 (1957).
Pflüger, E. F. W. *Das Glykogen und seine Beziehungen zur Zuckerkrankheit*, Bonn, 2nd edition (1905).
Polglase, W. J., Brown, D. M. and Smith, E. L. *J. Biol. Chem.* **199**, 105 (1952).
Polglase, W. J., Smith, E. L. and Tyler, F. H. *J. Biol. Chem.* **199**, 97 (1952).
Putzeys, P. and Verhoeven, L. *Rec. trav. chim.* **68**, 817 (1949).
Rall, T. W., Sutherland, E. W. and Berthet, J. *J. Biol. Chem.* **224**, 463 (1957).
Rall, T. W., Sutherland, E. W. and Wosilait, W. D. *J. Biol. Chem.* **218**, 483 (1956).
Randle, P. J. and Smith, G. H. *Biochem. J.* **70**, 490, 501 (1958).
Robbins, P. W., Traut, R. R. and Lipmann, F. *Proc. Nat. Acad. Sci.* **45**, 6 (1959).
Roberts, P. J. P. and Whelan, W. J. *Biochem. J.* **76**, 246 (1960).
Schoenheimer, R. *Z. physiol. Chem.* **182**, 148 (1929).
Seifter, S., Dayton, S., Novic, B. and Muntwyler, E. *Arch. Biochem.* **25**, 191 (1950).
Slein, M. W., Cori, G. T. and Cori, C. F. *J. Biol. Chem.* **186**, 763 (1950).
Staub, A., Sinn, L. and Behrens, O. K. *J. Biol. Chem.* **214**, 619 (1955).
Staudinger, H. J., *Makromol. Chem.* **64**, 2349 (1942).
Staudinger, H. J. *Makromol. Chem.* **2**, 88 (1948).
Steiner, D. F. and Williams, R. H. *J. Biol. Chem.* **234**, 1342 (1959).
Stetten, M. R., Katzen, H. M., and Stetten, D. *J. Biol. Chem.* **222**, 587 (1956).
Stetten, M. R., Katzen, H. M., and Stetten, D. *J. Biol. Chem.* **232**, 475 (1958).
Sulkin, N. M. *J. Neurochemistry* **5**, 231 (1960).
Sumner, J. B. and Howell, S. F. *J. Biol. Chem.* **115**, 583 (1936).
Sumner, J. B. and O'Kane, D. J. *Enzymol.* **12**, 251 (1948).

Sutherland, E. W., Colowick, S. P. and Cori, C. F. *J. Biol. Chem.* **140,** 309 (1941).

Sutherland, E. W. and Rall, T. W. *J. Amer. Chem. Soc.* **79,** 3608 (1957).

Sutherland, E. W. and Wosilait, W. D. *J. Biol. Chem.* **218,** 459 (1956).

Swanson, M. A. and Cori, C. F. *J. Biol. Chem.* **172,** 815 (1948).

Velick, S. F. and Wicks, L. F. *J. Biol. Chem.* **190,** 741 (1951).

Vestling, C. S., Mylroif, A. K., Irish, U. and Grant, N. H. *J. Biol. Chem.* **185,** 789 (1950).

Villar-Palasi, C. and Larner, J. *Arch. Biochem. Biophys.* **86,** 61 (1960).

Walker, G. J. and Whelan, W. J. *Biochem. J.* **67,** 548 (1957).

Walker, G. J. and Whelan, W. J. *Biochem. J.* **76,** 257, 264 (1960).

Whelan, W. J. and Roberts, P. J. P. *Nature,* **170,** 748 (1952).

Whelan, W. J. and Roberts, P. J. P. *J.* 1298 (1953).

Wolfrom, M. L., Lassettre, E. N. and O'Neill, A. N. *J. Amer. Chem. Soc.* **73,** 595 (1951).

Wolfrom, M. L. and Thompson, A. *J. Amer. Chem. Soc.* **79,** 4212 (1957).

Wosilait, W. D., and Sutherland, E. W. *J. Biol. Chem.* **218,** 469 (1956).

Yim, R., MacLaughlin, J. and Bessman, S. P. *Amer. J. Diseases Children* **96,** 549 (1958).

Yunis, A. A., Fischer, E. H. and Krebs, E. G. *J. Biol. Chem.* **234,** 3163 (1960).

Chapter 2

HYALURONIC ACID

Occurrence

HYALURONIC acid is a sulphate-free polysaccharide containing equimolar proportions of N-acetyl D-glucosamine and D-glucuronic acid residues and is widely distributed throughout the tissues of animals and humans. Hyaluronic acid was first isolated from bovine vitreous humour by Meyer and Palmer (1934). Further investigation revealed its presence in human umbilical cord (Meyer and Palmer, 1936a), bovine aqueous humour and the vitreous humour of pig eyes (Meyer and Palmer, 1936b). Other sources of the polysaccharide were bovine and human synovial fluid (Meyer, Smyth and Dawson, 1939), a human mesothelioma (Meyer and Chaffee, 1940), two cases of human synovioma (Meyer, 1947), the Rous and Fujinami tumours of chicken (Pirie, 1942) and a filterable fowl tumour (Kabat, 1939). Its presence in pig skin (Meyer and Chaffee, 1941), calf skin (Meyer and Rapport, 1952), cock's comb (Boas, 1949), several pathological human sera (Deutsch and Morton, 1956) and in proteolytic digests or normal human plasma (Schiller and Dewey, 1956) has also been reported. Hyaluronic acid is also a minor component of the polysaccharides present in growing bone, the lower ends of the long bones of calf, containing shaft and cancellous bone, cartilage and the epiphyses (Meyer, 1957).

Function

Hyaluronic acid is one of the constituents of ground substance. Meyer (1947) has ascribed to hyaluronic acid the functions of binding water in interstitial spaces, holding cells together in a jelly-like matrix and serving as a lubricant and shock-absorber in joints. He believes (Meyer, 1957) that hyaluronic acid is sited in the interfibrillar spaces where, according to Day (1952), it forms the waterproofing of the fabric.

Fessler (1960) has investigated the contribution of hyaluronic acid to the structure of Wharton's jelly of human umbilical cord. He showed that a combined structure of hyaluronic acid, water and collagen fibres could be made which had a definite resistance to compression.

Methods of Isolation

(a) Protein–hyaluronic acid complexes

Ogston and Stanier (1950) isolated the hyaluronic acid complex from ox synovial fluid by a filtration process. In one version of this (Ogston and

37

Stanier, 1953), the ox synovial fluid was cleared by centrifuging, dialysed against a $NaCl$—KH_2PO_4—Na_2HPO_4 buffer (pH 7·3) and then filtered through sintered glass (average pore diameter 1 to 1·5 μ). Repeated re-solution in water or 0·2M-$NaCl$ followed by re-filtration ensured complete removal of free protein. A more detailed account of this method (Blumberg and Ogston, 1957a) recommends that the initial centrifugation be accomplished at 73000 g for 30 min in a Spinco Model L ultracentrifuge. The initial dialysis was dispensed with and the phosphate buffer used for washing the complex on the sintered glass filter. The final stage of purification involved ultracentrifugation of the re-dissolved complex at 105000 g for 180 min followed by dialysis.

Cetylpyridinium chloride has been used by Scott (1955) as a precipitant for acidic mucopolysaccharides. Blumberg and Ogston (1957b) in using this reagent added cetylpyridinium chloride (0·5% in water) slowly to ox synovial fluid which had been previously dialysed against water for 1–2 days. When the clot formation produced was complete, the clot was washed thoroughly with water and redissolved in a methanol-saturated sodium chloride–water mixture (10:33:57). After absorption of the excess detergent on Fuller's earth and dialysis against a suitable buffer, final isolation in a pure form of the hyaluronic acid–protein complex was achieved by ultracentrifugation at 73000 g for 45 min.

Ogston and Sherman (1958) have used an electrodialysis apparatus to accomplish the removal of free protein from ox synovial fluid.

The apparatus consisted of three cylindrical chambers (diameter 3 cm). The two end chambers contained circular platinum electrodes and were separated from the central chamber by 'Millipore' HA membranes of pore diameter 0·4 μ. The transfer of electrode products to this central compartment was prevented by a carefully directed flow of fresh buffer through the two end chambers. Electrodialysis in the cold room (at 2°C) using 0·025M-phosphate buffer pH 7·0 and a current of about 37 ma effected the removal of free protein in 22 hours.

The protein contents of the hyaluronic acid complexes obtained by the filtration, cetylpyridinium chloride and electrodialysis methods were 25·7%, 23·3–29·8% and 30% respectively. Ogston and Sherman (1959) found that trypsin and chymotrypsin together can remove 65% of the protein from the complex without any loss of viscosity by the complex. This suggested that the protein, or a considerable part of it, was not important in determining the physico-chemical properties of hyaluronic acid in solution. Papain, too has a proteolytic activity on the complex but appears, as a reducing agent, to cause more general degradation as well. A most interesting observation was that ethylenediaminetetraacetic acid (EDTA) aided the degradation of the hyaluronic acid complex. Its use therefore in the preparation of hyaluronic acid from tissues is most undesirable. Balazs and Sundblad (1959) have confirmed the effect of

EDTA on hyaluronic acid and have further shown that protein content has no influence on the anomalous viscosity index or intrinisic viscosity of hyaluronic acid solutions. Indeed protein-free ($< 1\%$) hyaluronic acid showed the same viscosity characteristics as hyaluronic acid containing up to 30% protein or as the original tissue fluid, provided no degradation of hyaluronic acid occurred. Such results appear to exclude proteolysis as a cause of the pathological changes in the viscous behaviour of synovial fluid hyaluronic acid, as postulated by Blumberg and Ogston (1958).

Native hyaluronic acid in acid solution precipitates with protein in a fibrous clot (Blix and Snellman, 1945). The state of the hyaluronic acid in various preparations can be judged by observing the nature of the clot (Ropes and Bauer, 1953) and these have been graded as group I, firm ropy clot with complete clearing of the supernatant solution; group II, clot formed, but not so firm as in group I, wispy edges to the clot, incomplete clearing of the supernatant; group III, no clot but a dispersed white precipitate. Group I clots were given by whole ox synovial fluid and with the hyaluronic acid complexes obtained by the use of cetylpyridinium chloride or filtration. The protein present in the hyaluronic acid complex of ox synovial fluid is believed to be mainly an α-globulin (Curtain, 1955).

Hamerman and Sandson (1960) have utilized zone electrophoresis to isolate hyaluronate from small quantities of normal human synovial fluid. The weight ratio protein/hyaluronate in the isolated products was $0 \cdot 02 – 0 \cdot 12$. Two samples were found to form a precipitin line against anti γ-globulin. After injection into rabbits, antibodies to α_2-globulin as well as γ-globulin were detected by the tanned cell haemagglutination technique.

(b) Hyaluronic acid

A discussion on the isolation of hyaluronic acid is given in the paper by Kaye and Stacey (1951).

Isolation of free hyaluronic acid from fluids (vitreous humour, synovial fluid, etc.) or tissues (umbilical cord) has been widely accomplished using the successive procedures of mucin clot formation, deproteinization and fractional precipitation. With most fluids clot formation is achieved simply by dilution with 2–5 volumes of water and acidification to pH 4 with 50% acetic acid. Such precipitation may be incomplete where vitreous humour is used as the source unless the protein present is supplemented by addition of horse or cattle serum (Meyer, 1947). After standing at 0° for 24 hr the clot is washed with cold water and extracted with 5–10% sodium, potassium or calcium acetate.

When proceeding from solid tissues these are generally ground, dried with acetone and the resultant powder extracted with 5–10% sodium acetate. Acidification to pH 4 followed by precipitation with $1 \cdot 5$ volumes of ethanol and resolution in acetate gives an extract which can be treated thereafter by a procedure similar to that used with the extract from e.g. synovial fluid.

Most of the protein can be removed from these extracts by repeated partition with chloroform-amyl alcohol. Alternatively protein can be removed by digestion with pepsin at pH 1·5 and with trypsin at pH 7·5 (Grossfeld, Meyer, Godman and Linker, 1957). Addition of 10% zinc acetate and neutralization to pH 7·2 yields a precipitate of zinc hydroxide on which further impurities are absorbed. The crude hyaluronic acid is recovered from the supernatant by precipitation with alcohol.

The remaining problem is mainly to free the hyaluronic acid from other polysaccharide impurities. Glycogen can be removed by digestion with α-amylase and subsequent dialysis. Separation from chondroitin sulphate etc., is accomplished by fractional precipitation with alcohol of a solution of the polysaccharides in 10% calcium acetate or chloride (Meyer, Davidson, Linker and Hoffman, 1956). Salting out in the presence of pyridine has also been used to purify hyaluronic acid (Hadidian and Pirie, 1948; Alburn and Williams, 1950; Jeanloz and Forchielli, 1950).

In an attempt to provide a more rapid method of isolation, Cifonelli and Mayeda (1957) have utilized the observations of other workers that charcoal strongly absorbs proteins and nucleic acids but is a weak adsorbent for highly charged molecules and neutral polysaccharides. Pads of Darco G-60 and cellulose powder (equal weights) were used to filter suitable 0·15M-saline extracts of human umbilical cords. Absorption of the hyaluronate on the charcoal was minimized by the prior addition of one-tenth volume of ethanol. Dialysis of the eluate, Seitz filtration and precipitation with four volumes of ethanol yielded hyaluronic acid in a yield of 3·5–4%. From certain sources where absorption at 280 mμ still persisted in the hyaluronic acid preparation further purification was accomplished by passage of a solution of the crude hyaluronic acid down a column of Dowex 1, chloride (220–400 mesh, 2% cross-linked). The hyaluronic acid was subsequently eluted from the resin, having suffered little apparent degradation, by washing with 2M-NaCl. Markowitz, Cifonelli and Dorfman (1958) have also reported the removal of ultraviolet absorbing material from hyaluronic acid preparations by passage down a column of Norite A-20% stearic acid. The hyaluronic acid was then precipitated from solution as its cetylpyridinium chloride complex. Recovery was achieved by extraction of the washed complex with methanol and precipitation of the hyaluronic acid with one volume of glacial acetic acid. Laurent (1957) has described an interesting method for the separation of hyaluronic acid from chondroitin sulphate based on an observation by Scott (1956). Chondroitin sulphate was precipitated with an excess of cetylpyridinium chloride (in which the hyaluronic complex redissolves) and was removed by centrifugation. The hyaluronic acid fraction is precipitated from the supernatant by 70% ethanol, dissolved in distilled water and re-precipitated with cetylpyridinium chloride. To convert to the sodium salt it is redissolved in 0·4M-sodium chloride, reprecipitated with 70% ethanol, dialysed, centrifuged and lyophilized. The successful separation of the hyaluronic acid from bovine vitreous body into fractions with molecular weights ranging from $7·7 \times 10^4$ to $1·7 \times 10^6$ has been reported by Laurent, Ryan and Pietruskiewicz (1960).

The hyaluronic acid was isolated as cetylpyridinium hyaluronate which was redissolved in 2M-sodium chloride. Cetylpyridinium chloride and protein impurities were removed by addition of Micro-cel E (Johns Manville Co.) and the dialysed sodium hyaluronate precipitated by the addition of three volumes of ethanol. Fractionation was accomplished by mixing cetylpyridinium chloride (1·77 g in 0·25N-Na₂SO₄ [50 ml.]) with sodium hyaluronate (1·24 g) dissolved in 205 ml. of the same medium. The first fraction was collected by centrifugation of the turbid solution at 75000 xg and thereafter the precipitates formed by progressive dilution to sodium sulphate concentrations of 0·190, 0·174, 0·165, 0·155, 0·130, and 0·060N were recovered.

Ringertz and Reichard (1959) have demonstrated that mucopolysaccharides of differing types can be separated on columns of Ecteola cellulose (Peterson and Sober, 1956) washed with 0·5M NaOH, 3M NaCl and 0·1M NaCl—HCl (1:1). After adsorbing the polysaccharides onto the column they were eluted in the order hyaluronic acid first, chondroitin sulphate A and β-heparin together and finally heparin by washing the column with increasing concentrations of chloride from 0·1–2·5M. Under such conditions heparin could be recovered with full retention of its anticoagulant activity. The elution of the polysaccharides was detected by the carbazole method (Dische, 1947).

Determination of Hyaluronic Acid

(a) Turbidimetric method

This method, applicable either to the determination of hyaluronic acid or hyaluronidase, was developed by Seastone (1943) and by Kass and Seastone (1944). It depends on the observation that undegraded hyaluronate at pH 4·2 gives a fairly stable colloidal suspension with dilute serum which can be determined turbidimetrically. The turbidity read at 580 mμ is proportional to hyaluronic acid concentration only over a narrow range. The application of this method is not always straightforward (Meyer, 1947). Most pathological fluids and normal vitreous humour precipitate as a stable turbidity but normal human and cattle synovial fluid are precipitated as a coherent fibrous clot. Meyer (1947) recommends that these normal fluids be first incubated with 0·01 units of hyaluronidase. This amount of enzyme is too little to decrease the apparent hyaluronate concentration but prevents clot formation and allows the hyaluronic acid to be determined turbidimetrically. Later workers (Grossfield, Meyer and Godman, 1955) recommend prior incubation with 0·02 units of testicular hyaluronidase.

(b) *Chemical method*

This depends on the determination of the hexosamine present in hyaluronic acid and is applicable to the determination of hyaluronic acid in those normal fluids (e.g. vitreous humour) where this is the only hexosamine-containing polysaccharide present and where the protein concentration is very low and so contributes very little to the total hexosamine content. It has been used by Meyer, Smyth and Gallardo (1938) for the determination of the hyaluronic acid content of the ocular fluids from various species. The hyaluronic acid content of the vitreous humour varied from 9 mg per cent in the eye of the cat to about 48 mg per cent in cattle eyes.

(c) *Refractive index*

Blumberg, Ogston, Lowther, and Rogers (1958) have determined the specific refractive increment of protein-free hyaluronate obtained from *Streptococcus haemolyticus*. The value obtained, $1·44 \times 10^{-3}$ at 546 mμ, is close to that ($1·49 \times 10^{-3}$ at 546 mμ) of dextran recorded by Ogston and Woods (1954) but differs markedly from the values obtained by Blumberg and Oster (1954) [$1·8 \times 10^{-3}$ at 546 mμ] and by Laurent and Gergely (1955) [$1·7 \times 10^{-3}$ at 436 mμ]. The specific refractive increment is useful for determining the concentration of protein-free hyaluronic acid by measurement of the area of its boundary diagram in the ultracentrifuge.

Detection in Tissues

There has been much confusion among histochemists as to whether or not hyaluronic acid is PAS-(periodic acid–Schiff's reagent) positive (see Hale, 1957). From its postulated structure (Meyer, 1957) periodate would be expected to leave intact the N-acetylglucosamine residues, since these are linked through the 3-position, but would attack the glucuronic acid residues between positions 2 and 3 since these are linked through the 4-position. Three different groups of workers (Meyer, Fellig and Fischer, 1951; Blix, 1951; Jeanloz and Forchielli, 1951b) reported failure to oxidize hyaluronic acid by periodate. Although there is a need for reinvestigation of this problem one explanation could be that the acid conditions of the PAS test would favour the formation of a 3:6-lactone ring in the glucuronic acid residues thus rendering them immune to periodate attack.

Since its introduction into histochemistry (Manozzi-Torini, 1942), hyaluronidase has been used by numerous workers (e.g. Madinaveitia and Stacey, 1944). The specificity of various hyaluronidases is seen in

Table 2.I and suggests that the bacterial (streptococcal and pneumococcal) hyaluronidases are most specific for hyaluronic acid. Bunting (1950) reported that streptococcal hyaluronidase (18 hr incubation at 37°; 15 TRU/ml. 0·3% NaCl) removed metachromatic substance from acid mucopolysaccharides devoid of sulphate but failed to remove it where acid mucopolysaccharides containing sulphate were known to exist.

Table 2.I   Specificity of hyaluronidases

Substrate	Hyaluronidase from		
	Testes	Streptococcus	Pneumococcus
Hyaluronic acid	+	+	+
Chondroitin sulphate A	+	−	−
,, ,, B	−	−	−
,, ,, C	+	−	−
Heparitin sulphate	−	−	−

Substrate	Enzymes from flavobacterium:		
	Unadapted	Heparin-adapted	Chondroitin sulphate B adapted
Hyaluronic acid	+	+	+
Chondroitin sulphate A	+	+	+
,, ,, B			+
,, ,, C	+	+	+
Heparitin sulphate	−	+	
Heparin	−	+	

Hyaluronic acid in a concentration of 1% shows, in smears, typical metachromatic staining with toluidine blue (Meyer, 1947). This pheno-menon of metachromasia is encountered when a dye of a certain colour reacts with a substance to produce a dye complex with a colour different from that of the original dye. Although sulphated polysaccharides exhibit metachromasia to a much greater degree than hyaluronic acid, Sylvén and Malmgren (1952) could detect hyaluronic acid by this method in dried smears of fresh synovial, vitreous and aqueous humours. These authors suggested that an average hyaluronic acid concentration of at least 1·8% of the dry weight was required and therefore this method is a very insensitive one for the detection of hyaluronate in tissues.

Molecular Weight and Shape

Ox synovial fluid

Blix and Snellman (1945) who used mucin clot precipitation, removal of protein by Sevag separation and ethanol precipitation to prepare hyaluronic acid from ox synovial fluid, deduced a particle length of 4000–5000 Å and a molecular weight of 0.3×10^6 from streaming birefringence studies. The shape of the hyaluronic acid was believed to be that of a long asymmetric molecule. The hyaluronic acid-protein complex isolated by filtration of ox synovial fluid had a molecular weight of 10×10^6 (Ogston and Stanier, 1951) which on conversion to the free hyaluronic acid by papain digestion fell to 2×10^6 (Blumberg and Ogston, 1957a). Ogston and his co-workers deduced a random coil structure for hyaluronic acid from sedimentation, viscosity and streaming birefringence studies. Laurent (1957) found by light scattering measurements a molecular weight of 1.6×10^6 for hyaluronic acid isolated via precipitation as its cetylpyridinium complex. Values for the intrinsic viscosity $[\eta]_c$ of the above hyaluronic acid preparations varied from the order of 10 to 55, c being in g/100 ml.

Human synovial fluid

Examination of untreated human synovial fluid by sedimentation studies in an ultracentrifuge and viscosity measurements (Fessler, Ogston and Stanier, 1954; Johnston, 1955) indicated a random coil configuration for the hyaluronic acid present, molecular weights in the range 1.2–8.4×10^6 and intrinsic viscosities from 13–36.

Human umbilical cord

Except for the early value (0.5×10^6) of Blix and Snellman (1945) there is general agreement among recent workers that protein-free hyaluronic acid isolated from this source has a molecular weight in the range 2.8–8×10^6. Individual values deduced by light scattering measurements are 8×10^6 (prepared by proteolysis and ethanol precipitation; Blumberg and Oster, 1954), 2.8–4.3×10^6 (protein removed by Sevag separation, Laurent and Gergely, 1955) and 3.4×10^6 (Laurent, 1957) using the original method of Blix and Snellman (1945). Two other preparations obtained by Laurent (1957) using cetylpyridinium chloride precipitation had molecular weights of 3.0×10^6 and 5.8×10^6. Values for $[\eta]_c$ ranged from 9–33.6. Laurent (1957) believed that the different shapes deduced by the above workers could all be explained by a highly solvated coil structure which was easily deformed by a shearing force applied to an asymmetric particle.

Blumberg and Ogston (1958) have pointed out that the mutual repulsion between the ionized carboxylic groups in hyaluronic acid would cause an expansion and stiffening of the coil especially at low ionic strength. This, they believed, was reflected in the rapid increase of viscosity as the ionic strength was reduced below 0·1. Above an ionic strength of 0·2 where there was little dependence of viscosity on ionic strength this mutual repulsion was largely eliminated.

Vitreous humour

Most workers (Blix and Snellman, 1945; Laurent, 1955; Varga, 1955; Rowen, Brunish and Bishop, 1956) have found much lower values (0·2–1·3 × 10⁶) for the molecular weight of hyaluronic acid isolated from vitreous humour and this is probably because of the presence of some depolymerizing system. Blumberg and Ogston (1957 b) recommend injection of ethylene diamine tetraacetic acid into the eye shortly before death to prevent oxidative depolymerization of the hyaluronic acid by the copper ion-ascorbic acid system (Bárány and Woodin, 1955). The presence of hyaluronidase in the aqueous humour of cattle eyes has definitely been established (Meyer, 1947).

Structural Determination of Hyaluronic Acid

Analysis

Numerous determinations of the hexosamine and hexuronic acid contents of hyaluronic acid have indicated approximately equimolar proportions of these sugars. A polymer $(C_{14}O_{11}H_{21}N)_n$ with a N-acetylhexosamine-glucuronic acid repeating unit requires hexosamine, 47·2%, nitrogen, 3·7% and 11·6% CO_2 produced by decarboxylation of the hexuronic acid residues. Laurent (1957) in analyses of six preparations of hyaluronic acid from five different sources (human umbilical cord, ox vitreous humour and synovial fluid, cock's comb and pigskin) found total hexosamine, 41·7–44·5%, nitrogen, 4·1–4·6% and 11·2–11·9% CO_2. Individual analyses for hexosamine by separation on an ion exchange resin (Gardell, 1953) revealed that most of the total hexosamine was glucosamine as expected, but small amounts (0–3·1%) of galactosamine were also present depending on the source and method of purification. This galactosamine probably arose from some polysaccharide impurity. The high nitrogen values indicate that small amounts of protein still probably remained in the hyaluronic acid preparations. Cifonelli and Mayeda (1957) reporting analyses of hyaluronic acid samples prepared by the charcoal method and quoting values as ratios with the nitrogen value as 1·00 found uronic acid; hexosamine equivalents of 1·08; 0·91 for hyaluronic acid from bovine vitreous humour and 0·96; 0·85 and 1·05; 0·95 for two preparations from human umbilical cord. Ogston and Stanier (1953) found 30·6 g glucosamine (as N-acetyl glucosamine) and 35·9 g glucuronic acid per 100 g of hyaluronic acid–protein complex from synovial fluid. There appears from the above results to be a general trend to low glucosamine: glucuronic acid ratios contrary to the early findings of Meyer, Smyth and Dawson (1939). The six preparations of hyaluronic acid from synovial fluid made by these authors showed acetyl, 9·4–10·6%; uronic acid, 35·9–50·7%; hexosamine, 34·5–43·7% and nitrogen, 3·00–3·69%. Their optical rotations varied between −68·8° and −78·2°.

Infrared Spectrum

Orr and Harris (1952) from the infrared spectrum of the free acid (hyaluronic acid) have confirmed the presence of unionized carboxyl groups (1735 cm^{-1}) and a mono-substituted amide (1648 and 1560 cm^{-1}). The absence of absorption at 1735 cm^{-1} in the spectrum of the sodium salt showed that O-acetyl groups were absent.

Acid Hydrolysis Products

Meyer and Palmer (1936a) isolated crystalline D-glucosamine hydrochloride from acid hydrolysates (6 hr with 18% HCl in the presence of SnCl$_2$) of the hyaluronic acids from vitreous humour and umbilical cords. The D-glucosamine hydrochloride was identified by its equilibrium optical rotation ([α]$_D$ + 78·5°), and by conversion to D-glucosazone (m.p. 210°). D-glucosamine hydrochloride was also obtained in a similar manner by Meyer, Smyth and Dawson (1939) from synovial fluid hyaluronic acid. The identity of the hexosamine present in hyaluronic acid has also been established by ninhydrin degradation to arabinose (Stoffyn and Jeanloz, 1954). Oxidative hydrolysis (nitric acid) of the hyaluronic acids from vitreous humour and umbilical cord yielded crystalline potassium hydrogen saccharate (Meyer and Palmer, 1936a). The suspicion that this arose from D-glucuronic acid was confirmed by Meyer, Smyth and Dawson (1939) through the isolation of glucuronic acid thiosemicarbazone (m.p. 223–224°) from an enzymic hydrolysate (obtained using Type II *Pneumococcus* hyaluronidase) of synovial fluid hyaluronic acid.

Rapport, Weissmann, Linker and Meyer (1951) hydrolysed hyaluronic acid with testicular hyaluronidase and after discarding the precipitate obtained on addition of 2 volumes of ethanol the residual oligosaccharides were then hydrolysed with N-H$_2$SO$_4$ at 99° for 3 hr. Fractional crystallization of the products by addition of 1·0N-sodium carbonate to a 0·2N-hydrochloric acid solution yielded a crystalline disaccharide (overall yield as high as 61%) designated as hyalobiuronic acid having C, 40·01; H, 6·02; N, 3·99; hexosamine, 49·0; uronic acid, 54·3 and showing [α]$_D^{24}$ −31° in 0·1N-HCl. Its R$_F$ in butanol, acetic acid, water (38:12:50) was 0·13 compared with 0·29 for glucosamine and 0·43 for N-acetylglucosamine. The fact that hyalobiuronic acid reacted directly with the Elson–Morgan reagents suggested that it was a glucuronosyl-glucosamine. The remaining structural details of hyalobiuronic acid (see Fig. 2.1) have been established by the work of Weissmann and Meyer (1952) who also succeeded in obtaining the disaccharide, albeit in somewhat lower yield, by direct acid hydrolysis of umbilical cord hyaluronic acid. Treatment of hyalobiuronic

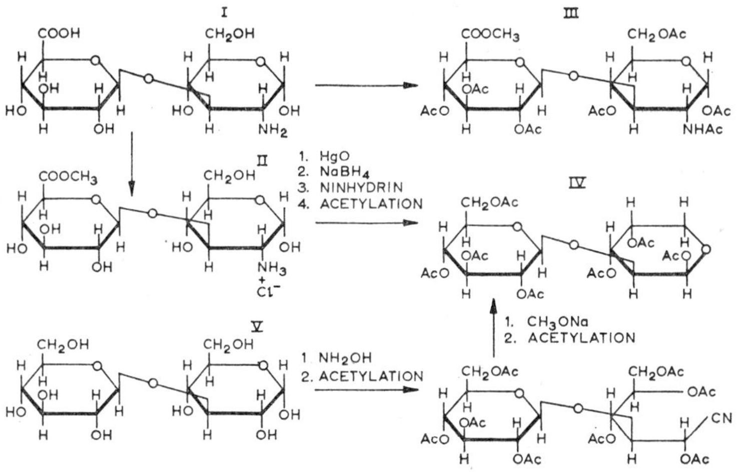

Fig. 2.1

acid (I) with cold methanolic hydrogen chloride gave a methyl ester hydrochloride (II) which when acetylated afforded a crystalline heptaacetyl-glucuronosyl-glucosamine methyl ester (III) [m.p. 120°, $[\alpha]_D^{22} + 25°$ in CHCl₃] containing one ethanol of crystallization. The same compound (III) could be obtained from hyalobiuronic acid by N-acetylation using ketene followed by treatment with cold methanolic hydrogen chloride and acetylating reagents as above. The methyl ester hydrochloride II could be degraded by the sequence of reactions illustrated to a glucosyl-arabinose whose hepta-acetate (IV) showed no depression of melting point on admixture with the hepta-acetate of 2-O-β-D-glucopyranosyl D-arabinose derived from laminaribiose (V) (3-O-β-D-glucopyranosyl-D-glucose). This established hyalobiuronic acid as 3-O-β-D-glucopyranuronosyl D-glucosamine (I).

Enzymic Hydrolysis

(a) Bacterial hyaluronidases

Pneumococcal hyaluronidase hydrolyses only glucosaminidic linkages in hyaluronic acid (Rapport, Linker and Meyer, 1951) to afford a product which has the reducing power of a disaccharide. Linker and Meyer (1954)

5

found that the disaccharide ([α]ᴅ − 20·0°) contained 42·3% hexosamine which was isolated as ᴅ-glucosamine hydrochloride in 74% yield and further characterized by preparation of its carbobenzoxy derivative. Its uronic acid content was 44·8% when determined by decarboxylation, but the disaccharide (I; see Fig. 2.2) did not contain glucuronic acid as such

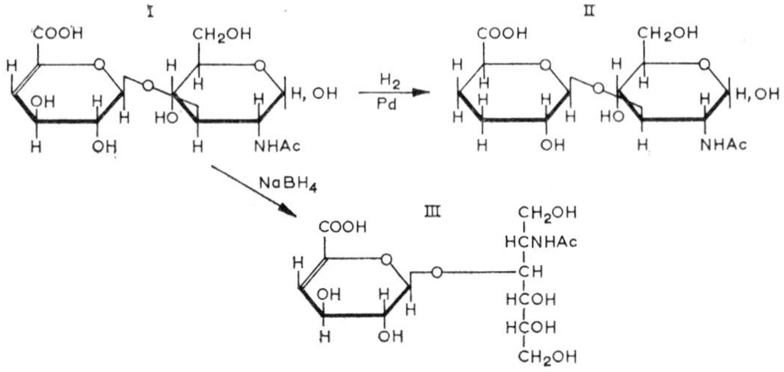

Fig. 2.2

since it consumed one mole of bromine and showed an absorption maximum at 230 mμ typical of αβ-unsaturated carbonyls. This was confirmed by ozonolysis of the disaccharide which yielded oxalic acid revealing the presence of a double bond in the 4:5 position of the uronic acid moiety. The disaccharide treated with acetic anhydride and pyridine yielded a crystalline hexaacetate (m.p. 190–192°) as would be expected from a structure such as I (see Fig. 2.2). Reduction of the disaccharide either with PtO/H_2 at room temperature or with Pd/charcoal/H_2 consumed approx. 2 moles of hydrogen/mole of disaccharide. This was explained by a conversion to II (Fig. 2.2) in which the unexpected second mole of hydrogen was used for the hydrogenolysis of the allylic hydroxyl group (carbon 3 of the uronic acid) yielding a disaccharide containing a 3:4-dideoxyuronic acid (Linker, Meyer and Hoffman, 1956). The palladium catalysed hydrogenated compound II had a reducing power either with ferricyanide or with hypoiodite equivalent to ca. 50% that of glucose as expected for a reducing disaccharide. It was now resistant to decarboxylation as evinced by uronic acid (CO_2) determination ($< 1\%$) and did not afford a colour with carbazole. No absorption was detectable in the ultraviolet. The structure II (Fig. 2.2) was also supported by the conversion of II to a crystalline pentaacetate, m.p. 248–251°. Reduction of the bacterial disaccharide I with sodium borohydride in 0·1ᴍ-borate buffer pH 8·1 afforded a non-reducing disaccharide alcohol (III) which still consumed 1 mole of bromine and showed an ultraviolet absorption spectrum identical with that of I. Its uronic acid content was 42% when determined by a decarboxylation procedure and 50% when determined by the carbazole method. III consumed one mole of hydrogen per mole of compound when reduced with Pd/charcoal/H_2. The above evidence supports the tentative assignment of the structure I to the bacterial disaccharide; the sole evidence for the assignment of the glycosidic linkage as 1:3 is by analogy with the known structure of hyalobiuronic acid (see above) and the fact that the N-acetylglucosamine moiety had not been modified. Furthermore the bacterial hyaluronidases have not been observed to show transglycosidation (Meyer, 1957), suggesting that the glycosidic linkage in the disaccharide was not modified by enzymic hydrolysis. The appearance of unsaturation in positions 4:5 of the uronic acid suggested that the glucosaminidic bond in hyaluronic acid was β-1:4 (see later). The same unsaturated disaccharide has been isolated by the action of staphylococcal and streptococcal hyaluronidases on hyaluronic acid.

(b) Testicular hyaluronidase

The main product of the action of testicular hyaluronidase on hyaluronic acid is a tetrasaccharide IV (at least 80%; see Fig. 2.3) together with small

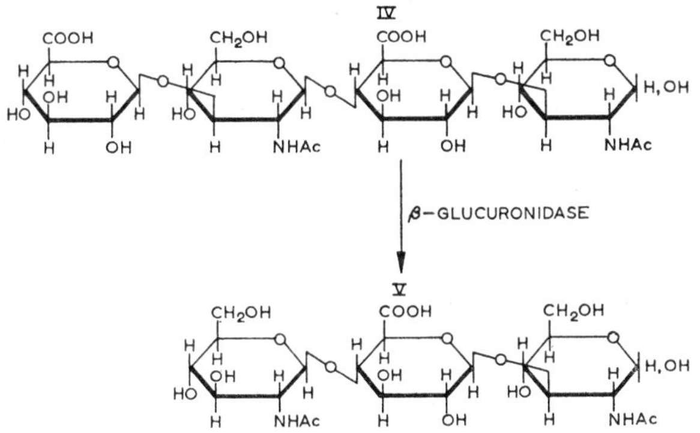

Fig. 2.3

amounts of N-acetyl hyalobiuronic acid (Weissmann, Meyer, Sampson and Linker, 1954). When incubated with pneumococcal hyaluronidase the tetrasaccharide gives equal amounts of N-acetyl hyalobiuronic acid and the unsaturated bacterial disaccharide I (Linker, Meyer and Hoffmann, 1956). The presence of glucuronosyl non-reducing terminal groups in the tetrasaccharide is indicated by the liberation of glucuronic acid when incubated with liver glucuronidase (Linker, Meyer and Weissmann, 1955). The resulting trisaccharide V has been methylated, the methyl ester group reduced with lithium aluminium hydride and the reduction product hydrolysed (Hoffmann and Meyer, 1957). The finding of 2:3-di-O-methyl glucose among the hydrolysis products establishes the glucosaminidic linkage in the trisaccharide, and also probably in hyaluronic acid, as through the 1:4 position. Some doubt must still exist regarding the glucosaminidic linkage in hyaluronic acid since testicular hyaluronidase has been found to exhibit transglycosidation properties (Hoffmann, Meyer and Linker, 1956).

The major product of the action of leech hyaluronidase on hyaluronic acid is a tetrasaccharide with the uronic acid at the free reducing end (Linker, Meyer and Hoffmann, 1960). This was deduced from the results of borohydride reduction and the conversion of the tetrasaccharide to a trisaccharide by β-glucosaminidase thus A–U–A–U → A + U–A–U (U, uronic acid; A, acetylhexosamine). The same tetrasaccharide was cleaved by treatment with lime water at room temperature to the trisaccharide U–A–U + anhydroacetyl-glucosamine. Hence leech hyaluronidase is an endoglucuronidase in contrast to the hyaluronidases of certain bacteria, snake venom and testis which are endohexosaminidases.

Periodate oxidation

Jeanloz and Forchielli (1951a) studied the periodate oxidation of methyl *N*-acetyl α-D-glucosaminide both at 25° with pH values between 2·3 and 6·8 and at 5° with pH values between 3·2 and 6·8. They concluded that oxidation at 5° and pH 4·5 in the dark eliminated side reactions and produced conditions under which the theoretical one mole of oxidant was consumed per mole of methyl *N*-acetyl α-D-glucosaminide. Under these conditions three hyaluronic acid preparations isolated by different methods from human umbilical cords but possessing the same purity consumed from 0·1–0·2 mole of periodate per repeating unit (i.e. 1 molecule of *N*-acetylglucosamine and 1 molecule of sodium glucuronate less 2 molecules of water) (Jeanloz and Forchielli, 1951b). A negligible amount of formic acid (0·08 mole) was liberated under these conditions. From these results the authors concluded that all structures in which the *N*-acetyl glucosamine residues are linked through the 6-position or in which the glucuronic acid residues are linked through position 2 or 4 can be eliminated. In our opinion only the former conclusion is valid since lactone formation might have occurred in the glucuronic acid residues at the acidic pH used for periodate oxidation. Meyer and Fellig (1950) obtained similar results for the periodate oxidation of undegraded hyaluronic acid. Hyaluronic acid reduced with potassium borohydride and submitted to periodate oxidation yields two moles of formaldehyde per end group oxidized. Molecular weights so obtained were very low (20–50,000) (Melby, Cyr, Unrau and Smith, 1960).

Tritylation

Treatment of hyaluronic acid in formamide with triphenylchloromethane in pyridine· gave a product which contained 0·95 trityl groups per disaccharide unit (Jeanloz and Forchielli, 1950). This indicated that it was highly improbable that the hydroxyl group in position 6 of the glucosamine moiety was involved in the linkage with glucuronic acid.

Methylation

Undegraded hyaluronic acid has proved extremely difficult to methylate. Kaye and Stacey (1951) succeeded however, in methylating umbilical cord mucin which had been depolymerized by dissolving in dilute potassium hydroxide, pH 8·5 and heating with barium carbonate for a few minutes and then after alcohol precipitation further degraded by heating for 6 hr with another aqueous suspension of barium carbonate at 80°. Several methylations of the depolymerized hyaluronic acid with dimethyl sulphate/35% sodium hydroxide in a two phase system of water and carbon tetrachloride followed by *N*-acetylation and further methylation with methyl iodide and silver oxide gave a product having OMe, 32·9% corresponding to *ca.* 4·2 methoxyl groups per disaccharide unit compared with the theoretical value of five methoxyl groups. Fractionation with chloroform/light petroleum (60–80°) yielded a fraction OMe, 33·7% which was subjected to methanolysis. This methanolysate was distilled *in vacuo* and the first distillate further methylated with methyl iodide/Ag₂O, re-esterified with diazomethane and treated with methanolic ammonia to yield crystalline methyl 2:3:4-tri-O-methyl α-D-glucuronoside acid amide. No amino sugar derivatives could be identified from the methylated hyaluronic acid, but Kaye and Stacey (1951) established that at least one-third of the glucuronic acid residues, and probably almost all, occupied positions other than those of non-reducing end groups. Methylation studies of hyaluronic acid have also been carried out by Meyer and Fellig (1950).

The combined evidence of the above workers establishes that hyaluronic acid is a polymer composed of alternate *N*-acetylglucosamine and D-glucuronic acid units linked β-glycosidically through positions 3 and 4 respectively.

Biosynthesis of Hyaluronic Acid

Analogy with previous syntheses of polysaccharides suggested that hyaluronic acid would be synthesized from substrates in which either *N*-acetyl glucosamine or glucuronic acid or both were bound glycosidically.

Compounds in this class include β-glucuronic acid 1-phosphate (Touster and Reynolds, 1952) and *N*-acetyl α-D-glucosamine 1-phosphate (Maley, Maley and Lardy, 1956) but the discovery of uridine nucleotides containing *N*-acetyl glucosamine (Cabib, Leloir and Cardini, 1953) and glucuronic acid (Dutton and Storey, 1954) and the demonstration that these could be used as glycosyl donors (Leloir and Cabib, 1953) has centred attention on this group as that most likely to provide the true substrate for the enzymic synthesis of hyaluronic acid.

Group A hemolytic streptococci have long been known to synthesize hyaluronic acid (Kendall, Heidelberger and Dawson, 1937) and have provided a convenient source of enzymes for the investigation of hyaluronic acid biosynthesis. Topper and Lipton (1953) showed that when the streptococci were cultured in the presence of glucose $1-C^{14}$ over 90% of the isotope contained in the glucosamine moieties of the hyaluronic acid resided in C_1. Independent studies by Roseman, Moses, Ludowieg and Dorfman (1953) confirmed these results and both groups interpreted these as an indication that the glucosamine moiety was derived directly from glucose without scission of the glucose molecule. Examination of the labelled hyaluronic acid obtained from the growth of the group A streptococci on glucose-6-C^{14} revealed that most of the C^{14} resided in C_6 of the glucuronic acid residues showing that these also arose from glucose without splitting the carbon chain (Roseman, Ludowieg, Moses and Dorfman, 1954). Other studies using $C^{14}N^{15}$-glucosamine have shown that glucosamine is incorporated into hyaluronic acid without previous deamination (Dorfman, Roseman, Moses, Ludowieg and Mayeda, 1955). Although growth on a medium containing carbonyl-labelled N-acetylglucosamine resulted in the incorporation of radioactivity in the acetyl group of hyaluronic acid it could not be concluded that N-acetylglucosamine was an intermediate in hyaluronic acid synthesis since the hemolytic streptococci were able to deacetylate N-acetylglucosamine and use the acetate for hyaluronic acid synthesis.

New impetus was given to these studies by the discovery of uridine diphosphoglucose, uridinediphospho-N-acetylglucosamine and uridinediphosphoglucuronic acid in extracts of group A streptococci (Cifonelli and Dorfman, 1957). Of particular interest was the discovery of one fraction which contained equimolar amounts of N-acetylhexosamine and uronic acid. Markowitz, Cifonelli and Dorfman (1958) using ^{3}H-labelled uridinediphosphoglucuronic acid and cell-free extracts of group A-streptococci have demonstrated that the glucuronic acid moiety can be incorporated into the hyaluronic acid in the presence of Mg^{++} and uridinediphospho N-acetylglucosamine and that this system also has a relative requirement for N-acetylglucosamine-1-phosphate and adenosine triphosphate. The inclusion of uridine triphosphate in the presence of N-acetylglucosamine 1-phosphate abolished the absolute requirement for uridinediphospho-N-acetylglucosamine. Uridinediphosphoglucuronic acid could likewise be replaced by diphosphopyridine nucleotide and uridinediphosphoglucose.

Progress in the elucidation of the mechanism of synthesis of hyaluronic acid in tissues has been less rapid although the work of Grossfeld, Meyer and Godman (1955) and Grossfeld, Meyer, Godman and Linker (1957) has established that hyaluronic acid can be produced in tissue culture. Production of hyaluronic acid by the synovial as well as by the periarticular tissues has also been studied in cultures by Hedberg and Moritz (1958). Yielding, Tomkins and Bunim (1957) using human synovial tissue have established that labelled hyaluronic acid may be synthesized from uniformly labelled glucose-C^{14} *in vitro*. Perhaps the most direct evidence that sugar nucleotides are involved in the synthesis of hyaluronic acid in tissues comes from the work of Glaser and Brown (1955), who demonstrated that Rous sarcoma* extracts brought about the incorporation of C^{14} into hyaluronic acid when uridinediphospho N-acetyl-glucosamine labelled in the acetyl group was used as a precursor. Strominger (1955) has reported the presence in oviducts of a uridinediphospho N-acetyl-glucosamine phosphate.

Pathological Conditions Involving Hyaluronic Acid

Deutsch (1957) has reported the presence of hyaluronic acid in the sera of two patients, one with a reticulum cell sarcoma, the other having a neuroblastoma.† In each case moving boundary electrophoresis in buffer pH 8·6 revealed the presence of a component having a mobility of $8·0 \times 10^{-5}$ cm^2 volt^{-1} sec^{-1} which constituted *ca.* 1·5% of the sera. This component was isolated from the non-dialysable serum components soluble in 50 per cent saturated $(NH_4)_2SO_4$ by electrophoretic separation and characterized as hyaluronic acid as follows. From electrophoretic mobility studies the component was shown to have a single species of acidic grouping with a pK near 2·6 close to that of a carboxyl group of the glucuronic acid type. Sulphate was absent and the failure of the material to show a positive mobility even at a very acidic pH indicated the absence of amino acids. Hydrolysis of the component with acid liberated *inter alia* glucosamine (34%) which was identified by paper chromatography and by ninhydrin degradation to arabinose. The ultraviolet absorption spectrum of the component showed no peak at either 280 or 260 mμ. When layered over acidified serum (pH 4·5) marked precipitation was observed. The precipitating ability of the component was destroyed by prior incubation with testicular hyaluronidase. No hyaluronic acid was found in sera of rats with Flexner-Jobling or Walker 256 carcinomas, Jensen sarcoma or azo dye hepatoma. Similar negative results were obtained in examination of ascites fluid and sera of mice with Ehrlich's ascites cell tumours or with carcinoma

---

* A tumour composed of embryonic connective tissue.

† A neuroblast is an embryonic nucleated cell from which the nerve fibres originate.

C755. Deutsch and Morton (1956) had earlier reported the presence of hyaluronic acid in several other pathological human sera.

Having previously isolated hyaluronic acid from the pleura and peritoneal fluid of a case of mesenthelioma (Meyer and Chaffee, 1940), Meyer and Stewart (quoted by Meyer, 1947) decided with a similar case to inject testicular hyaluronidase intraperitoneally to facilitate removal of a fluid of honey-like consistency. The viscosity of the fluid was lowered rapidly and was easily removed. After repeated injections and paracentesis the tumour did not seem to produce as much fluid as originally. Hyaluronic acid has been isolated from tumours in animals (Kabat, 1939; Pirie, 1942). In one case a chicken which had been injected with tumour virus particles developed a very large tumour in the right leg some ten weeks later. The polysaccharide isolated from the viscous fluid present in the tumour was identified as hyaluronic acid by its high negative optical rotation, sugar analysis, and susceptibility to pneumococcal hyaluronidase. Oxidative hydrolysis yielded crystalline potassium hydrogen saccharate. It is of interest that the polysaccharide showed no antigenic activity in rabbits. The polysaccharides isolated from Rous and Fujinami fowl tumours were sulphur free, contained uronic acid, hexosamine and acetyl moieties and were rapidly hydrolysed by testicular hyaluronidase. Warren, Williams, Alburn and Seifter (1949) have also reported the isolation of hyaluronic acid from Rous chicken sarcoma in a yield of 0·5 g/500 g of tumour tissue. Evidence has been presented (Warren, Horenstein and Gray, 1953) that the highly viscous component of the ascites mouse tumour MCIM is also hyaluronic acid.

Jensen (1954) has attempted to isolate hyaluronic acid from three ovarian cysts of the non-pseudomucinous type [Cystis simplex ovarii, Cystadenoma papilliferum ovarii and Cystadenoma serosum] and three of the pseudomucinous type [Cystadenoma pseudomucinosum ovarii I, Cystis pseudomucinosum ovarii II and Cystadenocarcinoma pseudomucinosum ovarii]. Hyaluronic acid (molecular weight $4·53$–$4·61 \times 10^5$) could only be isolated from the two pseudomucinous ovarian cysts I and II in yields of 42·9 mg/65 ml. fluid and 37·9 mg/98 ml. fluid respectively.

Maurer and Hudack (1952) have isolated a polysaccharide resembling hyaluronic acid from the callus tissue of healing rabbit fractures (7–9 day healing period). It had $[\alpha]_D - 95°$, contained 24·4% uronic acid, 23·6% hexosamine, 8·7% acetyl and only 0·3% sulphate and was attacked by pneumococcal hyaluronidase.

Ogston and Stanier (1953) have stressed the importance of the non-Newtonian viscosity of the hyaluronic acid complex in synovial fluid. They believed that it would endow a bearing structurally resembling the joints with the property of withstanding a pressure load nearly independent of its rate of movement over a considerable range. The changes of the volume of synovial fluid and of concentration of hyaluronic acid in it which occur in certain pathological conditions obviously affect the lubricant properties of the synovial fluid. Ragen and de la Mater (1942) reported a marked decrease in the viscosity of the fluid after injection of testicular hyaluronidase into the knee joints of patients with rheumatoid arthritis. The viscosity of the fluid returned to its original level after one week and no change was observed in the underlying disease. The concentration of hyaluronic acid in the knee synovial fluids of three patients with rheumatoid arthritis was 60, 132 and 206 mg per cent respectively (Meyer, 1947).

Johnston (1955) has compared the properties of normal and pathological (rheumatoid arthritis, acute trauma with large effusion) human synovial fluids from the point of view of viscosity, ultracentrifugal behaviour, mucin formation and hyaluronic acid molecular dimensions. He found that both the ultracentrifugal and viscosity behaviour was affected in abnormal fluids which had not lost the property of clot formation. A sensitive test of abnormality was to compare the extent of the viscosity anomaly of a fluid with its viscosity at a standard velocity gradient. Treatment of normal synovial fluid with hyaluronidase led to a steady decrease with time in the viscosity anomaly. The fluid passed through the range of the miscellaneous and rheumatoid arthritis fluids and finally showed less anomaly compared with its viscosity at a standard velocity gradient than any of the other fluids examined. Platt, Pigman and Holley (1959) have made an ultracentrifugal study of fifteen normal post-mortem human synovial fluids. All contained three major components: albumin, globulin and hyaluronic acid and six of the fluids contained additionally minor components with sedimentation constants ranging from 7·7 to 13·6S.

Ragan and Meyer (1949) suggested that the synovial fluid from patients with rheumatoid arthritis contained incompletely polymerized hyaluronic acid. An increased total amount of hyaluronate was also found.

Sunblad, Egelius and Jonsson (1954) have reported that local treatment of rheumatoid arthritis with hydrocortisone regularly resulted in the complete restoration to normal of the qualitative hyaluronic acid changes occurring in the joint fluids in this disease. The change in the degree of polymerization of the hyaluronic acid was manifested by a marked increase in both intrinsic viscosity and degree of flow anomalies. In a similar study reported earlier, Jessar, Ganzell and Ragan (1953) found an increase in viscosity and hyaluronic acid concentration (as determined by a turbidimetric method) after hydrocortisone treatment.

Ferrante (1957) reported that in patients with active untreated rheumatoid arthritis the daily urinary excretion of acid mucopolysaccharides (believed to be a mixture of hyaluronic acid and chondroitin sulphate) was higher than in normal individuals. After administration of sodium salicylate to these patients a decreased urinary excretion of acidic muco-polysaccharides was observed. In a comparison of three groups of patients (non-inflammatory, non-rheumatoid inflammatory and active rheumatoid) the acid mucopolysaccharide content of thrombocytes per unit of blood was significantly elevated in the inflammatory and rheumatoid groups (Kerby and Taylor, 1959). The polysaccharides were possibly a mixture of chondroitin sulphates B and C.

In connection with attempts to find the specific receptor substance of nerve and muscle which combines with quaternary ammonium com-pounds (e.g. acetylcholine, curare, etc.) when they produce their biological effects, Ehrenpreis and Kellock (1960) have investigated the interaction of some of these compounds with hyaluronic acid. While stilamidine was bound strongly to hyaluronic acid at pH 7·5, μ 0·1 no such binding was observed with curare (d-tubocurarine). This polysaccharide does not therefore appear essential for the pharmacological effects of curare on nerve impulse conduction. However, the curare-like compound, trieth-iodide of gallamine has been found associated with hyaluronic acid after *in vivo* injection.

REFERENCES

Alburn, H. E., and Williams, E. C. *Ann. N. Y. Acad. Sci.* **52,** 971 (1950).
Balazs, E. A., and Sundblad, L. *Acta. Soc. Med. Upsal.* **64,** 137 (1959).
Bàràny, E. H., and Woodin, A. M. *Acta physiol. Scand.* **33,** 257 (1955).
Blix, G. *Acta Chem. Scand.* **5,** 981 (1951).
Blix, G., and Snellman, O. *Arkiv. Kemi 19a,* No. 32 (1945).
Blumberg, B. S., and Ogston, A. G. *Biochem. J.* **66,** 342 (1957a).
Blumberg, B. S., and Ogston, A. G. *Biochem. J.* **68,** 183 (1957b).
Blumberg, B. S., and Ogston, A. G. *Chemistry and Biology of Mucopolysaccharides* p. 22 (1958).
Blumberg, B. S., Ogston, A. G., Lowther, D. A., and Rogers, H. J. *Biochem. J.* **70,** 1 (1958).
Blumberg, B. S., and Oster, G. *Science* **120,** 432 (1954).
Boas, N. F. *J. Biol. Chem.* **181,** 573 (1949).
Bunting, H. *Ann. N. Y. Acad. Sci.* **52,** 977 (1950).
Cabib, E., Leloir, L. F., and Cardini, C. E. *J. Biol. Chem.* **203,** 1055 (1953).
Cifonelli, J. A., and Dorfman, A. *J. Biol. Chem.* **228,** 547 (1957).
Cifonelli, J. A., and Mayeda, M. *Biochim. Biophys. Acta.* **24,** 397 (1957).
Curtain, C. C. *Biochem. J.* **61,** 688 (1955).
Day, T. D. *J. Physiol.* **117,** 1 (1952).
Deutsch, H. F. *J. Biol. Chem.* **224,** 767 (1957).
Deutsch, H. F., and Morton, J. I. *Fed. Proc.* **15,** 242 (1956).
Dische, Z. *J. Biol. Chem.* **167,** 189 (1947).
Dorfman, A., Roseman, S., Moses, F. E., Ludowieg, J., and Mayeda, M. *J. Biol. Chem.* **212,** 583 (1955).
Dutton, G. J., and Storey, I. D. E. *Boichem. J.* **57,** 275 (1954).
Ehrenpreis, S., and Kellock, M. G. *Biochim. Biophys. Acta.* **45,** 525 (1960).

Ferrante, N. *J. Clin. Invest.* **36**, 1516 (1957).
Fessler, J. H., Ogston, A. G., and Stanier, J. E. *Biochem. J.* **58**, 656 (1954).
Gardell, S. *Acta Chem. Scand.* **7**, 207 (1953).
Glaser, L., and Brown, D. *Proc. Nat. Acad. Sci.* **41**, 253 (1955).
Grossfeld, H., Meyer, K., and Godman, G. *Proc. Soc. Exp. Biol. Med.* **88**, 31 (1955).
Grossfeld, H., Meyer, K., Godman, G., and Linker, A. *J. Biophys. Biochem. Cytology* **3**, 391 (1957).
Hadidian, Z., and Pirie, N. W. *Biochem. J.* **42**, 260 (1948).
Hale, A. J. *Int. Rev. of Cytology* VI. 193 (1957).
Hamerman, D., and Sandson, J. *Nature* **188**, 1194 (1960).
Hedberg, H., and Moritz, U. *Proc. Soc. Exp. Biol. Med.* **98**, 80 (1958).
Hoffmann, P., and Meyer, K. *The Harvey Lectures* LI. 88 (1957).
Hoffmann, P., Meyer, K., and Linker, A. *J. Biol. Chem.* **219**, 653 (1956).
Jeanloz, R., and Forchielli, E. *J. Biol. Chem.* **186**, 495 (1950).
Jeanloz, R., and Forchielli, E. *J. Biol. Chem.* **188**, 361 (1951a).
Jeanloz, R., and Forchielli, E. *J. Biol. Chem.* **190**, 537 (1951b).
Jensen, C. E. *Acta pharmacol. et toxicol.* **10**, 83 (1954).
Jessar, R. A., Ganzell, M., and Ragan, C. *J. Clin. Invest.* **32**, 480 (1953).
Johnston, J. P. *Biochem. J.* **59**, 626 (1955): **59**, 633 (1955).
Kabat, E. A., *J. Biol. Chem.* **130**, 143 (1939).
Kass, E. H., and Seastone, C. V. *J. Exp. Med.* **79**, 319 (1944).
Kaye, M. A. G., and Stacey, M. *Biochem. J.* **48**, 249 (1951).
Kendall, F. E., Heidelberger, M., and Dawson, M. H. *J. Biol. Chem.* **118**, 61 (1937).
Kerby, G. P., and Taylor, S. M. *J. Clin. Invest.* **38**, 1059 (1959).
Laurent, T. C. *J. Biol. Chem.* **216**, 263 (1955).
Laurent, T. C. *Arkiv. för Kemi* **11**, (No. 54) 487 (1957).
Laurent, T. C., and Gergley, J. *J. Biol. Chem.* **212**, 325 (1955).
Laurent, T. C., Ryan, M., and Pietruskiewicz, A. *Biochim. Biophys. Acta.* **42**, 476 (1960).
Leloir, L. F., and Cabib, E. *J. Amer. Chem. Soc.* **75**, 5445 (1953).
Linker, A., Hoffman, P., Meyer, K., Sampson, P., and Korn, E. D. *J. Biol. Chem.*, **235**, 3061 (1960).
Linker, A., and Meyer, K. *Nature* **174**, 1192 (1954).
Linker, A., Meyer, K., and Hoffmann, P. *J. Biol. Chem.* **219**, 13 (1956).
Linker, A., Meyer, K., and Hoffmann, P. *J. Biol. Chem.* **235**, 924 (1960).
Linker, A., Meyer, K., and Weissmann, B. *J. Biol. Chem.* **213**, 237 (1955).
Madinaveitia, J., and Stacey, M. *Biochem. J.* **38**, 413 (1944).
Maley, F., Maley, G. F., and Lardy, H. A. *J. Amer. Chem. Soc.* **78**, 5303 (1956).
Manozzi-Torini, L. *Med. spar. Arch. ital.* **10**, 25 (1942).
Markowitz, A., Cifonelli, J. A., and Dorfman, A. *Biochim. Biophys. Acta.* **28**, 453 (1958).
Maurer, P. H., and Hudack, S. S. *Arch. Biochem. Biophys.* **38**, 49 (1952).
Melby, J. C., Cry, M., Unrau, A., and Smith, F. *Fed. Proc.*, **19**, 91 (1960).
Meyer, K. *Physiological Reviews* **27**, 335 (1947).
Meyer, K. *The Harvey Lectures LI*, 88 (1957).
Meyer, K., and Chaffee, E. *J. Biol. Chem.* **133**, 83 (1940).
Meyer, K., and Chaffee, E. *J. Biol. Chem.* **138**, 491 (1941).
Meyer, K., Davidson, E., Linker, A., and Hoffman, P. *Biochim. Biophys. Acta.* **21**, 506 (1956).
Meyer, K. H., and Fellig, J. *Experientia* **6**, 186 (1950).

58   HYALURONIC ACID

Meyer, K. H., Fellig, J., and Fischer, E. H. *Helv. Chim. Acta.* **34,** 939 (1951).
Meyer K., Godman, G., and Linker, A. J. *Biophys. Biochem. Cytology* **3,** 391 (1957).
Meyer, K., and Palmer, J. W. *J. Biol. Chem.* **107,** 629 (1934).
Meyer, K., and Palmer, J. W. *J. Biol. Chem.* **114,** 689 (1936a).
Meyer, K., and Palmer, J. W. *Am. J. Ophth.* **19,** 859 (1936b).
Meyer, K., and Rapport, M. M. *Science* (1952).
Meyer, K., Smyth, E. M., and Dawson, M. J. *J. Biol. Chem.* **128,** 319 (1939).
Meyer, K., Smyth, E. M., and Gallardo, E. *Am. J. Ophth.* **21,** 1083 (1938).
Meyer, K., and Stewart, quoted in *Physiol. Rev.* **27,** 335 (1947).
Ogston, A. G., and Sherman, T. F. *Biochem. J.,* **72,** 301 (1959).
Ogston, A. G., and Sherman, T. F. *Nature* **181,** 482 (1958).
Ogston, A. G., and Stanier, J. E. *Biochem. J.* **46,** 364 (1950).
Ogston, A. G., and Stanier, J. E. *Biochem. J.,* **49,** 591 (1951).
Ogston, A. G., and Stanier, J. E. *Faraday Soc. Dis.* No. **13,** 275 (1953).
Ogston, A. G., and Woods, E. F. *Trans. Faraday Soc.* **50,** 635 (1954).
Orr, S. F. D., and Harris, R. J. C. *Nature* **169,** 544 (1952).
Peterson, E., and Sober, H. A. *J. Amer. Chem. Soc.* **78,** 751 (1956).
Pirie, A. *Brit. J. Exp. Path.* **23,** 277 (1942).
Platt, D., Pigman, W., and Holley, H. L. *Arch. Biochem. Biophys.* **79,** 224 (1959).
Ragan, C., and de la Mater, A. *Proc. Soc. Exp. Biol. Med.* **50,** 349 (1942).
Ragan, C., and Meyer, K. *J. Clin. Invest.* **28,** 56 (1949).
Rapport, M. M., Linker, A., and Meyer, K. *J. Biol. Chem.* **192,** 283 (1951).
Rapport, M. M., Weissmann, B., Linker, A., and Meyer, K. *Nature* **168,** 996 (1951).
Ringertz, N. R., and Reichard, P. *Acta Chem. Scand.* **13,** 1467 (1959).
Ropes, M. W., and Bauer, N. *Synovial Fluid Changes in Joint Diseases* Harvard University Press (1953).
Roseman, S., Ludowieg, J., Moses, F. E., and Dorfman, A. *J. Biol. Chem.* **206,** 665 (1954).
Roseman, S., Moses, F. E., Ludowieg, J., and Dorfman, A. *J. Biol. Chem.* **203,** 213 (1953).
Rowen, J. W., Brunish, R., and Bishop, F. W. *Biochim. Biophys. Acta* **19,** 481 (1956).
Schiller, S., and Dewey, K. F. *Fed. Proc.* **15,** 348 (1956).
Scott, J. E. *Biochim. Biophys. Acta* **18,** 428 (1955).
Scott, J. E. *Biochem. J.* **62,** 31p (1956).
Seastone, C. V. *J. Exp. Med.* **77,** 21 (1943).
Stoffyn, P. J., and Jeanloz, R. W. *Arch. Biochem. Biophys.* **52,** 373 (1954).
Strominger, J. L. *Biochim. Biophys. Acta* **17,** 283 (1955).
Sundblad, L., Egelius, N., and Jonsson, E. *Scand. J. Clin. Lab. Invest.* **6,** 295 (1954).
Sylvén, B., and Malmgren, H. *Lab. Invest.* **1,** 413 (1952).
Topper, Y. J., and Lipton, M. M. *J. Biol. Chem.* **203,** 135 (1953).
Touster, O., and Reynolds, V. H. *J. Biol. Chem.* **197,** 863 (1952).
Varga, L. *J. Biol. Chem.* **217,** 651 (1955).
Warren, G. H., Horenstein, E., and Gray, J. *Arch. Biochem. Biophys.* **44,** 107 (1953).
Warren, G. H., Williams, E. C., Alburn, H. E., and Seifter, J. *Arch. Biochem.* **20,** 300 (1949).
Weissmann, B., and Meyer, K. *J. Amer. Chem. Soc.* **74,** 4729 (1952).
Weissmann, B., Meyer, K., Sampson, P., and Linker, A. *J. Biol. Chem.* **208,** 417 (1954).
Yielding, K. L., Tomkins, G. M., and Bunim, J. J. *Science* **125,** 1300 (1957).

Chapter 3

CHONDROITIN AND CHONDROITIN SULPHATES A, B AND C

Chondroitin

Chondroitin was first detected during a study of bovine cornea* by Meyer, Linker, Davidson and Weissmann (1953). It was composed of equimolar quantities of N-acetylhexosamine and uronic acid and was hydrolysed by bacterial and testicular hyaluronidases at a rate comparable to that of hyaluronic acid. However, chondroitin $[\alpha]_D - 20°$ had a much lower negative rotation than hyaluronic acid ($-65°$ to $-78°$). The main step in the purification of chondroitin was the removal of highly sulphated polysaccharide contaminants by passage down Dowex 1 (Cl^-). Chondroitin was eluted with water and N-HCl while the sulphated polysaccharides were strongly absorbed on the resin. A typical preparation ($[\alpha]_D^{22} - 20°$) had 36% uronic acid, hexosamine 28%, N 2·73% and SO_4 2·1%. The highly sulphated polysaccharides ($[\alpha]_D - 29°$) could be eluted from the ion exchange column with 3N-HCl and contained 32% uronic acid, 24% hexosamine, N 2·84% and SO_4 13·1%.

Acid hydrolysis of chondroitin afforded crystalline β-D-galactosamine hydrochloride further characterized as the Schiff's base formed by condensation with 2-hydroxynaphthaldehyde. Less drastic hydrolysis of chondroitin with N-H_2SO_4 at 100° for 4 hr gave the crystalline disaccharide chondrosine ($[\alpha]_D + 40°$, uronic acid 53%, hexosamine 44%, N 3·9%). The infrared spectra of the disaccharide was identical with that of crystalline chondrosine from cartilage chondroitin sulphate. Both chondroitin sulphate and chondroitin must therefore contain a high proportion of the same repeating unit. It is therefore probable that chondroitin represents the precursor of chondroitin sulphate A and C (See Figs. 3.3 and 3.4).

Chondroitin Sulphates A and C: Structural Studies

Because of their similarity and the confusion that exists in the literature it is appropriate that these two chondroitin sulphates should be discussed together. Early workers regarded chondroitin sulphate as a single entity, but many of their findings can be reinterpreted in the light of later results.

---

* The transparent part of the fibrous coat at the front of the eye.

Chondroitin sulphate was first isolated by Fischer and Boedeker (1861). Krukenberg (1884) and Mörner (1889) also reported the presence of chondroitin sulphate in cartilage. Hebting (1914) demonstrated that hydrolysis of chondroitin sulphate with oxalic acid gave a sulphate-free and acetyl-free disaccharide called chondrosine which he could convert to a crystalline ethyl ester hydrochloride. Levene and La Forge (1913) had also earlier postulated that chondrosine was a disaccharide. Further evidence in support of this contention was presented by von Fürth and Bruno (1937).

Further structural work (see Fig. 3.1) by Levene (1941) was carried out on the crystalline methyl ester hydrochloride of chondrosine (I)

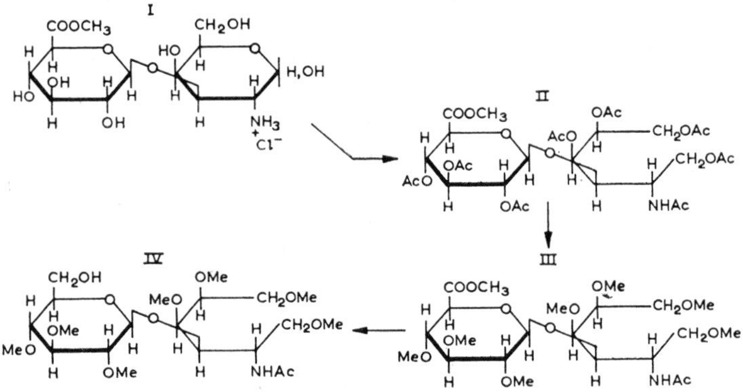

Fig. 3.1

($[\alpha]_D^{30} + 39 \cdot 2°$ in methanol; m.p. 165–170°) which analysed correctly for $C_{13}H_{24}O_{11}NCl$. Reduction of this methyl ester hydrochloride using Raney nickel and hydrogen under pressure at 75° for 48 hours at 2500 lb/sq in. gave a product which, on acetylation, yielded a crystalline hepta-O-acetate II (m.p. 122°; $[\alpha]_D^{25} - 21 \cdot 3°$ in ethanol) analysing for $C_{29}H_{41}O_{19}N$. Methylation of this hepta-O-acetate gave a crystalline hepta-O-methyl ether III (m.p. 67°; $[\alpha]_D^{25} - 4 \cdot 8°$ in ethanol) which analysed as $C_{22}H_{41}O_{12}N$. Reduction of this heptamethyl ether in the presence of a copper chromite catalyst afforded the corresponding alcohol IV (m.p. 55–57°, $[\alpha]_D^{30} - 44 \cdot 2°$ in $CHCl_3$) which analysed for $C_{21}H_{41}O_{11}N$. Although these experiments only provided evidence that chondrosine was composed of a hexosamine and a hexuronic acid residue, Levene (1941) believed mistakenly that chondrosine was a galactosaminidoglucuronic acid in which the linkage was β-1:4.

D-Glucuronic acid and D-galactosamine were firmly established as constituents of chondroitin sulphate by Bray, Gregory and Stacey (1944).

These workers isolated chondroitin sulphates from nasal septa* ($[\alpha]_D^{17} - 26°$), bovine trachea* ($[\alpha]_D^{17} - 25°$), human trachea* ($[\alpha]_D^{17} - 25°$ and human cartilage* ($[\alpha]_D^{17} - 19°$). The chondroitin sulphate was degraded with acid and the product acetylated and finally methylated. Acid hydrolysis of this methyl ether gave derivatives of glucuronic acid and galactosamine characterized as methyl 2:3:4-tri-O-methyl α-D-glucuronoside and methyl 3:4:6-tri-O-methyl 2-acetamido 2-deoxy α-D-galactoside. Wolfrom, Madison and Cron (1952) carried out a very detailed study of the crystalline methyl ester hydrochloride of chondrosine obtained from electrophoretically homogeneous cartilage chondroitin sulphuric acid ($[\alpha]_D^{30} - 24°$ in water). Unfortunately these authors interpreted their results on the basis of Levene's incorrect formula. For the sake of clarity we have therefore reinterpreted their results on the basis of the correct formula for chondrosine. The methyl ester hydrochloride of chondrosine (I) Fig. 3.1 was reduced with Raney nickel and hydrogen, esterified, acetylated and than treated with ammonia in ethanol to yield the glycitol (V) Fig. 3.2. Periodate oxidation of V initially left the uronic acid residue

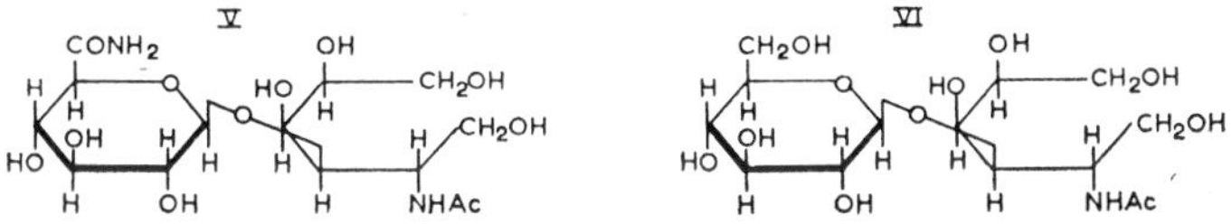

Fig. 3.2

intact and liberated one mole each of formic acid and formaldehyde with the consumption of two moles of periodate during the attack on the reduced moiety of the disaccharide. Prolonged action of periodate led to the consumption of one more mole of periodate (theoretically two moles should be used) in an attack on the uronic acid moiety. The chondroitin sulphate itself consumed one mole of periodate per disaccharide unit in an attack on the uronic acid portion.

Because of the controversy aroused by the structure postulated for chondrosine by Wolfrom et al. (1952) and others proposed by Meyer, Odier and Siegrist (1948) and by Masamune, Yoshizawa and Maki (1951) further investigation of the structure of chondrosine was undertaken by Davidson and Meyer (1954b). These workers succeeded in crystallizing

* The nasal septum or medial wall divides the nasal cavity into two halves. The trachea or windpipe contains from sixteen to twenty incomplete rings of hyaline cartilage. Hyaline cartilage has a pearly bluish colour and except where it coats the ends of the bones it is covered by a membrane called the perichondrium. Cartilage occurs wherever it is necessary to have rigidity and strength combined with a certain degree of elasticity.

chondrosine for the first time ($[\alpha]_D^{24} + 40°$ in 0·05N-HCl) and converted it to the crystalline methyl ester hydrochloride. The melting point and optical rotation of this material was similar to those described by Levene (1941) and by Wolfrom et al. (1952).

Chondrosine was reduced with sodium borohydride, esterified and acetylated to yield methyl-(hepta-O-acetyl)-3(?)-(β-D-glucopyranosyluron-ate)-2-acetamido 2-deoxy D-galactitol (II) (Fig. 3.1) having physical constants identical with those described by Levene (1941) and by Wolfrom et al. (1952). Chondrosine methyl ester hydrochloride was reduced with sodium borohydride and N-acetylated with acetic anhydride and Dowex-1 (CO$_3^-$) to give 3(?)-(β-D-glucopyranosyl)-2-acetamido 2-deoxy D-galacti-tol (VI). The β-glucosidic linkage in VI (Fig. 3.2) was confirmed by its susceptibility to emulsin (β-glucosidase). The presence of a glucose moiety in VI was confirmed by hydrolysis of VI and isolation of the glucose as β-D-glucose pentaacetate. This data proved unequivocally

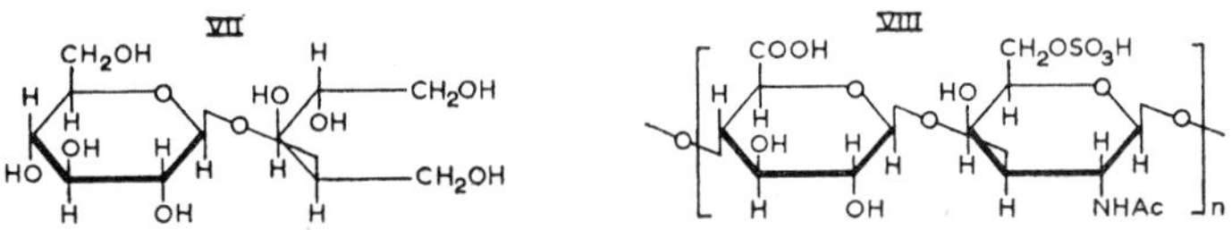

Fig. 3.3

that chondrosine was a β-D-glucuronosyl-D-galactosamine and reinter-pretation of the evidence of Wolfrom et al. (1952) strongly favoured linkage through the 3-position. Unequivocal evidence as to this feature was provided by Davidson and Meyer (1955) by ninhydrin degradation of the methyl ester hydrochloride of chondrosine to give a glucurono-syllyxose. Re-esterification and reduction with sodium borohydride in cold methanol-borate buffer yielded a glucosidopentitol (VII) (Fig. 3.3) isolated as a crystalline octaacetate. Periodate oxidation of VII consumed 4 moles of periodate and liberated one mole of formaldehyde and two moles of formic acid. These data require a 1:2 linkage in the glycosi-dolyxitol and therefore a 1:3 linkage in chondrosine.

Wolfrom and Juliano (1960) have converted chondroitin sulphate A to its methyl ester using the method of Kantor and Schubert (1957). Reduction with sodium borohydride and two further esterifications and reduction cycles gave the fully reduced chondroitin sulphate A ($[\alpha]_D + 11°$ in dimethyl sulphoxide). Partial acid hydrolysis of this product and subsequent fractionation afforded D-glucose, N-acetyl D-galactosamine and the disaccharide 3-O-β-D-glucopyranosyl 2-acetamido 2-deoxy α-D-galactose dihydrate. The structure of this disaccharide was deduced from (a) the products of acid hydrolysis, D-glucose and D-galactosamine,

(b) its ready degradation by alkali to D-glucose and 'anhydro N-acetyl D-galactosamine' and (c) its positive reaction with the Morgan–Elson reagents. The disaccharide on treatment with sodium borohydride gave a product (VI) (Fig. 3.2) identical with that derived from chondrosine methyl ester hydrochloride.

Little evidence as to the nature of the hexosaminidic linkage in chondroitin sulphate is available but Davidson and Meyer (1955) favoured linkage through the 1–4 positions and suggested that the probable repeating unit of cartilage chondroitin sulphate was VIII (Fig. 3.3).

Chondroitin sulphate can be desulphated by treatment at $-10°$ with almost absolute sulphuric acid followed by acetylation. Wolfrom and Montgomery (1950) reported a yield of about 30% of the desulphated acetylated product using this method. Kantor and Schubert (1957) claimed higher yields by treatment of dry potassium chondroitin sulphate with methanolic hydrogen chloride (0·06M-solution) at room temperature for a day. Their product was non-dialysable with no ester sulphate but with esterified carboxylic acid groups.

It was not until 1951 that Meyer and Rapport reported that two types of chondroitin sulphate, A and C, were present in hyaline cartilage. The properties of A and C were summarized by Meyer, Davidson, Linker and Hoffmann (1956) as follows:

Chondroitin sulphate A had $[\alpha]_D$ -28 to $-32°$, required 30–40% ethanol to precipitate its calcium salt, was hydrolysed by testicular hyaluronidase, contained equimolar amounts of D-galactosamine and D-glucuronic acid (whether determined as CO_2 or by the carbazole method) and gave a 15% reducing sugar equivalent after 1 hour at $100°$ with $N\text{-}H_2SO_4$. Fifty per cent of the sulphate was liberated after hydrolysis for 1 hour at $100°$ with N-HCl.

Chondroitin sulphate C had $[\alpha]_D$ $-16°$ to $-22°$, required 40–50% ethanol to precipitate its calcium salt, was hydrolysed by testicular hyaluronidase, contained equimolar amounts of D-galactosamine and D-glucuronic acid (whether determined as CO_2 or by the carbazole method) and gave a 22% reducing sugar equivalent after 1 hour at $100°$ with $N\text{-}H_2SO_4$. Fifty per cent of the sulphate was liberated after hydrolysis for 1 hour at $100°$ with N-HCl.

Both A and C were devoid of anticoagulant activity. One explanation advanced for their different optical rotations and solubility properties was that C had a lower molecular weight than A. Samples of crystalline chondrosine having identical infrared spectra were obtained from both A and C so the difference does not lie in the glucuronosyl-galactosamine glycosidic linkage.

Mathews (1958) reported that chondroitin sulphates A and C could be differentiated by their infrared spectra in the fingerprint region

700–1000 cm^{-1} where chondroitin sulphate C has unique bands at 1000 cm^{-1}, 820 cm^{-1} and 775 cm^{-1} while chondroitin sulphate A has bands at 928 cm^{-1}, 852 cm^{-1} and 725 cm^{-1}. Following an earlier assignment by Orr (1954), Mathews (1958) suggested that in A the sulphate group occupied an axial position while in C the sulphate group was in the equatorial position. This prompted the interpretation that in chondroitin sulphate A the sulphate was attached to the C_4 of the hexosamine moiety while in chondroitin sulphate C it was attached to the C_6 of the hexosamine moiety (see VIII). On the basis of published spectra, Mathews (1958) considered that the mucopolysaccharide from *nuclei pulposi** called 'chondroitin sulphuric acid-B' (Orr, 1954) and the chondroitin sulphate from shark cartilage (Nakanishi, Takahashi and Egami, 1956) could also be considered as the C sulphate.

The earlier infrared studies of Orr (1954) were also valuable because he distinguished in the spectra of the chondroitin sulphates (1) absorption at 1736 cm^{-1} in the spectra of the free acid (attributable to the C=O stretching of the —COOH group) which was absent in the spectra of the salt (indicating absence of *O*-acetyl groups) (2) the —NH deformation and C=O stretching of the *N*-acetyl groups at 1560 cm^{-1} and 1648 cm^{-1} respectively and (3) intense bands at *ca.* 1240 cm^{-1} due to the S=O stretching vibrations of the sulphate groups.

Hoffman, Linker and Meyer (1958) have produced further evidence regarding the position of the sulphate linkage in chondroitin sulphate A and C. Chondroitin sulphate A and C were treated with testicular hyaluronidase and the sulphated tetrasaccharides isolated. The tetrasaccharides ($[\alpha]_D - 9°$) from A contained 24% hexosamine and gave values of 31% and 21% for uronic acid when estimated by the carbazole and orcinol methods respectively. The tetrasaccharide ($[\alpha]_D - 8°$) from C contained 23% hexosamine and gave values of 31% and 20% for uronic acid when estimated by the carbazole and orcinol methods respectively. Both tetrasaccharides with liver β-glucuronidase gave free glucuronic acid and sulphated trisaccharides with identical R_F values. Hence it was concluded that the sulphate group in both A and C must be on the galactosamine residue and that the difference in A and C must be due to its point of substitution.

Chondroitin sulphate A and C were desulphated and shown to have the following properties: desulphated A ($[\alpha]_D - 27°$) contained 31% hexosamine and gave values of 41 and 29% when the uronic acid content was determined by the carbazole and orcinol methods respectively; desulphated C ($[\alpha]_D - 21°$) also contained 31% hexosamine and gave values

---

* The *nucleus pulposus* is the soft pulpy highly elastic substance in the centre of each intevertebral disc.

of 43 and 28% when the uronic acid content was determined by the carbazole and orcinol methods respectively. In a comparison of the infrared spectra of the sulphated and desulphated products there was a marked disappearance of absorption bands in the 850 cm^{-1} region for A and 820 cm^{-1} region for C confirming that these bands are due to sulphate groups. Since chondroitin sulphate B on desulphation showed a disappearance of absorption in the 850 cm^{-1} region and is known by methylation studies to have its sulphate group attached to C_4 of its galactosamine residues (Jeanloz and Stoffyn, 1958) the American workers argued that A had a C_4-galactosamine linked sulphate and C had a C_6-galactosamine linked sulphate. Hence chondroitin sulphate C is as depicted in VIII (Fig. 3.3) while chondroitin sulphate A is as shown in IX (Fig. 3.4).

Barium chondroitin sulphate A heated with hydrazine at 100° for 10 hr yields a partially desulphated (desulphation 39–53%) and highly (59–68%) N-deacetylated polymer (Wolfrom and Juliano, 1960). The yield of such a polymer could be increased from 43% to 67% by reduction of the terminal carbonyl with sodium borohydride. This result was consistent with the suppression of β-elimination in the alkaline medium. Sulphation of chon-

Fig. 3.4

droitin sulphate A and its N-deacetylated analogues gave products with anticoagulant activities up to 15% that exhibited by heparin. This could be attributed in part to the introduction of N-sulphate groups which could be specifically detected by the absence of 1560 cm^{-1} absorption in the infrared spectra of the sulphated polysaccharides. This absorption band was absent also in 2-deoxy 2-sulphoamino D-glucose (sodium salt) and in 2-hydroxyethylsulfamic acid hydrogen sulphate, disodium salt trihydrate but was present in the infrared spectra of sulfamic acid H_3N^+—SO_2—O^- indicating that this property was exclusive to mono N-substituted sulfamates R—NH—$SO_2^-Na^+$.

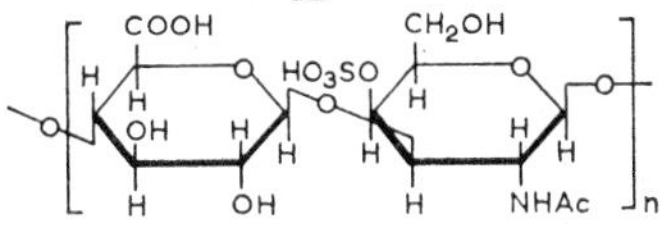

In studies of the crystallinity of calcium chondroitin sulphate A, Bettelheim and Philpott (1960) have encountered a new chondroitin sulphate. One of the fractions (Ca salt) isolated from bovine trachea was dissolved in water, clarified by centrifugation at 6000 r.p.m. for 20 min and the supernatant precipitated with 3 volumes of absolute ethanol. The highly crystalline fraction had C, 33·34%; H, 6·08%; N, 2·96%; S, 2·05% and Ca, 2·7%. A new type of hydrated calcium chondroitin sulphate sulphated only at every third chondroitin unit and having the formula $C_{42}O_{33}H_{22}N_3SO_3Ca$ 15H$_2$O would require C, 33·02%; H, 6.03%; N, 2·75%; S, 2·09% and Ca, 2.62%. By contrast normal chondroitin sulphate A fractions isolated as their calcium salts analysed correctly for

$C_{14}H_{20}NSO_{14}Ca\ 5H_2O$. Both chondroitin sulphates yielded glucuronic acid and galactosamine on acid hydrolysis. Distinct differences were detected in their infrared spectra. The new chondroitin sulphate showed a spectrum in which the sulphate band at 725 cm^{-1} was absent and the 928 cm^{-1} band had shifted to 955 cm^{-1}. The sulphate band at 1240 cm^{-1} was also much less intense. The fact that the new chondroitin sulphate precipitated with the smallest concentration of ethanol indicated that it was less polar than chondroitin sulphate A.

Although the chondroitin sulphate isolated from shark cartilage has an infrared spectrum identical with that of chondroitin sulphate C, the shark chondroitin sulphate has an unusually high sulphur content (S, 7·6% $\equiv$ 1·3 sulphate groups per acetylgalactosamine moiety). Since the two poly-saccharides also differ as acceptors in enzymatic sulphation, Suzuki (1960) has designated the chondroitin sulphate from shark cartilage as chondroitin sulphate D. Enzymatic degradation of chondroitin sulphate D with *Proteus vulgaris* chondroitinase gave *inter alia* Δ 4,5-glucuronido acetylgalactosamine 6-sulphate and a disaccharide disulphate in which the second sulphate residue was attached to the 2- or 3-position of the uronic acid. Δ 4,5-glucuronido acetylgalactosamine 4-sulphate was among the products characterized in digests of chondroitin sulphate A and B incubated with *Proteus vulgaris* chondroitinase (Suzuki, 1960).

Isolation from Normal and Pathological Tissues

Meyer, Davidson, Linker and Hoffmann (1956) have reviewed the general occurrence of the polysaccharide constituents of ground substance. They reported that chondroitin sulphate A had been isolated from tracheal cartilage, bovine cornea, bone, bovine nasal septum, rib cartilage of newborn babies, ox ligamentum nuchae* and bovine aorta†. Chrondroitin sulphate C was a minor constituent of cartilage and bone, of tendon, heart valves, of umbilical cord and of culture fluids from tissue cultures of fibroblasts derived from bone, human skin and rat subcutaneum. A chondroitin sulphate isolated from the electric organ of an electric eel was also probably C. A human chordoma originating in the mesopharynx‡ contained C as the only acid mucopolysaccharide. Chondroitin sulphate C was obtained from a human chondrosarcomata—the material used was a bloody viscous fluid obtained by aspiration of a cyst of a histologically

---

* The ligamentum nuchae is a fibrous membrane part of which connects together the apices of the spines from the seventh cervical vertebra to the sacrum.

† The aorta joins the left ventricle to the abdominal cavity and conveys the oxygenated blood to the tissues of the body.

‡ The pharynx is the part of the digestive tube behind the nasal cavities, the mouth and the larynx.

verified sarcoma. Only chondroitin sulphate A was obtained from another human chondrosarcomata—the material was resected from pubic bone and contained some bone and osteoid tissue. The finding in the two tumours of chondroitin sulphates A and C respectively, not accompanied by the other, strengthened the American workers' belief in the differentiation of these two chondroitin sulphates.

Badin, Schubert and Vouras (1955) and Bassiouni (1955) reported that acidic polysaccharides were present in normal human plasma. Bassiouni (1955) found that one of the two acid polysaccharides detected migrated on paper electrophoretograms at the same rate as the chondroitin sulphuric acid of cartilage while the other possessed a slower mobility. Two components staining metachromatically with toluidine blue were also detected on paper chromatograms by Bollet, Seraydarian and Simpson (1957). The chromatographic behaviour of one resembled chondroitin sulphate A of cartilage. Schiller (1958) has characterized a sulphated mucopolysaccharide from normal human plasma as chondroitin sulphate A. Normal human plasma was dialysed and the precipitate formed suspended in 0·1M-phosphate buffer, pH 7·8 and submitted to digestion with crystalline trypsin. After dialysis and removal of residual protein with trichloracetic acid, the crude polysaccharides present were precipitated with alcohol. After electrophoresis, the faster migrating component was further purified and analysed. Nitrogen, hexosamine, uronic acid and ester sulphate analyses indicated molecular ratios of 1·30, 1·00, 1·00 and 1·24. The hexosamine was identified by ninhydrin degradation as galactosamine. In its electrophoretic mobility, its optical rotation ($-31\cdot6° \pm 0\cdot5°$) and infrared spectrum the polysaccharide was identical with that of chondroitin sulphate A. Like chondroitin sulphate A, the sulphated mucopolysaccharide of plasma was devoid of anticoagulant activity. At most, approx. 1·5 mg of chondroitin sulphuric acid A was isolated from one litre of human plasma.

Several workers (Moernier, 1895; Addis, 1927–28; Kobayashi, 1938) have isolated mucopolysaccharides from normal human urine. Astrup (1947) precipitated the acidic mucopolysaccharides by addition of benzidine hydrochloride and reported that these were non-dialysable in a cellophane membrane and gave a metachromatic reaction with toluidine blue. Paper chromatographic examination of the acidic mucopolysaccharide revealed that it had the same mobility as chondroitin sulphate (Kerby, 1954). Craddock and Kerby (1955) reported that it was not depolymerized by testicular hyaluronidase and that the ratio of hexosamine to glucuronic acid was somewhat higher than that of chondroitin sulphate.

Ferrante and Rich (1956) precipitated the acidic mucopolysaccharides from normal urine by adjusting this to pH 5 and adding a 10% solution of cetyltrimethylammonium bromide. After further purification involving removal of proteins by trypsin and papain treatment the acidic poly-saccharide had N 3·91%, S 5·65%, uronic acid 39·7% and hexosamine 31·7%. Ninety per cent of the hexosamine present was identified as gal-actosamine and 9·8% as glucosamine. The polysaccharide behaved in a manner identical to that of bovine nasal septa chondroitin sulphate on paper chromatography and paper electrophoresis and both had identical infrared spectra. It showed only a single broad peak in the ultracentrifuge. It had $[\alpha]_D^{27} - 18·3 \pm 2·0°$ and in this case was depolymerized by testi-cular hyaluronidase as was the reference chondroitin sulphate. It was concluded that it must be either chondroitin sulphate A or C.

A sensitive method of detecting the acidic mucopolysaccharides in normal human urine has been described by Heremans, Vaerman and Heremans (1959).

This involves paper electrophoretic separation of the concentrated urine in a veronal-acetate buffer (pH 8·6; μ 0·1) on Whatman No. 1. After twelve hours at a potential of 3 V/cm three acidic mucopolysaccharides could be detected on the paper after treatment with a 1% solution of alician blue (Gurr) in a 9:1 mixture of acetic acid and water (5 min) followed by alternate washings with acetic acid and tap water. Using this technique as little as 0·5 μg of heparin or 2 μg of chondroitin sulphate A can be detected. None of the polysaccharides detected in urine could be stained with protein dyes.

Pernis and Clerici (1957) have studied the chemical composition of hyaline plaques from arteriosclerotic aortae and compared it with that of a normal aortic wall. In the study, analyses were carried out on nine different normal aortic walls of men aged 20–40 years and compared with those of hyaline plaques of nine different cases of arteriosclerosis. Each sample was severed into three fractions (Neuman and Logan, 1950), FI, FII and FIII which contained mainly collagen, heterogenous proteins and elastin respectively. The results of several determinations are given in Table 3.I

Table 3.I. Comparison of normal and pathological aorta

Determination of:	Fraction	Normal aorta	Pathological aorta
Hexoses	FI	1·357 ± 0·033	2·464 ± 0·163
	FII	traces	0
Methyl pentoses	FI	0·987 ± 0·400	0·840 ± 0·276
	FII	0·351 ± 0·126	0·380 ± 0·220
Hexosamines	FI	1·173 ± 0·293	0·260 ± 0·136
	FII	traces	0
Hexuronic acids	FI	1·122 ± 0·170	0
	FII	0	0
SO_4—	Whole sample	+ + +	+ −

and all values are expressed as g per 100 g of proteins of the corresponding fraction and the mean of nine cases.

These results suggested that the chondroitin sulphate type of mucopolysaccharide (chondroitin sulphate A has been reported in bovine aorta) decreases markedly during arteriosclerotic disease. The increased hexose content of Fl in the arteriosclerotic plaques may be due to the accumulation of e.g. keratosulphate. It is significant in this connection that metachromatic staining substances disappear only in the early stages of the disease during the serious imbibition of the intima, but show again, to an even larger degree, at a later period, in the constituted arteriosclerotic lesions, either coming from the blood stream or being newly synthesized from the arterial wall.

Kyrk and Dyrbyye (1957) have isolated mucopolysaccharides from human arterial tissue by treating a homogenate of the tissue successively with pepsin, trypsin and α-amylase and precipitating the residual polysaccharides with alcohol. On average 4·9 mg mucopolysaccharide/g wet tissue were isolated from the aortas of children 0–9 yrs, 4·8 mg/g from individuals aged 20–59 yrs and 2·4 mg/g from individuals aged 60–76 yrs. The mean mucopolysaccharide yields for the 30 aortic samples studied were 33·1% on the basis of hexosamine analyses and 60·9% on the basis of the sulphate determinations. The mean concentrations in the mucopolysaccharide samples were 24·8% total hexosamine, 33·4% uronic acid (decarboxylation) and 12·2% sulphate. Galactosamine averaged 79% of the total hexosamine content and glucosamine 21%. No correlation with age was observed in the total hexosamine, uronic acid and sulphate contents of the samples. It was concluded that chondroitin sulphate A or C constituted the major part of the mucopolysaccharides since hydrolysis by testicular hyaluronidase occurred.

The mucopolysaccharides of bovine heart valves have been studied by Deiss and Leon (1954, 1955). The heart valves were extracted with 0·01N-sodium hydroxide and most of the proteins removed by pepsin and trypsin digestion. After partition with chloroform-amyl alcohol, the residual mixture was treated with zinc hydroxide to remove other nitrogenous impurities. Dialysis and alcohol precipitation afforded a crude polysaccharide mixture which was fractionated by alcohol precipitation of the calcium salts of the polysaccharides. Fraction I, precipitated at 20% ethanol, showed the properties of chondroitin sulphate B, i.e. $[\alpha]_D - 69·8°$ and contained N 2.92%, acetyl 10·58%, sulphate 15·43%, galactosamine 24·3% uronic acid (decarboxylation) 28%, uronic acid (carbazole) 12·6%. Fraction II precipitated at 50% ethanol was further fractionated from $(NH_4)_2SO_4$ solution by addition of pyridine to precipitate fraction IIA and leave in solution IIB. Fraction IIA showed the properties of hyaluronic acid, i.e. $[\alpha]_D - 74·7°$ and contained N 3·94%, acetyl 13·03%, sulphate

< 0·1, glucosamine 35·81%, uronic acid (carbazole) 34·88%. Fraction IIB showed the properties of chondroitin sulphate C in that it had $[\alpha]_D - 22\cdot9°$ and contained N 3·33%, acetyl 4·76%, sulphate 11·15%, galactosamine 25·71%, uronic acid (carbazole) 23·38%. Fraction I was resistant to both pneumococcal and testicular hyaluronidases, while fraction IIA was hydrolysed by both of these enzymes. Fraction IIB was hydrolysed by testicular but not by pneumococcal hyaluronidase. The three acidic polysaccharides were present in bovine heart valves in approximately equal amounts.

Dunphy and Udupa (1955) have studied the processes that occur in wound healing in rats by a series of chemical and histochemical techniques. During the early stages of wound healing there was a rapid increase in hexosamine content of the wound (e.g. normal skin, 450 mg; 3-day wound, 956 mg; 6 day wound, 790 mg; 9 day wound, 505 mg; 12 day wound, 475 mg; 15 day wound 466 mg/100 g dry tissue) followed by a fall back to normal levels. During this initial increase (the productive phase) marked changes were observed in the ground substance and metachromasia (toluidine blue staining) reached its peak about the fifth or sixth day. At that stage the first chemical and histological evidence was obtained of the formation of collagen fibres. As these increased (the collagen phase) there was a progressive fall in the hexosamine content and metachromasia. This period was also accompanied by a marked rise in tensile strength. In scorbutic guinea-pigs the 'productive phase' was greatly extended and there was no 'collagen phase'. The concentration of mucopolysaccharides rose progressively until by the twelfth or fourteenth day they were far in excess of that seen at the peak observed in normal wounds about the fifth day. The mucopolysaccharide produced did not stain metachromatically and was therefore abnormal. In less than 48 hours after the administration of ascorbic acid such a wound passed into the 'collagen phase'. Rats fed on a non-protein diet for five days before wounding showed a different pattern of wound healing. Here the productive phase was prolonged and the peak levels were below normal. The collagen phase did not begin until the seventh or eighth day and progressed more slowly than normal. This pattern of healing could be shifted towards normal by addition of methionine to the diet.

The subcutaneous injection of carrageenin (50 mg) in guinea-pigs causes the formation of large amounts (10–20 g of granuloma tissue/guinea-pig) of easily separated connective tissue (Robertson and Schwartz, 1953). Slack (1957, 1958) has taken two groups of guinea-pigs one of which was maintained on an ascorbic acid deficient diet for 7 or 10 days before injection with carrageenin and killed at intervals from 6 to 12 days later. The other group of normal guinea-pigs were given ascorbic acid supplements during the periods of granuloma production. The granulomata were removed from each group at intervals, digested with papain and the residual polysaccharides fractionated using cetylpyridinium chloride. The basis of the fractionation was that on treatment of a $0 \cdot 2\text{M-Na}_2\text{SO}_4$ solution of the crude polysaccharide mixture with the quaternary ammonium salt only chondroitin sulphate was precipitated while hyaluronic acid remained in solution. Using this technique it was demonstrated that scorbutic animals showed a greatly increased production ($2\frac{1}{2}$–6 times) of total polysaccharides in comparison with that from normal animals. The major part of this increase was due to the production of hyaluronic acid. Production of the chondroitin sulphate fraction was generally slightly reduced in the scorbutic granuloma in comparison with the normal animals. The chondroitin sulphates isolated from both normal and scorbutic animals were attacked by testicular hyaluronidase, and both contained galactosamine although in the case of the fractions from scorbutic animals small amounts of glucosamine were also detected. From the results of alcohol precipitation it was concluded that the chondroitin sulphates were a mixture of A and C.

Lorincz (1960) has carried out an investigation into hereditary deforming chondrodysplasia (diaphysial aclasis). Large quantities of acidic mucopolysaccharides were found to be excreted in the urine. This mucopolysaccharide, which tended to slowly dialyse through cellophane, appeared to be similar to chondroitin sulphate A or C.

These findings indicate that this condition represents another heritable disorder of connective tissue mucopolysaccharide metabolism.

Isolation of Chondroitin Sulphate-Protein Complexes

Extraction of cartilage with neutral 10% calcium chloride (Blix and Snellman, 1945) yields relatively viscous preparations of chondroitin sulphate which Mathews (1955) has shown by light scattering methods have a molecular weight of 150,000 compared with values of 18000–48000 for alkali-extracted materials. Samples of chondroitin sulphate obtained in this way from layrngeal cartilage (the larynx extends from the root of the tongue to the trachea; there are nine cartilages in the human larynx) of six-month-old pigs and purified by precipitation with $\text{Co(NH}_3)_6\text{Cl}_3$ (Mathews and Dorfman, 1953) have been reported to contain $26 \cdot 3\%$ hexosamine and $14 \cdot 1\%$ sulphate (Muir, 1956). Such preparations appeared to be chondroitin sulphate complexes since on hydrolysis they yielded some aminoacids and were attacked by crystalline papain with a consequent loss of viscosity. Whereas the original preparation remained on the origin when chromatographed on Whatman No. 2 in 45% (v/v) n-propanol/55%, $0 \cdot 2\text{M}$-boric acid, the papain-digested material moved as a compact spot with an $R_F = 0 \cdot 58$ similar to that of an alkali-degraded preparation (Muir, 1956). The chondroitin sulphate complex was not attacked by crystalline trypsin, chymotrypsin or pepsin and was not coagulated by heating or the use of protein precipitants.

Muir (1957) claimed to have detected a new amino sugar in the hydrolysates of such chondroitin sulphate complexes particularly after prolonged hydrolysis with 2–6N-HCl. Paper chromatography showed that it was neither glucosamine nor galactosamine. The amino sugar, on ninhydrin degradation, gave a pentose which could not be distinguished from lyxose. Muir (1957) therefore suggested that it was probably talosamine the epimer of galactosamine which also gives lyxose on ninhydrin degradation.

Muir (1958) has obtained the chondroitin sulphate complex from pig cartilage electrophoretically homogeneous by precipitation with 5-aminoacridine hydrochloride at an acid pH. The pure complex showed $[\alpha]_D - 33°$, N 3·92%, hexosamine 27·5% and sulphate 14·5%.

After digestion of the chondroitin sulphate complex with papain it still contained half of the original amount of serine whereas the quantities of the other amino acids (glycine, alanine, aspartic acid, glutamic acid) which remained were very small. The untreated chondroitin sulphate complex contained glycine 0·67%, alanine 0·634%, valine 0·66%, serine 0·848%, threonine 0·504%, leucine 1·04%, isoleucine 0·496%, phenylalanine 0·69%, tyrosine 0·424%, proline 0·154%, arginine 0·536%, histidine 0·187%, lysine 0·302%, aspartic acid 0·938% and glutamic acid 1·407%.

Parallel studies have been carried out on chondromucoproteins from bovine and beef nasal cartilage*. These differ from the chondroitin sulphate complex of pig tracheal cartilage in not being resistant to trypsin. After treatment with trypsin pure chondroitin sulphate $[\alpha]_D - 29°$ could be isolated from bovine chondromucoprotein. Glutamic acid, a prominent feature of the pig chondroitin sulphate complex was absent from the ox cartilage complex (Webber and Bayley, 1956) which contained aspartic acid, ornithine, serine, glycine, threonine, lysine, alanine, proline, phenylalanine and leucine.

Shatton and Schubert (1954) suggested that in bovine nasal cartilage about one third of the chondroitin sulphate was bound to a protein different from collagen to form a mucoprotein (CS–P) while the remaining two-thirds was linked to collagen. Mathews and Lozaityte (1956) estimated CS–P to contain 60–75% chondroitin sulphate and 25–40% protein. Bernardi (1957) prepared a CS–P complex from beef nasal septa cartilage by extraction with 30% potassium chloride, filtration through cheese-cloth and centrifugation at 20,000 r.p.m. for 15 min. Examination of the supernatant in an analytical ultracentrifuge showed two components, the

* Free from all perichondrium; the membrane surrounding the cartilage.

concentration of the faster one being negligible compared to that of the slower component. The CS–P complex was further purified by dialysis of the supernatant and precipitation of the complex with two volumes of alcohol in the presence of 0·5% potassium acetate. On dissolving in M/15 phosphate buffer, the solution exhibited only a sedimenting boundary in the analytical ultracentrifuge. The CS–P hydrolysed with 6N-HCl at 120° for 18 hr gave aspartic acid, serine, glycine, glutamic acid, threonine, alanine, leucine, ornithine, lysine, valine, phenylalanine, histidine, tyrosine and proline. The proline was believed to arise from a trace contamination with collagen. Viscometric, ultracentrifugation, streaming birefringence and light scattering studies of CS–P prompted Bernardi (1957) to postulate an end to end arrangement of chondroitin sulphate linear chains and polypeptide chains. The CS–P, which showed Mw = $1·98 \times 10^6$, was pictured as exerting a stabilizing and cementing function on collagen.

Malawista and Schubert (1958) have described a new technique for isolating bovine nasal chondromucoprotein. By a single extraction of the cartilage with water for 1 day using a high speed VirTis 45 homogenizer (45000 r.p.m.) they were able to recover apparently undegraded chondromucoprotein accounting for over 80% of the total hexosamine initially present. The chondromucoprotein contained 17·4% hexosamine, 5·25% N, 3·9% S, no hydroxyproline, 1% proline and 8% moisture. Treatment of the potassium salt of chondromucoprotein with 0·18M-NaOH at 37° for 20 hr liberated free chondroitin sulphate ($[\alpha]_D^{25} - 20·1°$).

Gerber, Franklin and Schubert (1960) have separated bovine nasal chondromucoprotein into two distinct protein–polysaccharide fractions by ultracentrifugation. The lighter component obtained in 75% yield consisted of 15% protein and 85% chondroitin sulphate A. Its sedimentation constant was 10·55 at infinite dilution. The heavier fraction (13%) sedimenting easily at 10,000 g contained 50% protein and 50% chondroitin sulphate A.

Determination of Chondroitin Sulphate A

Meyer and Rapport (1950) have devised a turbidimetric method for the determination of chondroitin sulphate A. This depends on the appearance of turbidity (read at 580 mμ 30 min after mixing) when a buffered solution (0·1M acetate, pH 6·0) of chondroitin sulphate A is mixed with diluted horse serum. The serum was prepared by dilution with 0·5M-acetate buffer, pH 4·2 (9 vol.) and acidification to pH 3·1 with 4N-HCl. As recommended by Tolksdorf, McCready, McCullagh and Schwenk (1949) for hyaluronidase determination the diluted serum was heated for 30 min at 100°, cooled and filtered immediately before mixing. Standard curves were plotted for log per cent transmission against weight of chondroitin sulphate (30–300 mg).

The metachromatic activity of chondroitin sulphate could probably be used as a means of assay. Walton and Ricketts (1954) using a 0·005% (wt/vol.) solution of toluidine blue in 0·01N-HCl containing 0·2% (wt/vol) sodium chloride, obtained a linear relationship between the percentage of dye combined and concentration of bovine cartilage chondroitin sulphate used in the range 2·5–25 μg/ml. After addition of chondroitin sulphate the mixture was shaken with petroleum ether. This caused the metachromatic or bound component to separate at the interface and enabled the amount of dye bound to be determined by the diminished intensity observable in the aqueous phase at 630 mμ.

Enzymic Degradation of Chondroitin Sulphates A and C

Using bovine tracheal cartilage chondroitin sulphate (mainly A with small amounts of C) as the substrate, Dodgson, Lloyd and Spencer (1957) have shown that two enzymes obtained from *Proteus vulgaris* will collectively effect the degradation of the chondroitin sulphate to reducing substances and sulphuric acid. Only one of these enzymes, chondroitinase can use the intact chondroitin sulphate as a substrate. The other enzyme, chondro-sulphatase will liberate sulphuric acid from the sulphated oligosaccharides produced by the action of testicular hyaluronidase on cartilage chondroitin sulphates (Dodgson and Lloyd, 1957). The major product resulting from the action of chondroitinase on cartilage chondroitin sulphate has been isolated by fractionation on a charcoal-celite column (Dodgson and Lloyd, 1958). It had $[\alpha]_D^{20} - 14 \pm 2°$ in water and contained equimolar amounts of uronic acid, hexosamine and ester sulphate. Its structure was established as *N*-acetylchondrosine sulphate by (a) acidic hydrolysis to chondrosine and (b) enzymic hydrolysis by chondrosulphatase to *N*-acetylchondrosine. No evidence of unsaturation was obtained. Partial enzymic degradation of cartilage chondroitin sulphate with chondroitinase yielded a series of oligosaccharides which appeared to be di-, tetra-, hexa- and octa-saccharides containing *N*-acetylchondrosine sulphate as a repeating unit.

Although the isolation of saturated products has been confirmed by Linker, Hoffman, Meyer, Sampson and Korn (1960) using Dodgson and Lloyd's own enzyme, only unsaturated uronides were obtained when these workers used an enzyme prepared by themselves from *Proteus vulgaris* 4636. The unsaturated disaccharide obtained had the same composition and ultraviolet absorption as the unsaturated disaccharide obtained on treatment with the *Flavobacterium* enzyme discussed below.

The unadapted strains of a flavobacterium have been found to hydrolyse chondroitin sulphates A and C to a mixture of unsaturated di- and oligo-saccharides which were only partly sulphated (Hoffmann, Linker, Sampson and Meyer, 1957). These results can probably be attributed to the presence of two enzymes, the first concerned with the hydrolysis of hexosaminidic linkages and the production of unsaturation in the neighbouring uronic acid residues and the second, like the chondrosulphatase discussed above, with the hydrolysis of ester sulphate linkages. When incubated with the normal sulphated tetrasaccharide obtained by the action of testicular hyaluronidase on chondroitin sulphate A, the unadapted enzyme yielded one normal and one unsaturated disaccharide.

Flavobacterium grown in a medium containing chondroitin sulphate A yields enzymes which degrade chondroitin sulphate A to unsaturated and sulphated unsaturated disaccharides. Further degradation of the unsaturated disaccharide occurs to yield hexosamine and a new kind of α-ketouronic acid (Linker, Hoffman, Meyer, Sampson and Korn, 1960). Since this acid gave (a) positive reactions to tests for an α-keto acid, (b) yields formylpyruvic acid after periodate oxidation and (c) was derived from a Δ 4,5-unsaturated uronic acid the formula assigned to the new acid was a cyclic form of $CHO . CHOH . CHOH . CH_2 . CO . COOH$, i.e. a 4-deoxy 5-ketouronic acid. Further evidence was obtained from the semicarbazone spectrum which indicated the presence of an aldehyde group in addition to the α-keto group. These features were also suggested by a quantitative sodium borohydride reaction where approx. 2 moles of hydrogen per mole of compound were consumed.

Intact chondroitin sulphates A and C are resistant to hydrolysis by streptococcal and pneumococcal hyaluronidases but chondroitin is attacked to yield an unsaturated disaccharide (Davidson and Meyer, 1954).

The action of testicular hyaluronidase on chondroitin sulphate A or C yields sulphated tetrasaccharides of differing structures; as with the parent polysaccharides this difference probably resides in the point of attachment of the sulphate group in the galactosamine residues (Hoffman, Linker and Meyer, 1958). Like the products from the action of *Proteus vulgaris* chondroitinase they are the normal oligosaccharides with β-glucuronic acid residues as terminal non-reducing end-groups. Besides its function as a β-hexosaminidase, testicular hylauronidase is known to exhibit transglycosylation properties (Hoffman, Meyer and Linker, 1956). Testicular hyaluronidase has also been reported to attack desulphated chondroitin sulphate A to yield a tetrasaccharide (Hoffman, Linker and Meyer, 1957).

Biosynthesis of Chondroitin Sulphates A and C

Boström and Mänsson (1953) found that addition of a liver homogenate to a system containing slices of costal cartilage from young calves stimulated incorporation of S^{35}-labelled sulphate into the chondroitin sulphate (probably a mixture of A and C). Subsequent studies established that the stimulating activity was due to a ninhydrin-positive component (Boström,

Jorpes, Mänsson, Rodén and Vestermark, 1956) which Rodén (1956) identified as glutamine. Glutamine is well known as a donor of amino groups during transamination (Meister and Tice, 1950) and is believed to participate in glucosamine formation during hyaluronic acid biosynthesis (Lowther and Rogers, 1956). This knowledge prompted Rodén (1956) to try the effect of hexosamines on the incorporation of S^{35}-labelled sulphate and uniformly labelled C^{14}-glucose into cartilage chondroitin sulphate. Glucosamine enhanced the incorporation of S^{35}-labelled sulphate up to a maximum of three times the control value. Although galactosamine increased the S^{35} uptake to a maximum of twice the control value the amount required was 100 times larger than the glucosamine concentration which gave the same stimulation. Rodén (1956) presented a scheme of reactions whereby glucosamine was phosphorylated to glucosamine 6-phosphate and eventually uridinediphospho acetylglucosamine was converted to uridinediphospho acetylgalactosamine. The maximal stimulation of S^{35}-uptake by glucosamine, while not affected by addition of glutamine, was completely abolished by the presence of small concentrations of glucose. This could be explained from the knowledge that the phosphorylation of glucosamine by hexokinase is effectively inhibited by the presence of glucose. The incorporation of C^{14}-labelled glucose into chondroitin sulphate was increased at a low concentration of glucosamine but decreased at a high concentration in comparison with controls without glucosamine added. Analysis of the uronic acid moiety of the chondroitin sulphate showed that its radioactivity was increased at the low glucosamine concentration and decreased at the high concentration. By contrast the galactosamine moiety showed decreased radioactivity under both sets of conditions.

Rodén (1956) has made a similar study of the biosynthesis of chondroitin sulphate in pig *nucleus pulposus*. Again glutamine stimulated the incorporation of S^{35}-sulphate and was also found to increase the utilization of C^{14}-glucose for the synthesis of the galactosamine moieties.

Pogell (1959) has investigated the biosynthesis of the mucopolysaccharides in adult bovine corneas by incubating these with uniformly labelled C^{14}-D-glucose plus L-glutamine. The activity of the resulting C^{14}-labelled hexosamines incorporated in the mucopolysaccharides was assayed. It was demonstrated that this incorporation was considerably stimulated by the presence of the glutamine. Most of the hexosamine radioactivity was found in the acid-insoluble residue of cornea, presumably in the form of high molecular weight polysaccharides (Pogell and Koenig, 1959).

Maley and Maley (1959) have presented evidence that UDP-N-acetylglucosamine and UDP-glucosamine are converted to their corresponding galactosamine derivatives by a UDP glucosamine 4-epimerase.

Suzuki and Strominger (1959) have isolated a soluble enzyme from isthmus, a 2 cm long region of hen oviduct, which secretes the inner egg-shell membrane containing sulphated mucopolysaccharide. This soluble enzyme has the ability to catalyse the transfer of sulphate from ^{35}S-adenosine-3'-phosphate-5'-phosphosulphate to sulphated mucopolysaccharides in the presence of added primer (chondroitin sulphate A, B or C, or a sulphated heptasaccharide isolated from the liver of a patient with Hurler's syndrome). Transfer to acetylgalactosamine and its monosulphate has also been reported (Suzuki and Strominger, 1960).

D'Abramo and Lipmann (1957) showed that extracts of chick embryo condyles incorporated the sulphate group of ^{35}S-adenosine 3'-phosphate-5'-phosphosulphate into chondroitin sulphate A. Adams (1959a) later investigated the effect of the addition of various mucopolysaccharides on the biosynthesis of chondroitin sulphate in a particle-free enzyme system derived from chick embryo condyles. The enzyme was incubated with adenosine triphosphate and magnesium chloride in the presence of the added mucopolysaccharide and $Na_2{}^{35}SO_4$. The activity of the chondroitin sulphate formed was then assayed. Hyaluronic acid was without effect; umbilical cord chondroitin sulphate C and its protein complex stimulated to the same extent on a weight basis. Bovine trachea chondroitin sulphate A had a low degree of stimulation compared with chondroitin sulphate C, but this is probably explained by its presence already in the form of the mucoprotein in the enzyme system. Cartilage chondromucoprotein inhibited slightly the formation of chondroitin sulphate and when uridine diphosphoglucuronic acid was incubated with the chick condyle enzyme a suppression of chondroitin sulphate synthesis resulted. Adams (1959b) found that chondroitin did not act as a sulphate acceptor in the system described above.

Whitehouse and Lash (1961) have concluded from studies on the biogenesis of cartilage in tissue culture that cortisone, hydrocortisone and their chemical analogues inhibit the formation of acid mucopolysaccharides in connective tissue primarily by inhibiting the sulphation of the preformed polysaccharide.

Biosynthesis of Chondroitin Sulphate-Protein Complexes

Gross, Mathews and Dorfman (1959) have presented evidence suggesting that the chondroitin sulphate A–protein complex present in rat costal cartilage is metabolized as one unit. Rats were injected simultaneously with $Na_2S^{35}O_4$ and DL-lysine-1-C^{14} in order to label both polysaccharide and protein moieties. After various intervals up to 16 days the rats were sacrificed and the complex (20–23% protein; 77–80% chondroitin sulphate A) assayed. The radioactive sulphate was obtained after hydrolysis as $BaS^{35}O_4$ while C^{14} was isolated as $BaC^{14}O_3$ by means of a specific lysine decarboxylase. The time curve of disappearance of S^{35} closely paralleled that of C^{14}.

Chondroitin Sulphate B (β-Heparin): Structural Studies

Meyer and Chaffee (1941) in a study of the polysaccharides present in pig skin obtained a component which contained hexosamine, acetyl, uronic acid and sulphuric acid in equimolar ratios. Although this polysaccharide was thus superficially similar in composition to the chondroitin-sulphuric acid of cartilage it differed from the latter in its solubility and in its higher optical rotation ($[\alpha]_D - 53 \cdot 9°$, $-57 \cdot 9°$, $-55 \cdot 1°$). A typical preparation contained N, $2 \cdot 05$; hexosamine, $25 \cdot 1$; uronic acid, $30 \cdot 3$; acetyl, $7 \cdot 84$ and S, $5 \cdot 07\%$. The hexosamine present was isolated by the method of Meyer and Palmer (1936) and had $[\alpha]_D + 93 \cdot 6°$ (equil. after upward mutarotation) identical with that of chondrosamine hydrochloride. A polysaccharide with similar properties designated chondroitin sulphate B was later found (Meyer and Rapport, 1951) in tendon (pig and calf), heart valves and aorta. The chondroitin sulphate B (synonymous with β-heparin), isolated from beef lung during the fractionation of heparin by Marbet and Winterstein (1951) had $[\alpha]_D - 60°$ in water. Hydrolysis of the barium salt with 25% HCl for 12 hr under reflux afforded crystalline α-D-galactosamine hydrochloride ($[\alpha]_D^{20} + 122 \rightarrow + 92°$) further characterized as its Schiff's base with anisaldehyde.

Polysaccharide B isolated from hog gastric mucosa by Smith and Gallop (1953) was also probably identical with chondroitin sulphate B. It had $[\alpha]_D^{24°} - 52° \pm 3°$ in water and contained N, $2 \cdot 4\%$; S, $6 \cdot 1\%$; hexuronic acid (Lefevre-Tollens), $34 \cdot 6\%$; hexosamine (3N-HCl hydrolysis, 100°, 6 hr), $33 \cdot 6\%$ and N-acetyl, $8 \cdot 6\%$. The hexosamine was crystallized and shown to be chondrosamine hydrochloride. A definite conclusion as to the nature of the hexuronic acid was not reached. A significant finding however, was that the uronic acid determined by the Dische carbazole method was only $16 \cdot 6\%$. The number of moles of periodate consumed per 503 g of polysaccharide (the statistical polymer unit of uronic acid, acetylhexosamine and sulphate $1:1:1$) was $0 \cdot 8$ (24 hr), $1 \cdot 1$ (48 hr).

The first evidence as to the nature of the uronic acid in chondroitin sulphate B was provided by Hoffman, Linker and Meyer (1956). The ratio of the uronic acid values of chondroitin sulphate B obtained when determined with carbazole and orcinol reagents respectively is $0 \cdot 41$. Three reference uronic acids (L-iduronic acid, $0 \cdot 22$; D-mannurone, $0 \cdot 13$; L-gulurone, $0 \cdot 30$) had low carbazole/orcinol ratios when determined by these reagents while with two others (D-glucurone, $1 \cdot 0$; D-galacturonic acid, $0 \cdot 95$) the ratio was approximately unity. Hence it was concluded that neither glucuronic acid nor galacturonic acid was the major acid constituent of chondroitin sulphate B. Hydrolysis of chondroitin sulphate

B with Dowex 50 (H$^+$) at 100° and fractionation of the products on Dowex 1 (acetate) and paper chromatograms yielded disaccharide I, disaccharide II, and a hexuronic fraction the main constituent of which had an R$_F$ value identical with that of L-iduronic acid. The hexuronic acid fraction (carbozole/orcinol ratio, 0·32) also contained a small amount of glucuronic acid which accounts for its carbazole/orcinol ratio being somewhat higher than that of pure L-iduronic acid. Hydrolysis of disaccharide I, the major disaccharide product, gave galactosamine and iduronic acid while hydrolysis of disaccharide II afforded galactosamine and glucuronic acid. These results posed the problem as to whether the chondroitin sulphate 'B' fraction obtained from skin was a mixture of two different polysaccharides or a single molecular species. Studies of Hoffmann, Linker and Meyer (1957) favour the former possibility since fractions were obtained with a variable ratio of glucuronic acid to iduronic acid. Since, however, all fractions were resistant to testicular hyaluronidase no chondroitin sulphate A or C can be present.

Studies by Cifonelli, Ludowieg and Dorfman (1958) have shown that pure chondroitin sulphate B from beef lung contains only iduronic acid. The purified chondroitin sulphate B used by these workers had $[\alpha]_D{}^{25} - 85°$ and was not attacked by testicular hyaluronidase. The starting material was the β-heparin of Marbet and Winterstein (1951). This could be separated into two polysaccharides of which the major fraction (70%) was chondroitin sulphate B and the minor fraction was another new chondroitin sulphate having $[\alpha]_D{}^{22} + 10°$. When the β-heparin (1% solution) was mixed with 0·1 volume of saturated NaOH and 0·8 volume of qualitative Bendict's solution the chondroitin sulphate B was precipitated as a copper complex and the new chondroitin sulphate remained in the supernatant. The chondroitin sulphate B contained hexosamine, nitrogen and acetyl in the molar ratio of 1·00, 1·02 and 0·92 respectively. The uronic acid to hexosamine ratio, when the former was determined with carbazole (Dische, 1947), was only 0·40. In contrast this same ratio in the new chondroitin sulphate was 0·95.

Purified chondroitin sulphate B was hydrolysed with N-HCl at 100° for 1 hr and the products fractionated on charcoal by elution with water, 5%, 25% and 50% ethanol. The water eluate contained free hexosamine and a small amount of uronic acid. The alcohol eluates were further fractionated on Dowex 50 (H$^+$) to give a uronic acid fraction and an oligosaccharide fraction. The uronic acid fraction $([\alpha] + 30°)$ was characterized as L-iduronic acid by the scheme of reactions shown in Fig. 3.5.

The uronic acid was esterified by heating with 2% methanolic hydrogen chloride at 100° for 2 hr and the product reduced with sodium borohydride buffered with borate to give an initial pH of approximately 4·5. The product was an equilibrium mixture of L-idose and L-idosan separable

7

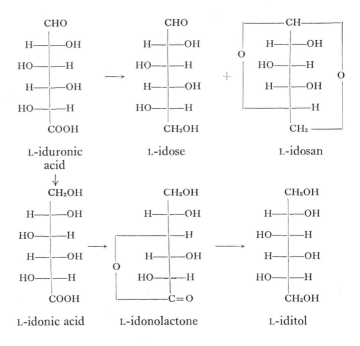

Fig. 3.5

on a charcoal column. Reduction of the uronic acid with unbuffered sodium borohydride gave idonolactone and iditol. The hexosamine was characterized as galactosamine by ninhydrin degradation (Stoffyn and Jeanloz, 1954b) to lyxose.

The disaccharide fraction ($[\alpha]_D^{20} + 38°$) behaved in the Elson–Morgan reaction as if it were a uronosyl-(1 → 3) hexosamine since analysis by this method (without hydrolysis) gave a chromogen with λ_{max} 510 mμ and a ratio of absorbancy at 540 mμ to that at 510 mμ of 0·35. This behaviour has been shown previously to be characteristic of a 3-substituted hexosamine (Cifonelli and Dorfman, 1958). The sequence of units in the disaccharide was indicated by the disappearance of the Elson–Morgan reaction following treatment with ninhydrin. Further evidence showed that the uronic acid in the disaccharide was iduronic acid.

Stoffyn and Jeanloz (1960) have added yet another synonym in describing chondroitin sulphate B as dermatan sulphate. Using material supplied by Marbet and Winterstein (1951) they succeeded in conclusively characterizing the uronic acid constituent of dermatan sulphate as L-iduronic acid (see also Jeanloz and Stoffyn, 1958). The dermatan sulphate was desulphated with an acetyl chloride–methanol mixture and the resulting polysaccharide (the methyl ester of desulphated dermatan sulphate) reduced with sodium borohydride. Hydrolysis of the product with 0.5N-H_2SO_4 at $100°$ for 7 hr yielded a mixture of sugars which were acetylated with acetic anhydride-pyridine. Chromatography on a silicic acid column eluted with benzene–ether (9:1) gave 2:3:4-tri-O-acetyl-1:6-anhydro-β-L-idopyranose in a yield of 33% and showing m.p. and rotation identical with that of a synthetic specimen obtained by synthesis from 1:2-O-isopropylidene L-idofuranose (Vargha, 1954).

Six methylations of chondroitin sulphate with dimethyl sulphate and sodium hydroxide at $0–5°$ gave a methyl ether (OCH_3, 16.04%) having N, 2.68%; S, 5.86% and acetyl CH_3CO, 7.17% in agreement with the values for a fully methylated polysaccharide (Jeanloz, Stoffyn and Tremege, 1957). Methanolysis of this product with 5% methanolic hydrogen chloride for 24 hr, N-acetylation and subsequent fractionation of the products on a silicic acid column gave three fractions I, II and III in the ratio of 1:1:2. Fraction I gave a positive reaction for uronic acid and a negative reaction for uronic acid. Fraction II, which gave a negative reaction for uronic acid but a positive reaction for nitrogen, afforded crystalline methyl 2-acetamido 2-deoxy 6-O-methyl α-D-galactopyranoside (m.p. $207–208°$) further characterized as its 3:4-isopropylidene derivative m.p. $157–158°$.

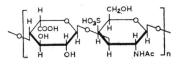

Fig. 3.6   *Structure of chondroitin sulphate B*

These data suggested that the sulphate group cannot be on position 6 of the galactosamine moiety and it is probably linked to position 4. This presumption is supported by the infrared studies of Mathews (1958) who on the basis of a previous assignment of bands by Orr (1954) suggested that the sulphate group in chondroitin sulphate B had an axial configuration. In more recent methylation studies Jeanloz and Stoffyn (1958) have hydrolysed the sodium salt of fully methylated desulphated β-heparin (OCH_3, 26.8%) and obtained crystalline methyl 2-acetamido 2-deoxy 4,6-di-O-methyl α-D-galactopyranoside identical with an authentic specimen obtained by synthesis (Stoffyn and Jeanloz, 1954a). This confirmed that the sulphate group is located on position 4 of the galactosamine residue and that the L-iduronic acid residues are attached to the galactosamine residues through C_3 as shown in Fig. 3.6.

Hoffman, Linker, Lippman and Meyer (1960) have produced evidence that chondroitin sulphate A and chondroitin sulphate B are stereoisomers differing only as C-5 uronic acid epimers. Identical unsaturated disaccharides were obtained from chondroitin sulphate A and chondroitin sulphate B by treatment with *Flavobacterium* enzymes. It is therefore concluded that chondroitin sulphate B contains α-1,3-L-idopyranosyluronic acid and

β-1,4-(2-acetamido 2-deoxy)-D-galactopyranosyl 4-O-sulphate as the repeating units in the polymer. A remarkable series of polysaccharides are thus encountered in connective tissue. Their inter-relationship is shown in Fig. 3.7.

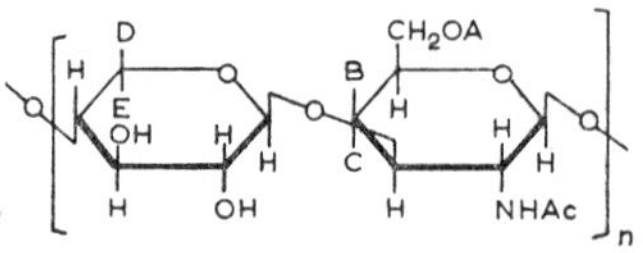

	A	B	C	D	E
Hyaluronic acid	H	H	OH	COOH	H
Chondroitin sulphate A	H	OSO₃H	H	COOH	H
Chondroitin sulphate B	H	OSO₃H	H	H	COOH
Chondroitin sulphate C	SO₃H	OH	H	COOH	H

Fig. 3.7

It can thus be seen that chondroitin sulphate A, chondroitin sulphate C and hyaluronate all form their repeating sequences with alternating β-1,3-D-glucopyranosyluronic acid and β-1,4-acetylhexosaminidic units. Chondroitin sulphate B differs from chondroitin sulphate A in that the D-glucopyranosyluronic acid moiety is replaced by its C-5 epimer, L-idopyranosyluronic acid.

Isolation from Normal and Pathological Tissues

Chondroitin sulphate B was first isolated from pig skin by Meyer and Chaffee (1941). This sulphated polysaccharide was accompanied in pig skin by hyaluronic acid from which it could be separated by alcohol fractionation in the presence of an excess of barium acetate or by preferential hydrolysis of the hyaluronic acid component using a *Pneumococcus* enzyme. Gardell, Gordon and Aquist (1950) demonstrated two components, presumably those reported above, in an extract of pig skin mucopolysaccharides. On slab electrophoresis, both moved towards the anode in 0·1M-acetate buffer, pH 4·7.

Meyer (1947) reported that, in pig skin, chondroitin sulphate B and hyaluronic acid were present in a ratio of 1·25:1. At term, the skin of pig embryos has a total mucopolysaccharide content very much higher than skin of the adult species but here the ratio of chondroitin sulphate B: hyaluronic acid is 1:5. Similar results were obtained (Loewi and Meyer, 1958) in a further comparison of the polysaccharide pattern of pig skin at various stages of embryonic development with that of adult pig skin. The differences between embryonic and adult skin were in accord with the correlation of chondroitin sulphate B with the coarse type of collagen bundles.

The presence of chondroitin sulphate B in rabbit skin was established by Schiller, Mathews, Jefferson, Ludowieg and Dorfman (1954).

The polysaccharides were extracted from the defatted skin with 2% NaOH at room temperature for 24 hr, the extracts dialysed and then digested with crystalline trypsin. After dialysis the crude polysaccharides were precipitated with 4 volumes of 95% ethanol in the presence of 1% sodium acetate. Separation of the polysaccharide components was effected by electrophoresis in a slab of Celite moistened with a mixture of 0·09M-NaCl and 0·01M-sodium phosphate buffer pH 7·0 saturated with thymol as a preservative. The apparatus devised was suitable for the separation of 200–300 mg quantities.

The chondroitin sulphate B from rabbit skin had $[\alpha]_D^{25} - 55°$ and the ratios of uronic acid:hexosamine:acetyl:sulphur were 0·94:0·91:0·94:0·96. While the uronic acid content determined by the manometric CO_2 method (Tracey, 1948) approached the theoretical value it was only 37% of theory when determined by the carbazole reaction (Dische, 1947). The hexosamine was identified by its X-ray diffraction pattern as chondrosamine hydrochloride. The polysaccharide was resistant to the action of streptococcal hyaluronidase but was attacked to the extent of some 30% by testicular hyaluronidase (compare with results above).

In the isolation of chondroitin sulphate B from tendon, heart valves and aorta (Meyer and Rapport, 1951) the tissues were extracted with 0·33–0·5N-NaOH at 0° and the extracts neutralized with acetic acid. The mucopolysaccharides present were freed from protein with amyl alcohol-chloroform, and from glycogen by digestion with amylase. The residual polysaccharides were fractionally precipitated from calcium acetate-acetic acid solution by alcohol at 0°. Under these conditions chondroitin sulphate B was precipitated at an alcohol concentration of 20%. It was resistant to both testicular and pneumococcal hyaluronidase.

Dorfman and Lorincz (1957) found that whereas normal urine contains only small amounts of chondroitin sulphate A, two patients with the Hurler syndrome (syn. gargoylism) excreted relatively large amounts of chondroitin sulphate B together with small amounts of heparitin sulphate. In a further study Meyer, Grumbach, Linker and Hoffman (1958) also found that the urine of 4 out of 5 patients with gargoylism contained both chondroitin sulphate B and heparitin sulphate with the former predominating. The urine of another patient yielded only heparitin sulphate. In these cases the chondroitin sulphate B fractions were recognized by their strongly negative rotation, a low carbazole/orcinol ratio in uronic acid determination and their resistance to testicular hyaluronidase.

Polatnick, La Tessa and Katzin (1957) have examined the acid mucopolysaccharides present in bovine cornea and sclera (the sclera is the opaque posterior fibrous coat of the eyeball). These two adjacent positions in the eye represent highly specialized forms of connective tissue arising embryologically from the same mesodermal area. However, whereas the cornea is transparent and contains an orderly arrangement of collagen fibres the sclera is opaque and the collagen fibres are coarser and interwoven in irregular bundles. Using analysis and fractionation techniques similar to those of Meyer, Linker, Davidson and Weissman (1953) these workers found that the mucopolysaccharides (2·2% of the dry weight) of the cornea were divided into chondroitin sulphate A, 22% chondroitin, 20% and keratosulphate, 52%. In contrast the bovine sclera in two fractionations afforded yields of 0·7 and 0·9% of the dry weight as mucopolysaccharides which were separated into a chondroitin sulphate B fraction, 50 and 56% and an undefined chondroitin sulphate A and C fraction, 48 and 40%. No keratosulphate was found in the sclera and only trace amounts of hyaluronic acid. The chondroitin sulphate B fraction had $[\alpha]_D^{26} - 62·5°$ in water, was not hydrolysed by testicular hyaluronidase and contained 13·2% sulphate; 30·9% hexosamine and gave values of 36·0% and 12·6% uronic acid when estimated by the orcinol and carbazole methods respectively. The hexosamine was established as galactosamine by ninhydrin degradation. The unidentified chondroitin sulphate A and C fractions $[\alpha]_D - 24·5°$, $- 23·7°$, $- 23·1°$ were all hydrolysed by testicular hyaluronidase, contained 12·9%, 14·8% and 13·4% sulphate respectively and showed carbazole/orcinol uronic acid ratios of 0·81, 1·4 and 1·4 respectively.

Anticoagulant Studies

Chondroitin sulphate B (Marbet and Winterstein, 1951) exerts anticoagulant activity which is greatly dependent upon the coagulation system

Table 3.II. *Anticoagulant activity of chondroitin sulphate B preparations*

Polysaccharide tested	Method of assay				
	Studer and Winterstein (1951)	Ox blood in vitro	British Pharmacopoeia 1953	U.S.P. xiv 1950	In vivo
Chond. sulph. B (sheep lung)	50·4, 49·9; 56·3, 51·6; 49·1	3·4 4·2	0	< 2	3 (cat) 3–4 (dog)
Chond. sulph. B (ox lung)	24·6; 25·7; 24·3; 24·3	8·3	3–4	< 2	6–8 (cat) 8 (dog)

in which it is measured (Yamashina, 1954). Anticoagulant activity is high when measured by the thrombin method but only small if determined *in vitro* using the methods described by Blombäck, Blombäck, Corneliusson, and Jorpes (1953) or by an *in vivo* determination. Examples are given in Table 3. II.

Grossman and Dorfman (1957) have shown that chondroitin sulphate B surpasses heparin in antithrombic potency at low thrombin concentrations but has little or no antithrombic properties at high thrombin concentrations.

Biosynthesis of Chondroitin Sulphate B

Rodén and Dorfman (1958) isolated hyaluronic acid and chondroitin sulphate B from rat skin after administration of glucose-6-C^{14} and have studied the distribution of radioactivity in these polysaccharides. In chondroitin sulphuric acid B 43% of the activity was found in the galactosamine moiety and 43% in the C-6 of the L-iduronic acid moiety, 5% was found in the acetyl group. It was concluded that the L-iduronic acid of chondroitin sulphuric acid B arises from glucose without splitting of the carbon chain.

Enzymic Degradation of Chondroitin Sulphate B

Neither chondroitin sulphate B itself nor the product derived from it by desulphation is attacked by testicular or pneumococcal hyaluronidase (Hoffman, Linker and Meyer, 1957). Extracts derived from a flavobacterium grown on chondroitin sulphate B as a carbon source contain at least two and probably three or four enzymes concerned with the degradation of chondroitin sulphate B (Hoffman, Linker, Sampson, and Meyer, 1957). Such extracts have only a negligible action on chemically desulphated chondroitin sulphate B. One of the enzymes in the extract is heat-labile (inactivated by heating at 56° for 5 min) and will attack the 4:5-unsaturated disaccharides prepared from hyaluronic acid or chondroitin causing the disappearance of uronic acid (detected by the carbazole reagent) and liberation of free *N*-acetyl hexosamines. Its function in the degradation of chondroitin sulphate B is also probably to degrade the Δ4:5-unsaturated disaccharides formed by the remaining enzymes in the extract since the intact extract produces initially an increase in reducing power, a higher carbazole value and the appearance of absorption at 230 mμ associated with unsaturation. Thereafter the carbazole colour and ultraviolet absorption decrease in a parallel fashion and free *N*-acetyl galactosamine is liberated. Heated extracts yield a mixture of unsaturated (sulphated and desulphated) di- and oligosaccharides when incubated with chondroitin sulphate B.

Detection of Chondroitin Sulphates in Tissues

Wolfrom, Madison and Cron (1952) established that cartilage chondroitin sulphate $(A + C)$ consumed one mole of periodate per disaccharide unit in oxidizing the glucuronic acid residues between C_2–C_3 and hence can be detected in tissues by its PAS-positive reaction. Smith and Gallop (1953) reported a similar periodate consumption by chondroitin sulphate B. Metachromatic staining with toluidine blue is exhibited by cartilage chondroitin sulphate (Walton and Ricketts, 1954) and almost certainly by chondroitin sulphate B although no specific report of this has been encountered. The specific detection of the chondroitin sulphates must rest on the use of (a) streptococcal or pneumococcal hyaluronidase to distinguish all of them from hyaluronic acid and (b) testicular hyaluronidase to distinguish chondroitin sulphates A and C from chondroitin sulphate B. Use of an extract of the chondroitin sulphate B adapted strain of flavobacterium will then provide final confirmation.

REFERENCES

Adams, J. B. *Nature* **184**, 275 (1959a).
Adams, J. B. *Biochim. Biophys. Acta* **32**, 559 (1959b).
Addis, T. *Harvey Lectures Ser.* **23**, 222 (1927–28).
Astrup, P. *Acta Pharmacol. Toxiol.* **3**, 165 (1947).
Badin, J., Schubert, M., and Vouras, M. *J. Clin. Invest.* **34**, 1317 (1955).
Bassiouni, M. *Ann. Rheumatic Diseases* **14**, 288 (1955).
Bernardi, G. *Biochim. Biophys. Acta* **26**, 47 (1957).
Bettelheim, F. A. and Philpott, D. E. *Nature* **188**, 564 (1960).
Blix, G. and Snellman, O. *Ark. Kemi Min. Geol.* **A19**, 32 (1945).
Blombäck, M., Blombäck, B., Corneliusson, E. V., and Jorpes, J. E. *J. Pharm. Pharmacol.* **5**, 1031 (1953).
Bollet, A. J., Seraydarian M. W., and Simpson, W. F. *J. Clin. Invest.* **36**, 1328. (1957).
Boström, H., Jorpes, E., Månsson, B., Rodén, L., and Vestermark, A. *Ark. Kemi* **8**, 469 (1956).
Boström, H., and Månsson, B. *Acta Chem. Scand.* **7**, 1014 (1953).
Bray, H. G., Gregory, J. E., and Stacey, M. *Biochem. J.* **38**, 142 (1944).
Cifonelli, J. A. and Dorfman, A. *J. Biol. Chem.* **231**, 11 (1958).
Cifonelli, J. A., Ludowieg, J. and Dorfman, A. *J. Biol. Chem.* **233**, 541 (1958).
Craddock, J. G. and Kerby, G. P. *J. Lab. Clin. Med.* **46**, 193 (1955).
D'Abramo, F. and Lipmann, F. *Biochim. Biophys. Acta* **25**, 211 (1957).
Davidson, E. A. and Meyer, K. *J. Biol. Chem.* **211**, 605 (1954a).
Davidson, E. A. and Meyer, K. *J. Amer. Chem. Soc.* **76**, 5686 (1954b).
Davidson, E. A. and Meyer, K. *J. Amer. Chem. Soc.* **77**, 4796 (1955).
Deiss, W. P. and Leon, A. S. *J. Biol. Chem.* **206**, 375 (1954).
Deiss, W. P. and Leon, A. S. *J. Biol. Chem.* **215**, 685 (1955).
Dische, Z. *J. Biol. Chem.* **167**, 189 (1947).
Dodgson, K. S. and Lloyd, A. G. *Biochem. J.* **65**, 4p (1957); **66**, 532 (1957).

Dodgson, K. S. and Lloyd, A. G. *Biochem. J.* **68,** 88 (1958).
Dodgson, K. S., Lloyd, A. G. and Spencer, B. *Biochem. J.* **65,** 131 (1957).
Dorfman, A. and Lorincz, A. E. *Proc. Nat. Acad. Sciences* **43,** 443 (1957).
Dunphy, J. E. and Udupa, K. N. *New Eng. J. Med.* **253,** 847 (1955).
Ferrante, N. Di. and Rich, C. *Clin. Chim. Acta* **1,** 519 (1956).
Fischer, G. and Boedeker. *Annalen* **117,** 111 (1861).
von Fürth, O. and Bruno, T. *Biochem. Z.* **294,** 153 (1937).
Gardell, S., Gordon, A. H. and Åqvist, S. *Acta Chem. Scand.* **4,** 907 (1950).
Gerber, B. R., Franklin, E. C. and Schubert, M. *J. Biol. Chem.* **235,** 2870 (1960).
Gross, J., Mathews, M. and Dorfman, A. *Fed. Proc.* **18,** 239 (1959).
Grossman, B. J. and Dorfman, A. *Pediatrics* **20,** 506 (1957).
Hebting, J. *Biochem. Z.* **63,** 353 (1914).
Heremans, J. F., Vaerman, J. P. and Heremans, M. Th. *Nature* **183,** 1606 (1959).
Hoffman, P., Linker, A. and Meyer, K. *Science* **124,** 1252 (1956).
Hoffman, P., Linker, A. and Meyer, K. *Arch. Biochem. Biophys.* **69,** 435 (1957).
Hoffman, P., Linker, A. and Meyer, K. *Biochim. Biophys. Acta* **30,** 184 (1958).
Hoffman, P., Linker, A., Lippman, V. and Meyer, K. *J. Biol. Chem.* **235,** 3066 (1960).
Hoffman, P., Linker, A., Sampson, P. and Meyer, K. *Biochim. Biophys. Acta.* **25,** 658 (1957).
Hoffman, P., Meyer, K. and Linker, A. *J. Biol. Chem.* **219,** 653 (1956).
Jeanloz, R. W. and Stoffyn, P. J. *Fed. Proc.* **17,** 249 (1958).
Jeanloz, R. W., Stoffyn, P. J. and Tremege, M. *Fed. Proc.* **16,** 201 (1957).
Kantor, T. G. and Schubert, M. *J. Amer. Chem. Soc.* **79,** 152 (1957).
Kerby, G. P. *J. Clin. Invest.* **33,** 1168 (1954).
Kobayashi, T. *J. Biochem.* (Japan), **28,** 31 (1938).
Krukenberg, C. F. W. *Z. Biol.* **20,** 307 (1884).
Kyrk, J. E., and Dyrbyye, M. *J. Gerontology* **12,** 20, 23 (1957).
Levene, P. A. *J. Biol. Chem.* **140,** 267 (1941).
Levene, P. A., and La Forge, F. B. *J. Biol. Chem.* **15,** 155 (1913).
Linker, A., Hoffman, P., Meyer, K., Sampson, P., and Korn, E. D. *J. Biol. Chem.* **235,** 3061 (1960).
Loewi, G. and Meyer, K. *Biochim. Biophys. Acta* **27,** 453 (1958).
Lorincz, A. E. *Fed. Proc.* **19,** 148 (1960).
Lowther, D. J., and Rogers, H. J. *Biochem. J.* **62,** 304 (1956).
Malawista, I., and Schubert, M. *J. Biol. Chem.* **230,** 535 (1948).
Maley, F., and Maley, G. F. *Biochim. Biophys. Acta* **31,** 577 (1959).
Marbet, R., and Winterstein, A. *Helv. Chim. Acta* **34,** 2311 (1951).
Masamune, H., Yoshizawa, Z. and Maki, M. *Tohoku J. Exp. Med.* **55,** 47 (1951).
Mathews, M. B. *Fed. Proc.* **14,** 252 (1955).
Mathews, M. B. *Nature* **181,** 421 (1958).
Mathews, M. B. and Dorfman, A. *Arch. Biochem. Biophys.* **42,** 41 (1953).
Mathews, M. B. and Lozaityte, I. *Fed. Proc.* **15,** 1012 (1956).
Meister, A. and Tice, S. V. *J. Biol. Chem.* **187,** 173 (1950).
Meyer, K. *The Harvey Lectures* LI. **88** (1957).
Meyer, K. and Chaffee, E. *J. Biol. Chem.* **138,** 491 (1941).
Meyer, K., Davidson, E., Linker, A. and Hoffmann, P. *Biochim. Biophys. Acta* **21,** 506 (1956).
Meyer, K., Grumbach, M. M., Linker, A. and Hoffmann, P. *Proc. Soc. Exp. Biol. Med.* **97,** 275 (1958).
Meyer, K., Linker, A., Davidson, E. A. and Weissmann, B. *J. Biol. Chem.* **205,** 611 (1953).

Meyer, K. H., Odier, M. E. and Siegrist, A. E. *Helv. Chim. Acta* **31,** 1400 (1948).
Meyer, K. and Palmer, J. W. *J. Biol. Chem.* **114,** 689 (1936).
Meyer, K. and Rapport, M. M. *Arch. Biochem.* **27,** 287 (1950).
Meyer, K. and Rapport, M. M. *Science* **113,** 596 (1951).
Moernier, C. T. *Skand. Arch. Physiol.* **6,** 322 (1895).
Moernier, C. T. *Skand. Arch. Physiol.* **1,** 210 (1889).
Muir, H. *Biochem. J.* **62,** 26P (1956).
Muir, H. *Biochem. J.* **65,** 33P (1957).
Muir, H. *Biochem. J.* **69,** 195 (1958).
Nakanishi, K., Takahashi, N. and Egami, F. *Bull. Chem. Soc. Japan* **29,** 434 (1956).
Neuman, R. E. and Logan, M. A. *J. Biol. Chem.* **186,** 549 (1950).
Orr, S. F. D. *Biochim. Biophys. Acta* **14,** 173 (1954).
Pernis, B. and Clerici, E. *Experientia* **13,** 351 (1957).
Pogell, B. M. *Biochim. Biophys. Acta* **31,** 280 (1959).
Pogell, B. M. and Koenig, D. F. *J. Biol. Chem.* **234,** 2504 (1959).
Polatnick, J., La Tessa, A. J. and Katzin, H. M. *Biochim. Biophys. Acta* **26,** 361 (1957).
Robertson, W. B., and Schwartz, B. *J. Biol. Chem.* **201,** 689 (1953).
Rodén, L. *Ark. Kemi* **10,** 325, 333, 345, 383 (1956).
Rodén, L. and Dorfman, A. *J. Biol. Chem.* **233,** 1030 (1958).
Schiller, S. *Biochim. Biophys. Acta* **28,** 413 (1958).
Schiller, S., Mathews, M. B., Jefferson, H., Ludowieg, J. and Dorfman, A. *J. Biol. Chem.* **211,** 717 (1954).
Shatten, J. and Schubert, M. *J. Biol. Chem.* **211,** 565 (1954).
Slack, H. G. B. *Biochem. J.* **65,** 459 (1957).
Slack, H. G. B. *Biochem. J.* **69,** 125 (1958).
Smith, H. and Gallop, R. C. *Biochem. J.* **53,** 666 (1953).
Stoffyn, P. J. and Jeanloz, R. W. *J. Amer. Chem. Soc.* **76,** 563 (1954a).
Stoffyn, P. J. and Jeanloz, R. W. *Arch. Biochem. Biophys.* **52,** 373 (1954b).
Stoffyn, P. J. and Jeanloz, R. W. *J. Biol. Chem.* **235,** 2507 (1960).
Studer, A. and Winterstein, A. *Helv. Physiol. Pharmacol. Acta* **9,** 6 (1951).
Suzuki, S. *J. Biol. Chem.* **235,** 3580 (1960).
Suzuki, S. and Strominger, J. L. *Biochim. Biophys. Acta* **31,** 283 (1959).
Suzuki, S. and Strominger, J. L. *J. Biol. Chem.* **235,** 257, 267, 274 (1960).
Tolksdorf, S., McCready, M. H., McCullagh, D. R. and Schwenk, E. *J. Lab. Clin. Med.* **34,** 74 (1949).
Tracey, M. V. *Biochem. J.* **43,** 185 (1948).
Vargha, L. *Ber.* **87,** 1351 (1954).
Walton, K. W. and Ricketts, C. R. *Brit. J. Exp. Path.* **35,** 227 (1954).
Webber, R. V. and Bayley, S. T. *Can. J. Biochem. Physiol.* **34,** 993 (1956).
Whitehouse, M. W. and Lash, J. W. *Nature* **189,** 37 (1961).
Wolfrom, M. L. and Juliano, B. O. *J. Amer. Chem. Soc.* **82,** 1673, 2588 (1960).
Wolfrom, M. L., Madison, R. K. and Cron, M. J. *J. Amer. Chem. Soc..* **74,** 1491 (1952).
Wolfrom, M. L. and Montgomery, R. *J. Amer. Chem. Soc.* **72,** 2859 (1950).
Yamashina, I. *Acta Chem. Scand.* **8,** 1316 (1954).

Chapter 4

HEPARIN AND HEPARITIN SULPHATE

Heparin—Introduction

HEPARIN is an anticoagulant present in human connective tissue, where it appears to be localized in the mast cells. Such cells are believed to be the site of synthesis of heparin and in addition perform storage and excretory functions in relation to heparin. Heparin has been found useful in surgery and in the treatment of thrombosis. However, because of the low concentrations present in normal tissue, this expensive biological product has been 'copied' by organic chemists in such synthetic anticoagulants as dextran sulphate (Ricketts, 1953; James and Ricketts, 1954), laminarin sulphate (Adams and Thorpe, 1957) and other polysaccharide polysulphates. Heparin itself is a highly sulphated polysaccharide composed of D-glucuronic acid and D-glucosamine residues.

Methods of Isolation

Early methods developed by Howell undoubtedly resulted in only impure preparations. In the first of these (Howell, 1922–3; 1924) most of the fatty material in minced dog liver was removed with boiling methanol and the residue then extracted with physiological saline. Enzymic digestion of the extract sufficed to remove the glycogen present and most of the proteins were precipitated with cadmium chloride, to leave a crude preparation of heparin. Although this latter stage was improved using Lloyd's reagent (Howell, 1928) and the heparin was precipitated with excess barium hydroxide, it was the observation of Fischer and Schmitz (1932b, 1933) that laid the basis of the methods used in the next decade. These workers found that heparin combined with certain proteins near their isoelectric points to form complexes that could be dissociated by the addition of alkali. Charles and Scott (1933a) were thus enabled to employ as the main step in their purification procedure the precipitation of a heparin–protein complex at an acidic pH. Later, Charles and Scott (1936) succeeded in isolating heparin as its crystalline barium salt.

Purified heparin was first precipitated from its aqueous solution by addition of 5% benzidine hydrochloride. The methanol washed precipitate was heated in aqueous alkali at 75° until a clear brown solution was obtained. On cooling, the benzidine crystallized out and was removed. Addition of two volumes of methanol and then two volumes of ether, precipitated heparin containing only

0·7% ash. This heparin could then be crystallized from aqueous solution by addition of 5% barium acetate and glacial acetic acid.

An electrophoretically homogeneous preparation of heparin has been obtained (Wolfrom, Montgomery, Karabinos and Rathgeb, 1950), using an adaptation of this procedure. The crystalline barium salt has also been isolated directly from the commercial sodium salt (Wolfrom, Weisblat, Karabinos, McNeely and McLean, 1943). Numerous organic salts (piperidine, n-pentylamine, isopentylamine, dodecylamine, decamethylene diamine) of heparin have also been reported (Foster and Huggard, 1955).

Scott, Gardell and Nilsson (1957) have successfully fractionated crude heparin using cetylpyridinium chloride. The cetylpyridinium complexes formed were fractionated into (i) those insoluble in concentrations of potassium chloride > 1N (ii) those soluble in 1N-KCl but insoluble in 0·6N-KCl and (iii) the remainder soluble in 0·6N-KCl. Fraction (i) had 9·2% S, (ii) had 6·3% S and (iii) had 1·2% S. The presence of the purest heparin in fraction (i) was confirmed by the demonstration that (i) contained glucosamine (ii) glucosamine with a little galactosamine and (iii) considerable quantities of galactosamine with glucosamine. Fractions soluble only in the highest concentrations of potassium chloride (> 1·35N) were also found to have the highest anticoagulant activity. To obtain the polysaccharide from its complex the latter was dissolved in 33% saturated saline, treated with Fuller's earth to remove cetylpyridinium ions, dialysed and freeze-dried.

Korn (1958) has used an adaptation of this method in the isolation of heparin from mouse mast cell tumour slices.

Homogenized heat-sterilized tissue was treated with pancreatin at pH 8·5 to remove the bulk of the protein. The dialysed centrifuged solution was then adjusted to a one molar concentration of sodium chloride and the heparin fraction precipitated by the addition of an excess of cetyltrimethylammonium bromide. The complex was dissolved in 4M-NaCl and reprecipitated by dilution to 1M-NaCl. After three repetitions of this procedure, the cetyltrimethylammonium ion was removed as its insoluble thiocyanate salt and the heparin remaining in the supernatant recovered by dialysis and freeze-drying.

Heparin was found to be absorbed readily on anion exchange resins such as Dowex 1, Dowex 2, Dowex 3, Amberlite CG-45 and Duolite A-4 when the latter were buffered at pH 6·0. However, when eluted with strong salt solutions, the eluates differed from the original preparations in having greater absorption at 400 mμ than 535 mμ when assayed by the carbazole reaction (Dische, 1955). Green (1960) has therefore used the ECTEOLA cellulose anion exchanger to resolve a commercial bovine heparin preparation into four major and one minor carbazole positive fractions each with λ_{max} 535 mμ. In this fractionation, 90% of the original material was recovered. Radioactive heparin isolated from a mast cell tumour gave only one peak when submitted to this procedure. This component, which was eluted with M-sodium chloride, constituted only 50% of the original.

Excellent recoveries of heparin and other polysaccharides have been reported following chromatography on ECTEOLA cellulose (Ringertz and Reichard, 1959); slight losses (105 initial → 100 final) in anticoagulant activity were encountered because of the weakly acid (0·05M-HCl) conditions of elution. By carrying out the chromatography at 4°C this slight inactivation was eliminated and excellent separations of hyaluronic acid, chrondroitin sulphate and heparin achieved (Ringertz and Reichard, 1960). The sodium chloride used in elution was removed by gel filtration through Sephadex. Heparins of different anticoagulant activity were eluted at different elution volumes—in general those with the highest anticoagulant activity tended to show the highest affinity for the column. ECTEOLA chromatography has been used to isolate heparin from mast cells (Ringertz, 1960).

Other Techniques for Heparin Separation

Jorpes (1946) reported that in free electrophoresis heparin had mobilities of -17 to -19 cm^2 V^{-1} sec^{-1} × 10^{-5} being considerably greater than those of hyaluronic acid (-12 cm^2 V^{-1} sec^{-1} × 10^{-5}) but of the same order as those of chondroitin sulphate (-16 cm^2 V^{-1} sec^{-1} × 10^{-5}). Reinits (1953) examined the migration of these polysaccharides on filter-paper strips when submitted to electrophoresis. Heparin had a slightly greater mobility than chondroitin sulphate at pH 6·7 in 0·1M-sodium phosphate buffer but could not be separated in a mixture. Under these conditions hyaluronic acid had a low mobility. The positions of the polysaccharides on paper were located either by elution and estimation or by staining with toluidine blue, azure A or periodate-fuchsin. The difficulty of locating the polysaccharides on paper has been overcome by Lewis and Smith (1957) who have used glass-fibre paper. While borate buffer pH 9–10 is satisfactory for the separation of polysaccharides which have entirely different structures the use of 2N-sodium hydroxide offers many advantages. The movement of the polysaccharides appears to depend on the ionization of the alcoholic groups under the influence of the alkaline electrolyte since there can be no possibility of complexes between the polysaccharides and the glass fibre paper. When examined in this way heparin, hyaluronic acid and chondroitin sulphate behaved as homogeneous polymers and could be separated from each other with relative ease. Ascending paper chromatography with 25% (v/v) n-propanol in M/15 sodium phosphate buffer pH 6 has been used to separate heparin (Kerby, 1953) and dextran sulphates (Ricketts, Walton and Saddington, 1954). In the case of the latter, with preparations of similar sulphate content, the R$_F$ value was dependent on molecular size. Other separations of heparin preparations have been achieved with the Craig counter-current machine (O'Keeffe, Russo-Alesi, Dolliver and Stiller, 1949) and by adsorption front analysis (Snellman, Jensen and Sylvén, 1949).

Distribution of Heparin in the Tissues

Charles and Scott (1933b) determined the heparin contents of various tissues by isolation. Highest concentrations (mg/kg of tissue) were found in liver (beef, 190; hog, 340; dog, 330) and muscle (beef, 600) but beef thymus, spleen and lung also contained quite large amounts (310, 230, 230 respectively). Small amounts of heparin were found in beef heart (54 mg) and blood (66 mg). The amounts of heparin extracted from various tissues with 0·5M-potassium thiocyanate varied from less than 4 units in rabbit intestine to 4800 units/100 g tissue in the liver of a hypophysectomized dog (Monkhouse, 1956). Jaques, Waters and Charles (1942) compared the anticoagulant activities of the crystalline barium salts obtained from tissues of various mammalian species and reported activities of heparins from dog, beef, pork and sheep in the ratio of 10:5:2:1. These workers could detect no chemical difference between the heparins. They showed similar optical rotations and sulphur contents and gave similar values when assayed with toluidine blue and titrated against salmine (for protein-binding power). Species differences in heparin have also been reported by Bell and Jaques (1956).

Mast cells are now generally accepted as the sites of heparin storage although it has been reported that the distribution of heparin in rat and rabbit tissues and the mast cell counts did not always follow the same pattern (Marx, Rucker, Ruggeri and Freeman, 1957). The availability of mouse mast cell tumours makes possible a study of the metabolism of heparin in mast cells (Korn, 1958).

The mast cell occurs in tumours in the loose reticular tissue surrounding small blood vessels and underlying epithelial serous and synovial membranes. In the rabbit the majority of these cells are found in the blood. A mass of evidence has also accumulated correlating the mast cell with histamine production.

Examination of the polysaccharide pattern in mouse mast cell tumours has shown that in addition to heparin they contain a series of glucosamine- and galactosamine-containing polysaccharides of different sulphate content (Ringertz, 1960). It has been suggested that the former are precursor polysaccharides for heparin.

Mast cells have been shown to be released from rat mesentery into the peritoneal fluid. The average concentration of heparin in peritoneal fluid of rats was 14 mg/100 g fluid (Mergenthaler and Paff, 1956). Bloom and Ringertz (1960) have isolated the mast cells from peritoneal washings from rats and mice by a gradient centrifugation technique. After digestion with proteolytic enzymes a crude polysaccharide fraction was recovered by alcohol precipitation. About 80–100% of the total polysaccharide content was heparin; no hyaluronic acid was found. Heparin has also been found in the mast cells of human umbilical cord (Moore and Schoenberg, 1957). The secretion of heparin by mast cells following injury has been incorporated in a theory postulated as to the mechanism of the initiation of the inflammatory process (McGovern, 1957). Negatively charged heparin was believed to repel negatively charged leucocytes.

Dog mastocytomas were found to contain large quantities of heparin (Oliver, Bloom and Mangeri, 1947). In addition Magnusson and Larsson (1955) reported a polysaccharide fraction which was probably a mixture of chondroitin sulphate and heparin monosulphate. A more recent fractionation (Ringertz and Bloom, 1960) revealed that about 70% of the polysaccharide in the tumours was heparin while 30% was present as a non-sulphated fraction containing the amino sugars glucosamine and galactosamine in the ratio 3:1 and < 0·3 moles of sulphate/mole aminosugar and uronic acid. Heparin has been demonstrated to exist in combined form in dog blood using radioactive sulphate (Eiber and Danishefsky, 1957a).

In an evaluation of the heparin activity of mother and foetal plasma very similar values (0·39, 0·40) were found which increased in puerperium but became normal in 8 days (Maneschi and Rio, 1957). The heparin activity of the cord blood (40 cases) has been found to be a little lower than that of the mother (De Bellis, 1954). Guarini (1955) reported average heparin activities of 0·042, 0·042 and 0·034 mg% in blood from 15 normal individuals, 7 compensated heart patients and 18 heart patients with chronic circulatory insufficiency. Serafin (1957) assayed heparin in human plasma by a method which involved the initial precipitation of the heparin present as its octylamine salt. In normal subjects an average value of 9·8 mg heparin/100 ml. plasma was found (range 48–13·8 mg). An average concentration of 1·6 mg heparin/100 g serum has been reported for rats (Mergenthaler and Paff, 1956).

For assay of heparin in tissues, where it is tightly bound to protein, a procedure involving denaturation of heparinase, proteolysis under conditions of simultaneous dialysis, lipid removal, etc., was adopted (Freeman, Posthuma, Gordon and Marx, 1957). Treatment with cortisone has been reported to reduce the quantity of heparin in the skin (Monkhouse, MacKneson and Bambers, 1957).

The virulence-enhancing factors of hog gastric mucin for bacteria have been extensively investigated by Smith (1950, 1951). It was found that this activity was due to a synergic action between a particulate residue, a viscous medium and a soluble third factor (Smith, Harris-Smith and Stanley, 1952). Fractionation of the crude third factor gave polysaccharides

A, B and C two of which (A and C) were involved in virulence enhancement (Smith, Gallop and Stanley, 1952).

Polysaccharide A, identified as heparin, was a powerful anticoagulant for blood and had a strong anticomplementary effect in a system involving sheep haemolysis. No such activity was displayed by polysaccharide C. Polysaccharide B appeared to be the mucoitin monosulphuric ester of Meyer, Smyth and Palmer (1937).

Heparin has also been isolated from the scales of carp *Cyprinus carpio* (Veil and Quivy, 1950) and from sea clams (Frommhagen, Fahrenbach, Brockman and Stokstad, 1953).

Structure of Heparin

Analyses

Many of the early preparations of heparin were impure or analysis was not carried out on anhydrous material and therefore should be discounted. More reliable analyses published by Wolfrom, Weisblat, Karabinos, McNeely and McLean (1943) are as follows. Crystalline BaH heparinate: C, 20·19; H, 2·85; N (Dumas), 1·94; S (acid hydrolysable), 11·31; ash, 40·41; anhydrohexuronic acid, 17·9; Ba, 23·78; anhydrohexosamine, 17·3 ± 1·2%. This particular preparation had $[\alpha]_D^{25} + 47\cdot5°$ (water), gave a negative biuret test, and had a neut. equiv. of 750. No acetyl, N-methyl or O-methyl groups were present. Heparin therefore contains anhydrohexosamine and anhydrohexuronic residues in the approximate molar ratio of 1:1. The N:S:Ba ratio is 2:6:3.

Nature of aminosugar constituent

Jorpes (1935) showed that the nitrogen present in heparin was incorporated in a hexosamine residue which was later characterized by Jorpes and Bergström (1936) as glucosamine. The sugar amine was later isolated as the copper salt of D-glucosaminic acid ($[\alpha]_D^{18} - 19° \pm 2$ in 2·5% hydrochloric acid) during the oxidative hydrolysis of heparin (Wolfrom and Rice, 1946). Korn (1958) has hydrolysed heparin with 6N-hydrochloric acid and then subjected the hydrolysate to ninhydrin degradation. Paper chromatograms revealed that arabinose (derived from glucosamine) was present. The optimum conditions for liberation of the aminosugar are hydrolysis with 4N-HCl at 100° for 10 hr. Under these conditions glucosamine hydrochloride was recovered in 83% yield and after one recrystallization this showed $[\alpha]_D^{25} + 72°$ (water) (Wolfrom, Weisblat, Karabinos, McNeely and McLean, 1943).

Nature of uronic acid constituent

Heparin was first suspected to contain uronic acid residues by Howell (1928) and this supposition was in part confirmed by Jorpes (1935) who measured the amounts of carbon dioxide liberated during acid hydrolysis. Wolfrom and Rice (1946) presented evidence that the uronic acid was D-glucuronic acid based upon the isolation of potassium hydrogen D-glucosaccharate after oxidative hydrolysis of heparin. It was considered that much of the acidic decarboxylation of the uronic acid would be avoided if this was oxidized as it was liberated. To accomplish this a mixture of bromine/strong sulphuric acid at 3° for one week was used. The crystalline potassium acid saccharate isolated had $[\alpha]_D + 10°$ in water indicating the D-configuration. No potassium acid D-glucosaccharate was isolated from a hydrolysis in which bromine was absent.

Final confirmation as to the nature of the uronic acid constituent was obtained by Foster, Olavesen, Stacey and Webber (1961). Successive removal of N-sulphate groups and selective N-acetylation gave a product $[\alpha]_D + 54°(H_2O)$; S, $8·25\%$ corresponding to $2·68$ sulphate groups per tetrasaccharide unit. Subsequent hydrolysis with $2N-H_2SO_4$ at 95–100° for 3 hr gave *inter alia* D-glucuronic acid (10% yield). This was characterized by conversion to 1, 2-O-*iso*propylidene-D-glucofurano-3 →6-lactone (m.p. 119–120°, $[\alpha]_D + 69°$ in water).

Evidence for O-sulphate groups

Wilander (1938) prepared the free acid of heparin by electrodialysis. Such a product consumed 4 equivalents of alkali, three within the range below pH 3 corresponding to three sulphuric acid groups and the fourth between pH 3 and 7. Since only one of these sulphate groups could be attached to nitrogen—see later (N:S ratio 1:3) the remainder must be attached as O-sulphate groups. Further evidence of this linkage accrues from the greater acid stability of these groups (2N-HCl at 100° required for hydrolysis). Model carbohydrate sulphates such as methyl 2-amino 2-deoxy N-sulpho tri-O-sulpho β-D-glucopyranoside dibarium salt require 20 minutes to lose the N-sulphate and 12 hours to lose the O-sulphate groups when heated in 0·004N-hydrochloric acid (Wolfrom, Shen and Summers, 1953).

Absence of N-acetyl groups

There was much controversy among the earlier workers as to whether or not a N-acetyl grouping was present in heparin. Varying acetyl contents were found by Charles and Todd (1940), and Jorpes and Bergström (1937). However, following assertions by Masamune, Suzuki and Kondoh (1940) and Wolfrom, Weisblat, Karabinos, McNeely and McLean (1943) that the amino group was not acetylated this point was further investigated by Meyer and Schwartz (1950). These workers found that one heparin preparation could be resolved into two components by electrophoresis. The fast-moving component, which contained all the anticoagulant activity contained no acetyl whereas the immobile component which was biologically inactive contained 19% acetyl. Heparin shows no infrared absorption at 1560–1508 cm–1 attributable to the N–H deformation mode of a N-acetyl group (Barker, Bourne and Whiffen, 1956).

Evidence for N-sulphate groups

Following the exclusion of N-methyl groups, Wolfrom and McNeely (1945) suggested that a sulphamic acid type linkage was present. However, probably because of the severity of the conditions, no correspondence could be found between liberated sulphuric acid and free amino nitrogen following acid hydrolysis. Some success in achieving such a correlation was obtained by Jorpes, Böström and Mutt (1950) and Meyer and Schwartz (1950). The former workers first treated their heparin with boiling N-sodium hydroxide for 1 hr under which conditions N-sulphate linkages were relatively stable (while 25% of the ester sulphate groups were liberated) and then carried out a mild acid hydrolysis. The nitrogen of heparin was set free as amino nitrogen after hydrolysis in 0·04N-HCl at 100° for about 3 hrs—under these conditions exactly equivalent amounts of sulphate and amino nitrogen were liberated. A substituted amidosulphuric acid-$NHSO_2OH$ group was therefore postulated. An alternative procedure for checking the correlation between amino groups and sulphate release has been adapted with success by Foster, Martlew and Stacey (1954). As the hydrolysis proceeded the free amino groups were reacted with 1-fluoro 2:4-dinitrobenzene and then determined from the characteristic λ_{max} 358 mμ of the N-2:4-dinitrophenyl group. The sulphate liberated was calculated from the sulphur contents of the N-(2:4-dinitrophenyl) heparins.

Periodate oxidation of heparin

Wolfrom, Montgomery, Karabinos and Rathgeb (1950) oxidized sodium heparinate at 28° with sodium metaperiodate. Titration showed that there was initial rapid consumption of one mole of periodate per tetrasaccharide unit but no formic acid or formaldehyde was liberated. Furthermore N-acetyl desulphated heparin consumed 1 mole of periodate per disaccharide unit at 3–6° again without formation of formaldehyde or formic acid and with destruction of the hexuronic acid portion only. Partial acid hydrolysis of heparin (0·5N-H_2SO_4 at 100° for 18 hr.) gave a disaccharide designated heparosinsulphuric acid. This contained one hexosamine, one hexuronic acid group and one ester sulphate group. The sequence in the disaccharide was believed to be glucosamine-glucuronic acid on the somewhat flimsy evidence that it gave a yellow precipitate with barium hydroxide (cf. Levine and Christman, 1937). This disaccharide consumed 3 moles of periodate with the formation of 1 mole of formic acid but no formaldehyde. Both sugar residues were attacked. The corresponding N-acetyl derivative of the disaccharide consumed two moles of periodate per mole and again one mole of formic acid but no formaldehyde was produced. Structure (a) (Fig. 4.1) was therefore given to heparosin sulphuric acid and structure (b) (Fig. 4.1) to heparin. The acid stability of

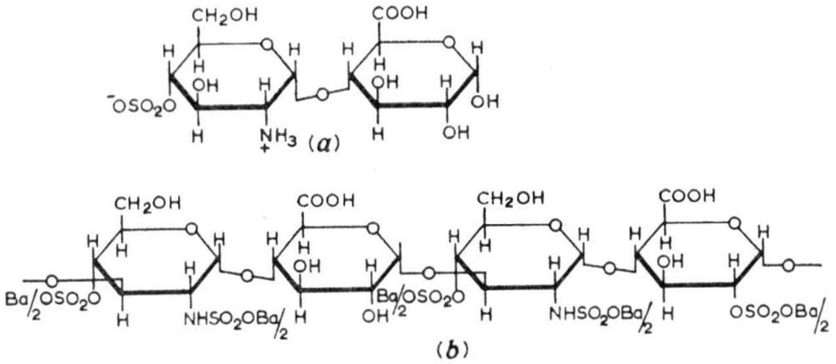

Fig. 4.1

heparin is in favour of pyranose rings while its positive rotation indicates α-glycosidic linkages.

The polysaccharide resulting from the desulphation of heparin with 0·6M-anhydrous methanolic hydrogen chloride contained equimolar amounts of sulphur and nitrogen (Danishefsky, Eiber, and Carr, 1960). After N-acetylation and further methanolysis an additional sulphate group was cleaved from each tetrasaccharide unit. The resulting product contained N, S, CH_3CO and OCH_3 in the ratio of 2:1:2:2. Since it is more susceptible to acidic hydrolysis than heparin itself it has been recommended as more suitable for structural studies as excessive destruction of uronic acid is thus avoided.

Enzymic Degradation of Heparin

Payza and Korn (1956) have shown that a soil bacterium *Flavobacterium heparinum* is able to utilize heparin as its sole source of carbon, nitrogen and sulphur. This organism is an obligate aerobe which grows best at 24° and pH 6·5–7·0. To overcome the expense of using heparin in the culture media, the organism can be first grown on trypticase–phytone–glucose medium and the cells then adapted to heparin by suspending in phosphate buffer, casein hydrolysate and sodium heparinate, and vigorously aerating the suspension at 24°. After 2–4 hr, about two-thirds of the heparin is found to be degraded. Such degradation can be followed by the decrease in metachromasia with azure A (Jaques, Monkhouse and Stewart, 1949) measured at 490 mμ.

Cell-free extracts prepared from the heparin-adapted bacteria (Korn and Payza, 1956) were found to degrade heparin optimally at pH 7–7·5 and to be inhibited by any salt at a relatively low molarity. Pyrophosphate and ethylene diamine tetraacetic acid inhibited at much lower molarities. Such extracts were believed to contain a sulfamidase, a sulfesterase and at least one glycosidase which together catalysed the degradation of heparin since incubation resulted in (1) loss of metachromasia (2) liberation of reducing groups and aminosugars and (3) an increase in susceptibility to periodate. The optimum temperature for heparin degradation is 24° (Korn, 1957). Hoffman, Linker, Sampson, Meyer and Korn (1957) have shown that the extracts do not degrade desulphated heparin indicating that a sulphate group is essential for the glycosidic cleavage. The action of the extract on heparin liberates oligosaccharides possessing glucosamine reducing end-groups one of which appears to be an unsaturated disaccharide.

Biosynthesis of Heparin

Little is yet known of the mechanism of synthesis of heparin. Eiber and Danishefsky (1957b) have demonstrated that $Na_2S^{35}O_4$ injected intraperitoneally gives a maximum incorporation of S^{35} in dog liver heparin after about 28 hr. We thus have at our disposal a radioactive heparin suitable for metabolic studies since about 52 mg of barium acid salt of heparin ($[\alpha]_D^{20} + 48°$) was obtained per kilo of liver. Jorpes, Odeblad and Boström (1953) earlier showed that exogenous sulphate is taken up into mast cells. The synthesis of heparin in mouse mast cell tumour slices has been studied by Korn (1958) since these are subcutaneous masses of essentially homogeneous tissue. Incubation of the tissue slices with either C^{14}-glucose or S^{35}-sulphate gave rise to labelled heparin. Approximately equal incorporation of the sulphate into amide (N-sulphate) and ester (O-sulphate) groups was deduced since hydrolysis of S^{35}-labelled heparin in 2N-HCl at 100° for 1 hr removed 95% and hydrolysis in 0·04 N-HCl at 100° for 2·5 hr. 47% of the original radioactivity. The latter hydrolysis conditions would suffice only to remove the N-sulphate groups.

Ringertz (1960) has concluded from *in vitro* experiments with transplantable mouse tumours that the nucleotide adenosine-5'-phosphosulphate is an intermediate in the sulphation of heparin. In a cell-free enzyme system it was found that heparin and heparin-like polysaccharides were sulphated rapidly while chondroitin sulphate A was sulphated only very slowly. Hyaluronic acid was completely inactive as a sulphate acceptor.

Biological Activity of Heparin

Among the other important biological functions of heparin is its ability to inhibit ribonuclease. Roth (1953) demonstrated that crystalline pancreatic ribonuclease was inhibited by heparin in concentrations which had been already shown by other workers (Heilbrunn and Wilson, 1949; Harding, 1951) to inhibit cell division. Since ribonuclease is important in the anabolism and catabolism of ribonucleic acid of the cytoplasm and nucleus, these properties are probably related. Autoclaving heparin had no effect on its inhibiting action and heparin had no effect on the precipitability of ribonucleic acid. A somewhat puzzling finding was that this inhibition was not related to its coagulating ability since sometimes heparin samples with the greatest coagulatory power inhibited less than others with less coagulating ability. Inhibitory power varied with pH, e.g. 55% at pH 6·0; 34% at pH 8·5. Ribonuclease activity in rat kidney and liver was also inhibited.

Further evidence for the inter-relationship between ribonuclease and heparin has been obtained by growth of cells in tissue cultures containing heparin. Such cells accumulated large quantities of ribonucleic acid but divided slowly or not at all (Paff, Sugiura, Bocher and Roth, 1952). Hence although the inhibition of ribonuclease by heparin *in vitro* is not great with low concentrations, *in vivo* the effect of heparin may be much more pronounced.

Heparin has been shown (Warren and Graham, 1950) to be bacteriostatic in concentrations of 100 ppm or greater when tested in a protein-free medium containing sodium chloride-dipotassium phosphate-ammonium sulphate-glucose-asparagine. The test organisms used were *Bacterium stewartii* and *Micrococcus pyogenes* var. *aureus*. With the former organisms those that had been left in contact with heparin sometimes developed colonies of an unusual rough type that failed to revert to the original type on subsequent sub-culturing. Heparin is not bacteriostatic in an organic medium probably because the heparin reacts with and is rendered inactive by the proteins of the medium.

Levy and Swank (1954) have demonstrated that heparin is important in lipid transport and metabolism. The disappearance of particulate fat on intravenous administration of heparin was first observed by Hahn (1943) and later confirmed by numerous other workers (Weld, 1944; Anderson and Fawcett, 1950; Swank, 1951). Such effects only occurred *in vivo* and heparin had no such action when mixed *in vitro* with lipemic plasma. Several suggestions to explain these effects have been made including the formation of a heparin-phospholipid complex possessing surface activity (Anderson and Fawcett, 1950) and the possibility that heparin causes the formation of a chylolytic substance which is responsible for dissolution of the chylomicrons. It was observed, however (Graham, Lyon, Gofman, Jones, Yankley and Simonton, 1951) that intravenous injection of heparin produced a marked change in the lipoprotein spectrum which was not observed *in vitro*. These changes could, however, be accomplished *in vitro* by sera obtained from human subjects after intravenous injection of heparin. This prompted the suggestion that the *in vitro* lipemia-clearing action of post-heparin plasma was the result of the enzymic conversion of one lipoprotein class into another (Boyle, Bragdon and Brown, 1952). Indeed Shore, Nichols and Freeman (1953) found that post-heparin plasma liberated fatty acids and glycerides from egg lipoproteins. Meng, Hollett and Cole (1954) found that the clearing factor of post-heparin plasma of dogs was thermolabile but relatively stable at 0–5°C. It had optimal clearing action at pH 6·4–7·0 and 35–40°C. Korn (1954) has obtained a factor from rat heart which catalyses the hydrolysis of chylomicrons with a marked increase in the reaction in the presence of heparin. This factor was termed lipoprotein lipase. This enzyme and the clearing factor are distinguished from other blood lipases and esterases in that the latter in man are not increased by heparin (Spitzer, 1952) or inhibited by glyco-cholate (Nikkila and Haahti, 1954), protamine (Korn, 1954) and high ionic strengths (Brown, Boyle and Anfinsen, 1953). The last mentioned workers pictured the overall reaction as (1) Plasma precursor protein + heparin + tissue factor ⟶ clearing factor, (2) Low density lipoproteins + plasma

$$\text{coprotein} \xrightarrow[\text{factor}]{\text{clearing}} \text{smaller low density lipoproteins} + \alpha_1\text{-lipoproteins.}$$

Robinson and French (1957) in a review of the heparin clearing reaction have pointed out that the turbidity of the plasma in alimentary lipaemia is due to visible lipid particles which include chylomicra and low density lipoprotein complexes. Such particles are composed primarily of trigly-ceride. The lipase released into the blood of an animal following heparin injection hydrolyses the triglyceride moieties to non-esterified fatty acids, mono- and diglycerides and glycerol. Shore, Colvin and Shore (1959) have presented data indicating that of the triglycerides likely to be present in human serum lipoproteins, the lipase prefers triolein to trilinolein, tripalmitin or tristearin as its substrate.

Riley, Shepherd and West (1955) suggested that since both heparin and histamine are now known to be concentrated in the mast cells the release of histamine caused by damage to the mast cells would be accompanied by the release of heparin and a consequent increase in the clotting time of the blood. However, although this phenomena has been observed in the dog following intravenous injection of a histamine liberator the clotting time of rats' blood after similar injection remained unchanged. In this respect the rat appears to be similar to the rabbit and guinea-pig. These workers therefore suggested that the function of heparin was probably more con-cerned with events in the tissues than with the coagulability of circulating blood. Amann and Werle (1956) have reported the formation of complexes by heparin with histamine and other di- and polyamines.

Anticoagulant Activity of Heparin

The complicated series of events occurring in the coagulation of blood has been admirably reviewed by Seegers (1955). A more recent review on the plasma procoagulants is that by Brinkhous (1959). Basically, however, the main events are (i) the transformation of fibrinogen to fibrin and co-fibrin by the enzyme thrombin and (ii) the transformation of prothrombin to thrombin. Heparin exerts its activity in step (ii) as do a host of other factors (calcium ions, thromboplastin, accelerator-globulin, platelet derivatives, platelet cofactor I, platelet cofactor II, antithromboplastin, together with other activators and other inhibitors). Only two aspects concern us here, the role of heparin and heparin cofactor.

The first extensive investigations of the anticoagulant activity of heparin were carried out by Howell and Holt (1918) who postulated that heparin releases an antithrombin from an inactive proantithrombin. Astrup and Darling (1943) found that for the formation of an antithrombic substance from heparin a thermolabile substance in blood plasma was required; this they termed a thrombin coinhibitor. This coinhibitor was destroyed after heating for five minutes at 56° and was not identical with the normal antithrombin of plasma and serum. Hence to distinguish between the normal antithrombin and the antithrombic substance formed from heparin the latter was called thrombin inhibitor. Thus whereas normally most of the thrombin added to defibrinated plasma is inactivated in about 30 min, the addition of heparin accelerates inactivation so that it occurs within 2 or 3 min. Astrup and Darling (1943) were also able to obtain from plasma a fraction whose chief antithrombin action was dependent upon the presence of heparin.

Fitzgerald and Waugh (1955) have defined heparin cofactor as a preparation which, with heparin, exhibits an antithrombic effect in excess of those given by heparin or cofactor alone. They separated such a heparin cofactor from bovine plasma and found that it had a molecular weight of the order of 15,000. Snellman, Sylvén and Julén (1951) have isolated from fresh ox liver capsules a nonsedimentable material containing heparin associated with a lipoprotein. The latter was composed of lipid (lecithin, 11–55%; cholesterol, 8% and neutral fats, 37%) together with a polypeptide of low molecular weight containing only six aminoacids. The Scandinavian workers were further able to demonstrate by electrophoresis of the whole complex that the heparin was linked to this special protein fraction (two other fractions were inert) which by clotting assay was found to be responsible for both the heparin and complement (heparin cofactor) activities. All three parts (heparin–lipid–protein) of the complex were required to produce the antithrombic effect.

The antihemophilic factor is a procoagulant plasma protein which possesses the property of correcting both the clotting defect and hemostatic defect in true hemophilia. Rizza and Walker (1957) have reported that heparin appears to prevent inactivation of this factor by thrombin.

Methods of Assay

Biological methods

One of the oldest methods of assay of heparin was based on the belief that it acted as an antiprothrombin by neutralizing thromboplastin. The rate of formation of thromboplastin determines, to a large extent, the clotting time. Using hen's plasma and an extract of chicken embryo as the source of thromboplastin, Fischer and Schmitz (1932a) found that the concentration of heparin added to plasma was directly proportional to the logarithm of the coagulation time. Later workers (Bertrand and Quivy, 1949) used an extract of human brain as a source of thromboplastin. However, Macmillan and Brown (1954) reported that brain extract was an incomplete thromboplastin and required serum containing factor VII for its activation. When left in contact with this activated brain extract heparin caused progressive destruction of thromboplastic activity.

Jorpes (1955) recommends whole ox blood as the best method for assaying heparin *in vitro*. In this method the coagulation times of mixtures of fresh ox blood, physiological saline and varying amounts of heparin are determined (Blombäck, Blombäck, Corneliusson and Jorpes, 1953).

The thrombin method of Studer and Winterstein (1951) utilizes citrated ox plasma and measures the action of heparin on thrombin. Such a method reveals interesting differences between heparin, β-heparin and other polysaccharides.

The official method of the United States Pharmacopoeia (U.S.P. xiv [1950]) is based on that of Kuizenga, Nelson and Cartland (1943) who reported that recalcified sheep plasma required a smaller increment in heparin for a transition from coagulation to fluidity than either recalcified beef or horse plasma. Mangieri (1947) described an improved heparin assay in which only 1 μg of standard heparin was required to effect this change. The British Pharmacopoeia 1953 method uses salted blood (one volume of 7% sodium sulphate solution with 5 volumes of ox blood). This blood is diluted with one volume of dilute heparin and mixed with one-fifth volume of a thrombokinase solution. A method for the *in vivo* assay of heparin was described by Jorpes, Blombäck and Blombäck (1954) and Jorpes (1955). In a comparison of the various methods of assay using new Swedish standard heparin, Jorpes (1955) found 110 I.U./mg (*in vivo* sheep), 108 I.U./mg. (fresh ox blood), 107 I.U./mg (thrombin method), 96 I.U./mg (USP 1950) and 103 I.U./mg (B.P. 1953).

Chemical Assays

Chargaff and Olsen (1937) discovered that protamine neutralized the anticoagulant effect of heparin on blood both *in vitro* and *in vivo*. This enabled Jaques and Waters (1941) to measure the rate at which heparin appeared in the blood of dogs following anaphylactic shock. Blood from the shocked animal was withdrawn and mixed with varying concentrations of protamine in isotonic saline. The amount of protamine required to neutralize the heparin in the blood was that amount which gave the lowest clotting time of the blood sample. Some confirmation of this method was provided by the ability to isolate crystalline heparin in good yield from the blood of dogs in anaphylactic shock but not from the blood of normal dogs. Since there was no liberation of heparin into the blood of hepatectomized dogs in anaphylactic shock it was concluded that the liver was the source of heparin in a normal animal suffering anaphylactic shock. Indeed the amount of heparin which could be extracted from the liver of dogs in anaphylactic shock was much less than that extracted from normal dog liver.

Since the protamine titration requires a clotting system, Jaques, Monkhouse and Stewart (1949) devised a direct method for blood-heparin determination. To precipitate the heparin octylamine was added to the citrated plasma. The stable octylamine heparin was then hydrolysed by heating to 70° in 0·1N-NaOH, the octylamine extracted with ether, and the heparin reprecipitated by addition of brucine at pH 5·5. The heparin present was then determined by its metachromatic activity with Azure A (Jaques, Mitford and Ricker, 1947). The method was checked by the addition of 0·02 to 0·36 mg of heparin to about 10 ml. of canine blood— the average recovery using the above method was 87–90%. Complete recovery of added heparin was obtained from plasma.

The use of toluidine blue in the assay of sulphated polysaccharides is discussed in chapter 3. Details of the purification of commercial toluidine blue samples have been reported by Ball and Jackson (1953).

Detection in Tissues

Histochemical methods are still too imperfect to permit any reliable distinction between different polysaccharides in single cells. However, the application of the autoradiographic technique using S^{35} sulphate permits at least the ability to distinguish sulphated polysaccharides, e.g. heparin from the non-sulphated variety, e.g. hyaluronic acid (Dziewiatkowski, 1956). Twenty-four hours after administration of S^{35}-sulphate the labelled materials in the tissues are mostly sulphated polysaccharides. Using this technique one has the added advantage of determining the relative amounts of such polysaccharides in different tissues as well as being able to assess their turnover.

Although heparin is attacked by periodate (Wolfrom, Montgomery, Karabinos and Rathgeb, 1950) there is some disagreement among histo-chemists as to whether it is detected in tissues by the PAS technique (Hale, 1957). It is known, however, that some mast cells are PAS positive (Lillie, 1950). In general, however, those cells which were strongly metachromatic were often PAS-negative; other cells which were PAS-positive were orthochromatic. Heparin is, of course, metachromatic with toluidine blue and hence these phenomena could be related to the degree of sulphation of the polysaccharides, i.e. the higher the degrees of sulphation the more resistant to periodate the polysaccharide becomes. The advent of heparinases discussed in an earlier section may help in the specific location of heparin in the tissues.

Heparitin Sulphate

Jorpes and Gardell (1948) were the first to discover a dextrorotatory polysaccharide resembling heparin but of low anticoagulant activity. This polysaccharide, which they named heparin monosulphuric acid, consti-tuted the main fraction of the easily soluble salts remaining in the mother liquor when protein-free heparin was isolated from ox liver and ox lung as its water-insoluble barium salt. The purest fraction from ox lung had $[\alpha]_D^{20} + 49 \cdot 4°$ (c, 2 in water), contained N, $2 \cdot 61\%$ and showed a sulphur content of $5 \cdot 42\%$ compared with that of $5 \cdot 38\%$ calculated for a heparin monosulphuric acid. On hydrolysis with boiling 20% hydrochloric acid for 7 hr it gave a hydrolysate from which crystalline α-D-glucosamine hydrochloride $[[\alpha]_D^{20} + 100°(2 \text{ min}) \rightarrow + 71°(\text{equil.})]$ could be isolated in 37% of the calculated amount. The heparin monosulphuric acid contained $28 \cdot 4\%$ uronic acid (calc., $32 \cdot 6\%$) and gave $7 \cdot 5\%$ acetic acid (calc. $10 \cdot 1\%$). These analyses were thus roughly in agreement with a polysaccharide with one sulphuric acid group for each disaccharide unit consisting of 1 mole of uronic acid, 1 mole of hexosamine (mostly D-glucosamine) and 1 mole of acetic acid. Because of its apparent similarity to heparin and its low anti-coagulant activity of 10 to 16 heparin units per mg the polysaccharide was assumed to be the monosulphuric ester of the heparin polysaccharide.

Meyer (1956) proposed that the name heparin monosulphuric acid be changed to heparitin sulphate since the acetic acid arose from N-acetyl groups which are known to be absent from heparin. Meyer, Davidson, Linker and Hoffman (1956) reported that fractions with different degrees of sulphation were encountered in human amyloid liver and in bovine and human aorta which appeared to be related to heparin. The hexosamine in the sulphated fractions from amyloid liver was predominantly glucos-amine together with some galactosamine. It was believed that the fractions were, in fact, mixtures. The purest fraction had $[\alpha]_D + 39°$, N, $2 \cdot 6\%$;

acetyl, 5·5%; and contained 29% hexosamine, 34% uronic acid and 16% sulphate. The polysaccharide was resistant to testicular hyaluronidase. Dorfman and Lorincz (1957) discovered that the urine of a patient with the Hurler syndrome (syn. gargoylism) contained small amounts of a polysaccharide having the properties of heparitin sulphate. It showed $[\alpha]_D^{20} + 39°$ based on hexosamine content. Analysis revealed that for each mole of hexosamine there was 0·87 mole of N-acetyl accompanied by 1·4 moles of uronic acid and 1·17 mole of ester sulphate. This heparitin sulphate was accompanied in the urine by relatively large amounts of chondroitin sulphate B. Available evidence indicates that normal urine contains only small amounts of chondroitin sulphate A.

Brante (1952) was the first worker to obtain evidence of the nature of the storage substance deposited in the liver of patients with gargoylism. He showed that 10% of the weight of the liver was composed of a polysaccharide having 27% hexosamine, 26% uronic acid and 3·9% sulphur. Stacey and Barker (1956) showed in another case investigated that this sulphated polysaccharide (fraction I S, 7·7% and $[\alpha]_D^{17} + 18·1°$; fraction II S, 6·3% and $[\alpha]_D^{17} + 37·2°$) exhibited a slight but definite blood anti-coagulant activity. Its structural similarity to heparin was stressed by the fact that on acid hydrolysis both heparin and the sulphated polysaccharide gave the same disaccharide (believed to be the heparosin sulphuric acid of Wolfrom, Montgomery, Karabinos and Rathgeb, 1950). In this case the spleen was not found to contain such a polysaccharide. Brown (1957) examined three cases of gargoylism. Some of the fractions obtained are listed in Table 4.I.

Table 4.I. *Heparitin sulphate fractions from gargoylism tissues*

Case	Tissue	Uronic acid/ glucosamine	S/N	Acetyl/N	$[\alpha]_D^{25}$
K.N.	Autopsy liver	1·11	1·7	0·75	+69·5°
	Autopsy spleen	1·30	1·7	—	—
G.H.	Autopsy liver	1·35	0·66	0·62	+57·0°
D.C.	Biopsy liver	1·29	1·31	0·73	+35·8°

The total content of storage substance (% wet weight) varied from 0·11 (in the spleen) to the range 0·4–1·4 found in the liver. When one heparitin sulphate fraction was examined one-third of its sulphate was hydrolysed in 30 min at 100° in 0·04N-HCl. This figure rose to 57% after 60 min. Such evidence indicated that part, at least, of the sulphate was present in the intact polysaccharide in a sulfamic-type (N-sulphate) linkage to the nitrogen of some of the glucosamine residues. In this feature it would resemble heparin (Jorpes, Boström and Mutt, 1950). Brown (1957) found that the heparitin sulphate fractions slowly dialysed through Visking sausage casing indicating that the size of these fractions is in the oligosaccharide range. Molecular weights calculated from sedimentation-diffusion data indicate the range 1200–2000. The anticoagulant activity of two of the fractions was less than 2% that of heparin on a weight basis. From the above evidence and from studies of the acid hydrolysis products Brown (1957) suggested the partial structure shown (that of a heptasaccharide; Fig. 4.2).

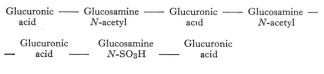

Fig. 4.2

The glycosidic bonds were designated as having the α-configuration. Such a substance would have a S/N ratio of 0·33. Other substances containing more sulphate residues would have S/N ratios of 0·66, 1·0, 1·33, etc.

Meyer, Grumbach, Linker and Hoffman (1958) have also studied the acidic mucopolysaccharides in the urine and liver of patients who had gargoylism. From the urine of four out of five patients both chondroitin sulphate B and heparitin sulphate were isolated with the former predominating. The urine of one patient and the liver of another, yielded only heparitin sulphate. The type of polysaccharide excreted by these patients had no obvious correlation with the severity of the disease or the postulated mode of inheritance suggested by the history. Linker, Hoffman, Sampson and Meyer (1958) have summarized the properties of the heparitin sulphate obtained from these and other sources. All fractions were dextrorotatory, contained variable amounts of sulphate, and had acetyl values which were approximately half of the theoretical for a N-acetylated disaccharide repeating unit. No O-acetyl groups were present. Although their fractions were found to dialyse through cellophane membranes at a very slow rate the low reducing value (1·5% of that glucose) and paper chromatographic properties suggested that they were larger than the heptasaccharide postulated by Brown (1957). Under conditions which have been shown to remove N-sulphate but not O-sulphate (Wolfrom and McNeely, 1948) heparitin sulphate lost one-half of its sulphate content concomitantly with the liberation of an equivalent amount of NH_2 groups. These workers concluded that one N-acetyl, one N-sulphate and, at most, one O-sulphate group were present per tetrasaccharide unit. All heparitin sulphate fractions were resistant to testicular, bacterial or leech hyaluronidase but were hydrolysed by enzymes obtained from a flavobacterium adapted either to heparin or to heparitin sulphate (Hoffman, Linker, Sampson, Meyer and Korn, 1957).

Crude heparitin sulphate, obtained as a side fraction during the commercial preparation of heparin, has been further separated into several fractions by the use of cetylpyridinium chloride. A family of substances appeared to be present containing variable numbers of sulphate and acetyl groups (Cifonelli and Dorfman, 1960). Similar fractions were obtained on refractionation of a heparin monosulphate fraction isolated from the liver of a patient with the Hurler syndrome. Using the Elson–Morgan reaction on the oligosaccharides released on hydrolysis of the polysaccharides it was concluded that neither heparin nor heparin monosulphate contain $1 \longrightarrow 3$ uronosyl-hexosamine linkages. The oligosaccharides obtained from both polysaccharides had mostly uronic acid at the reducing end.

REFERENCES

Adams, S. S. and Thorpe, H. M. *J. Pharm. Pharmacol.* **9,** 459 (1957).
Amann, R. and Werle, E. *Klin. Wochenschr.* **34,** 207 (1956).
Anderson, N. G. and Fawcett, B. *Proc. Soc. Exp. Biol. Med.* **74,** 768 (1950).
Astrup, T. and Darling, S. *Acta Physiol. Scand.* **5,** 13 (1943).
Ball, J. and Jackson, D. S. *Stain Technology* **28,** 33 (1953).
Barker, S. A., Bourne, E. J. and Whiffen, D. H. *Methods of Biochemical Analysis* **3,** 213 (1956).
Bell, H. J. and Jaques, L. B. *Bull. soc. chim. Belgies* **65,** 36 (1956).
Bertrand, I. and Quivy, D. *Acta int. Pharmacodyn.* **79,** 173 (1949).
Blombäck, B., Blombäck, M., Corneliusson, E. V. and Jorpes, J. E. *J. Pharm. Pharmacol.* **5,** 1031 (1953).
Bloom, G. and Ringertz, N. R. *Arkiv för Kemi* **16,** 51 (1960).
Boyle, E., Bragdon, J. H. and Brown, A. K. *Proc. Soc. Exp. Biol. Med.* **81,** 475 (1952).
Brante, G. *Scand. J. Clin. Lab. Invest.* **4,** 43 (1952).
Brinkhous, K. M. *Ann. Rev. of Physiology* **21,** 271 (1959).
Brown, R. K. *Proc. Nat. Acad. Sci. U.S.* **43,** 443 (1957).
Brown, R. K., Boyle, E. and Anfinsen, C. B. *J. Biol. Chem.* **204,** 423 (1953).
Chargaff, E. and Olsen, K. B. *J. Biol. Chem.* **122,** 153 (1937).
Charles, A. F. and Scott, D. A. *J. Biol. Chem.* **102,** 425 (1933a).
Charles, A. F. and Scott, D. A. *J. Biol. Chem.* **102,** 431 (1933b).
Charles, A. F. and Scott, D. A. *Biochem. J.* **30,** 1927 (1936).
Charles, A. F. and Todd, A. R. *Biochem. J.* **34,** 112 (1940).
Cifonelli, J. A. and Dorfman, A. *J. Biol. Chem.* **235,** 3283 (1960).
Danishefsky, I., Eiber, H. B. and Carr, J. J. *Arch. Biochem. Biophys.* **90,** 114 (1960).
De Bellis, L. *Quaderni clin. ostet. ginecol.* **9,** 487 (1954).

Dische, Z. *Methods of Biochemical Analysis* **2**, 313 (1955).

Dorfman, A. and Lorincz, A. E. *Proc. Nat. Acad. Sci. U.S.* **43**, 443 (1957).

Dziewiatkowski, D. D. *Int. Rev. of Cytology* **7**, 159 (1956).

Eiber, H. B. and Danishefsky, I. *Proc. Soc. Exp. Biol. Med.* **94**, 801 (1957a).

Eiber, H. B. and Danishefsky, I. *J. Biol. Chem.* **226**, 721 (1957b).

Fischer, A. and Schmitz, A. *Z. physiol. Chem.* **210**, 129 (1932a).

Fischer, A. and Schmitz, A. *Naturwissenschaften* **20**, 471 (1932b).

Fischer, A. and Schmitz, A. *Biochem. Z.* **259**, 61 (1933).

Fitzgerald, M. A. and Waugh, D. F. *Arch. Biochem. Biophys.* **58**, 431 (1955).

Foster, A. B. and Huggard, A. J. *J. Adv. Carb. Chem.* **10**, 335 (1955).

Foster, A. B., Martlew, E. F. and Stacey, N. *Abs. Papers Amer. Chem. Soc.* **126**, 6D (1954).

Foster, A. B., Olavsen, A. H., Stacey, M. and Webber, J. M. *Chem. Ind.* in the press (1961).

Freeman, L., Posthuma, R., Gordon, L. and Marx, W. *Arch. Biochem. Biophys.* **70**, 169 (1957).

Frommhagen, L. H., Fahrenbach, M. J., Brockman, J. A. and Stokstad, E. L. R. *Proc. Soc. Exp. Biol. Med.* **82**, 280 (1953).

Graham, D. M., Lyon, T. P., Gofman, J. W., Jones, H. B., Yankley, A. and Simonton, J. *Circulation* **4**, 666 (1951).

Green, J. P. *Nature* **186**, 472 (1960).

Guarini, G. *Il Progr. med.* **11**, 360 (1955).

Hahn, P. F. *Science* **98**, 19 (1943).

Hale, A. J. *Int. Rev. Cytology* **6**, 193 (1957).

Harding, D. *Exp. Cell Research* **2**, 403 (1951).

Heilbrunn, L. V. and Wilson, W. L. *Proc. Soc. Exp. Biol. Med.* **70**, 179 (1949).

Hoffman, P., Linker, A., Sampson, P., Meyer, K. and Korn, E. D. *Biochim. Biophys. Acta* **25**, 658 (1957).

Howell, W. H. *Amer. J. Physiol.* **63**, 434 (1922–23).

Howell, W. H. *Amer. J. Physiol.* **71**, 553 (1924–25).

Howell, W. H. *Bull. Johns Hopkins Hospital* **42**, 199 (1928).

Howell, W. H. and Holt, E. *Amer. J. Physiol.* **47**, 328 (1918).

James, A. E. and Ricketts, C. R. *Brit. Patent* 715,821 (1954).

Jaques, L. B., Mitford, M. and Ricker, A. G. *Rev. Canad. Biol.* **6**, 740 (1947).

Jaques, L. B., Monkhouse, F. C. and Stewart, M. *J. Physiol.* **109**, 41 (1949).

Jaques, L. B. and Waters, E. T. *J. Physiol.* **99**, 454 (1941).

Jaques, L. B., Waters, E. T. and Charles, A. F. *J. Biol. Chem.* **144**, 229 (1942).

Jorpes, J. E. *Acta Pharm. Toxicol.* **11**, 367 (1955).

Jorpes, J. E. *Biochem. J.* **29**, 1819 (1935).

Jorpes, J. E. *Heparin in the Treatment of Thrombosis*, 2nd ed. (1946). Oxford Medical Publications.

Jorpes, J. E. and Bergström, S. *Z. physiol. Chem.* **244**, 253 (1936).

Jorpes, J. E. and Bergström, S. *J. Biol. Chem.* **118**, 447 (1937).

Jorpes, J. E., Blombäck, M. and Blombäck, B. *J. Pharmacol.* **6**, 694 (1954).

Jorpes, J. E., Boström, H. and Mutt, V. *J. Biol. Chem.* **183**, 607 (1950).

Jorpes, J. E. and Gardell, S. *J. Biol. Chem.* **176**, 267 (1948).

Jorpes, J. E., Odeblad, E. and Boström, H. *Acta Haematol.* **9**, 275 (1953).

Kerby, G. P. *Proc. Soc. Exp. Biol. N.Y.* **83**, 263 (1953).

Korn, E. D. *Science* **120**, 399 (1954).

Korn, E. D. *J. Biol. Chem.* **226**, 841 (1957).

Korn, E. D. *J. Amer. Chem. Soc.* **80**, 1520 (1958).

Korn, E. D. and Payza, A. N. *J. Biol. Chem.* **223**, 859 (1956).

Kuizenga, M. H., Nelson, J. W. and Cartland, G. F. *Amer. J. Physiol.* **139**, 612 (1943).

Levene, P. A. and Christman, C. C. *J. Biol. Chem.* **122**, 204 (1937).

Levy, S. W. and Swank, R. L. *J. Physiol.* **123**, 310 (1954).

Lewis, B. A. and Smith, F. *J. Amer. Chem. Soc.* **79**, 3929 (1957).

Lillie, R. D. *Anat. Record* **108**, 239 (1950).

Linker, A., Hoffman, P., Sampson, P. and Meyer, K. *Biochim. Biophys. Acta* **29**, 443 (1958).

Macmillan, R. L. and Brown, K. W. G. *J. Lab. Clin. Med.* **44**, 378 (1954).

Magnusson, S. and Larsson, B. *Acta Chem. Scand.* **9**, 534 (1955).

Maneschi, M. and Rio, F. *Monit. ostet. ginecol.* **28**, 124 (1957).

Mangieri, C. N. *J. Lab. Clin. Med.* **32**, 901 (1947).

Marx, W., Rucker, P., Ruggeri, L. and Freeman, L. *Proc. Soc. Exp. Biol. Med.* **94**, 217 (1957).

Masmune, H., Suzuki, M. and Kondo, I. *J. Biochem. Japan* **31**, 343 (1940).

McGovern, V. J. *J. Pathol. Bact.* **73**, 99 (1957).

Meng, H. C., Hollet, C. and Cole, W. E. *Amer. J. Physiol.* **179**, 314 (1954).

Mergenthaler, D. D. and Paff, C. H. *Anat. Record* **126**, 165 (1956).

Meyer, K. *Abs. Amer. Chem. Soc. Meeting Sept.* p. 150 (1956).

Meyer, K., Davidson, E., Linker, A. and Hoffman, P. *Biochim. Biophys. Acta* **21**, 506 (1956).

Meyer, K., Grumbach, M. M., Linker, A. and Hoffman, P. *Proc. Soc. Exp. Biol. Med.* **97**, 275 (1958).

Meyer, K., Smyth, E. M. and Palmer, J. W. *J. Biol. Chem.* **119**, 73 (1937).

Meyer, K. H. and Schwartz, D. E. *Helv. chim. Acta* **33**, 1651 (1950).

Monkhouse, F. C. *Can. J. Biochem. Physiol.* **34**, 759 (1956).

Monkhouse, F. C., MacKneson, R. G. and Bambers, G. *Proc. Soc. Exp. Biol. Med.* **95**, 489 (1957).

Moore, R. D. and Schoenberg, M. D. *A.M.A. Arch. Pathol.* **64**, 39 (1957).

Nikkilä, E. A. and Haahti, E. *Acta chem. scand.* **8**, 363 (1954).

O'Keeffe, A. E., Russo-Alesi, F. M., Dolliver, M. A. and Stiller, E. T. *J. Amer. Chem. Soc.* **71**, 1517 (1949).

Oliver, J., Bloom, F. and Mangeri, C. *J. Exp. Med.* **86**, 107 (1947).

Paff, G. H., Sugiura, H. T., Bocher, C. A. and Roth, J. S. *Anat. Record* **114**, 499 (1952).

Payza, A. N. and Korn, E. D. *J. Biol. Chem.* **223**, 853 (1956).

Reinits, K. G. *Biochem. J.* **53**, 79 (1953).

Ricketts, C. R. *Brit. Patent* 695,789 (1953).

Ricketts, C. R., Walton, K. W. and Saddington, S. M. *Biochem. J.* **58**, 532 (1954).

Riley, J. F., Shepherd, D. M. and West, G. B. *Nature* **176**, 1123 (1955).

Ringertz, N. R. *Arkiv. för Kemi* **16**, 67 (1960).

Ringertz, N. R. *Acta Chem. Scand.* **14**, 312 (1960).

Ringertz, N. R. and Bloom, G. *Arkiv. för Kemi* **16**, 57 (1960).

Ringertz, N. R. and Reichard, P. *Acta Chem. Scand.* **13**, 1467 (1959).

Ringertz, N. R. and Reichard, P. *Acta Chem. Scand.* **14**, 303 (1960).

Rizza, C. and Walker, W. *Nature* **180**, 143 (1957).

Robinson, D. S. and French, J. E. *Quart. J. Exp. Physiol.* **42**, 151 (1957).

Roth, J. S. *Arch. Biochem. Biophys.* **44**, 265 (1953).

Scott, J. E., Gardell, S. and Nilsson, I. N. *Biochem. J.* **67**, 7P–8P (1957).

Seegers, W. H. *Adv. in Enzymol.* **16**, 23 (1955).

Serafin, J., *Amer. J. Med. Technol.* **23**, 171 (1957).

Shore, B., Colvin, O. M. and Shore, V. G. *Biochim. Biophys. Acta* **36**, 563 (1959).

Shore, B., Nichols, A. V. and Freeman, N. K. *Proc. Soc. Exp. Biol. Med.* **83,** 216 (1953).

Smith, H. *Biochem. J.* **46,** 352, 356 (1950); **48,** 441 (1951).

Smith, H., Gallop, R. C. and Stanley, J. L. *Biochem. J.* **52,** 15 (1952).

Smith, H. Harris-Smith, P. W. and Stanley, J. L. *Biochem. J.* **50,** 211 (1952).

Snellman, O., Jensen, R. and Sylvén, B. *Acta chem. Scand.* **3,** 589 (1949).

Snellman, O., Sylvén, B. and Julén, C. *Biochim. Biophys. Acta* **7,** 98 (1951).

Spitzer, J. J. *Amer. J. Physiol.* **171,** 492 (1952).

Stacey, M. and Barker, S. A. *J. Clin. Path.* **9,** 314 (1956).

Studer, A. and Winterstein, A. *Helv. Physiol. Pharmacol. Acta* **9,** 6 (1951).

Swank, R. L. *Amer. J. Physiol.* **164,** 798 (1951).

Veil, C. and Quivy, D. *Compt. rend. Soc. biol.* **144,** 1483 (1950).

Warren, J. R. and Graham, F. *J. Bact.* **60,** 171 (1950).

Weld, C. B. *Canad. M.A.J.* **51,** 578 (1944).

Wilander, O. *Scand. Arch. Physiol.* **81,** supp. 15 (1938).

Wolfrom, M. L. and McNeely, W. H. *J. Amer. Chem. Soc.* **67,** 748 (1945).

Wolfrom, M. L., Montgomery, R., Karabinos, J. V. and Rathgeb, P. *J. Amer. Chem. Soc.* **72,** 5796 (1950).

Wolfrom, M. L. and Rice, F. A. H. *J. Amer. Chem. Soc.* **68,** 532 (1946).

Wolfrom, M. L., Shen, T. M. and Summers, C. G. *J. Amer. Chem. Soc.* **75,** 1519 (1953).

Wolfrom, M. L., Weisblat, D. I., Karabinos, J. V., McNeely, W. H. and McLean, J. *J. Amer. Chem. Soc.* **65,** 2077 (1943).

Chapter 5

MISCELLANEOUS POLYSACCHARIDES

Introduction

THE remaining polysaccharides and polysaccharide sulphates known to occur in living tissues will now be discussed. In addition to keratosulphate, which is already known to be present, we may expect to find polysaccharides analogous to pneumogalactan and mucoitin sulphate in human tissues. The other polysaccharide sulphates from fish and snails are less likely to be found.

Keratosulphate

In a study of the mucopolysaccharides of bovine cornea (Meyer, Linker, Davidson and Weissman, 1953) a new polysaccharide, keratosulphate, was isolated. Bovine cornea were digested first with pepsin and then with trypsin to remove proteins and a crude mixture of polysaccharides precipitated from the filtered digest by addition of alcohol (1·2 volumes). Further purification and fractional precipitation of the calcium salts of the polysaccharides with alcohol gave a fraction (precipitated with 50% alcohol) which had $[\alpha]_D + 4\cdot5°$, and contained nitrogen, 3·24%, hexosamine 33·4%, hexose 36%, acetyl 10·4%, sulphate 18·4% and only 2% uronic acid. This polysaccharide, keratosulphate, on hydrolysis gave crystalline D-glucosamine hydrochloride further characterized as its N-carbobenzoxy derivative. Paper chromatographic analysis of the hydrolysate of keratosulphate indicated that the hexose was galactose and this was confirmed by isolation of its α-methylphenylhydrazone.

Keratosulphate appears therefore to be a polymer mainly composed of N-acetylglucosamine, galactose and sulphate in equimolar proportions. It does not cross-react with Type XIV anti-pneumococcus serum and gives a negative response when tested by complement fixation with anti-A and anti-B serum. Keratosulphate is resistant to testicular and bacterial hyaluronidases, emulsin, alfalfa β-galactosidase and a *Clostridium welchii* extract.

Keratosulphate has been obtained from *nucleus pulposus* (central part of the intervertebral disc) in a series of studies (Gardell and Rastgeldi, 1954; Gardell, 1957). The intervertebral discs were homogenized, freeze-dried and the powder extracted with boiling water. After digestion with pancreatic and intestinal glycerol extracts the crude polysaccharides were

9

precipitated with alcohol. The polysaccharides were dissolved in 0·3% aqueous barium acetate and fractionated on a cellulose column by elution with decreasing concentrations of aqueous alcohol (80 → 20%) containing 0·3% barium acetate. Complete separation into a keratosulphate (N 2·6%, S 5·45%, glucosamine hydrochloride 21·1%, galactosamine hydrochloride 0·3%, galactose 16·8%, fucose 2·3%) and a chondroitin sulphate (N 2%, S 4·83%, glucosamine hydrochloride 0·3%, galactosamine hydrochloride 22·8%) was obtained. Keratosulphate was separated from a mixture of the mucopolysaccharides of the cornea in a similar fashion.

Meyer, Hoffman and Linker (1958) have isolated keratosulphate in addition to chondroitin sulphate, from human costal cartilage obtained from two cases of Marfan's syndrome and from two young adults free of skeletal abnormalities. It will be recalled that Meyer, Davidson, Linker and Hoffman (1956) encountered no keratosulphate fraction in their work on hyaline mammalian cartilage including that of new-born infants. Also Hoffman, Linker and Meyer (1958) had shown that the rib cartilage of the new-born yielded only chondroitin sulphate A while in the adult it was predominantly chondroitin sulphate C. This information, as well as the knowledge that there is a shift from D-galactosamine to D-glucosamine with increasing age in epiphysial human cartilage (Kuhn and Leppelmann, 1958) prompted Kaplan and Meyer (1959) to study the distribution of chondroitin sulphate and keratosulphate in human rib cartilage of various age-groups.

Analyses showed that the chondroitin sulphate content per dry weight of cartilage appeared to decrease with age from 6–8% in new born to 1–2% at 60 to 80 years old. In contrast keratosulphate, which was negligible or absent in the very young, increased to reach a plateau at 20 to 30 years old which remained constant to the greatest ages investigated (70 to 80 years) where it represented approximately 50% of the total mucopolysaccharide. An interesting feature was that the ratio of keratosulphate to total mucopolysaccharide showed a linear relationship with age. The two cases of Marfan's syndrome cited above both had somewhat higher keratosulphate/total mucopolysaccharide ratios than normal. No correlation was found with sex, with the presence and degree of arteriosclerosis or the state of nutrition. As Kaplan and Meyer (1959) have pointed out the rib cartilage is almost an ideal tissue on which to study the effect of ageing since it is little affected by mechanical stresses, infection or nutritional status.

Shetlar and Masters (1955) have determined the uronic acid content of costal cartilage obtained at autopsy from human subjects of various age groups. They found the following values: foetal, 7·8%; new-born, 7·5%; 4 months, 7·0%; 6–11 yr, 3·6%; 25–40 yr, 3·3%; 41–55 yr, 2·4%; 56–70 yr, 1·6%; 71–88 yr, 1·3%. These values almost certainly parallel the decrease in chondroitin sulphate discussed above.

Hallén (1958) has concluded that analogous changes take place in the mucopolysaccharide pattern in the human *nucleus pulposus*. An increase was noted in the ratio of glucosamine/galactosamine from 0·5 at 15 years of age to 1·5 at 90 years indicative of an increase in the keratosulphate/ chondroitin sulphate ratio. Both of these polysaccharides have been detected previously in *nucleus pulposus*, chondroitin sulphate by Malmgren and Sylvén (1952) and keratosulphate by Gardell and Rastgeldi (1954). The total hexosamine content of *nucleus pulposus* decreased from 14% of dry weight at 15 years of age to 6% at 90 years.

Roden (1956) has separated the mucopolysaccharides present in *nuclei pulposi* from pigs by the use of detergents. In the presence of an excess of 1% cetyl pyridinium chloride only the chondroitin sulphate was precipitated and the keratosulphate remained in solution. An alternative procedure was to pass the polysaccharide mixture down a column of cellulose previously washed with water and 1 per cent cetyl pyridinium

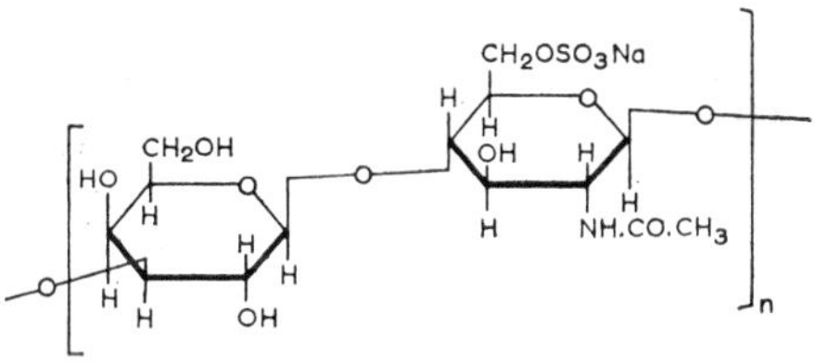

Fig. 5.1

chloride. When the column was washed with 1% cetyl pyridinium chloride and then subsequently with 1·5N-KCl the keratosulphate was eluted first and the chondroitin sulphate last. Using these techniques for separation Roden (1956) has demonstrated that *in vitro* the presence of glutamine stimulates the incorporation of S^{35}-sulphate into the keratosulphate of *nuclei pulposi*.

The keratosulphate of bovine cornea and its desulphated polymer have been methylated (Hirano, Hoffman and Meyer, 1960). Among the methyl ethers obtained on hydrolysis were 2:4-di-*O*-methyl D-galactose, 2:4:6-tri-*O*-methyl D-galactose, 2:3:4:6-tetra-*O*-methyl D-galactose, 2-acetamido 2-deoxy 3-*O*-methyl D-glucose and 2-acetamido 2-deoxy 3:6-di-*O*-methyl D-glucose. Assay of the methyl ethers obtained from the methylated keratosulphate and its methylated desulphated analogue showed that the sulphate was located on the glucosamine moiety. The identity of the methyl ethers and information gained from the study of the enzymic hydrolysis of keratosulphate (see below) enabled the American workers to postulate that keratosulphate had the repeating unit shown in Fig. 5.1.

A similarity between the structure of the keratosulphate of cornea and rib cartilage and the structure of the blood group polysaccharides has been reported (Rosen, Hoffman and Meyer, 1960) on the basis of cross reactions with anti-blood group sera. Extracts of a coccobacillus (Chase) were also found to hydrolyse keratosulphate to oligosaccharides, sulphate, D-galactose and N-acetylglucosamine. Since the enzymes responsible for the liberation of monosaccharides were a β-galactosidase and a β-glucosaminidase, keratosulphate must be linked β-glycosidically. The same extracts degraded blood group substances. These workers also reported that keratosulphate contained 1–2% methylpentose (cf. blood group substances which contain L-fucose).

Polyhexosamine Sulphate

An unusual polysaccharide, so far not found in higher animals, has been isolated from the hypobronchial gland of the snail Busycon canaliculatum L. (Bacila and Ronkin, 1952). Fresh mucus obtained from this gland was stirred with chloroform to denature proteins and the aqueous phase precipitated with ethanol to yield the crude polysaccharide. Partial acid hydrolysates of the polysaccharide treated with phenylhydrazine gave inter alia glucosazone and galactosazone. These appear to have arisen from glucosamine and galactosamine respectively since later workers (Shashoua and Kwart, 1959) detected both of these sugars in almost equivalent amounts in hydrolysates of the polysaccharide. The sulphur content of the polysaccharide (S, 7·2%) suggested that about two-thirds of the aminohexose units were sulphated. Analysis of the residue obtained on ashing the polysaccharide indicated that it was a mixed calcium–sodium salt. The infrared spectra of the polysaccharide showed the absence of N-acetyl and carboxylic acid groups.

In the mucus this polysaccharide is complexed with a protein (Kwart and Shashoua, 1958) which contains some 17 aminoacids, the most abundant of which are aspartic acid (11·27%), threonine (11·23%), leucine (9·22%) and glutamic acid (15·28%).

Charoninsulphuric Acid

The mucus of the mollusc Charonia lampas contains sulphated polyglucosans which have been extracted in high yield (Soda and Terayama, 1948). Evidence has been obtained which suggests that they are mixtures of amylose and cellulose sulphates (Egami, Asahi, Takahashi, Suzuki, Shikata and Nishizawa, 1955). When charoninsulphuric acid was desulphated with methanol-hydrochloric acid and dissolved in Schweitzer's reagent a portion neutralized with acetic acid gave a precipitate (fraction A). More precipitation occurred on addition of methanol to the supernatant (fraction B). Enzymic degradation of fraction A with Irpex cellulase liberated glucose and cellobiose while acetolysis of fraction A afforded cellobiose octaacetate. These properties are indicative of β-1:4-glucosidic linkages similar to those present in cellulose. By contrast fraction B stained red with iodine, gave glucose on acid hydrolysis and was hydrolysed by α- and β-amylase to give glucose and maltose. Some cellobiose was also reported. Attack by these enzymes is specific for α-1:4-glucosidic linkages. Periodate oxidation of fraction B confirmed the position of these linkages.

Further confirmation of the presence of both α- and β-linkages has been obtained from infrared spectra (Nakanishi, Takahashi and Egami, 1956). Further sulphation of charoninsulphuric acid has been found to occur in the presence of p-nitrophenylsulphuric acid (the sulphate donor) and an acetone dried extract of the mucous gland of *Charonia lampas* (Suzuki, Takahashi and Egami, 1957). Histochemical results indicate that in the mollusc itself incorporation of $S^{35}O_4^{--}$ into charoninsulphuric acid occurs near the nuclei granules of the glands cells in a layer bordered with connective tissues (Suzuki and Ogi, 1956).

Polyglucose Sulphate

The cartilage-like tissue of the marine snail *Busycon canaliculatum* differs from that of higher animals in that it does not contain chondroitin sulphate (Lash, 1957). The odontophore in snails supports the rasping organ (radula), and histologically exhibits a typical hyaline metachromatic matrix. Extraction of the fresh odontophore with water dissolved a large amount of myoglobin and left behind the chondroid matrix. Treatment of the latter with trypsin released the metachromatic substance (27% of the dried weight of odontophore) which was found to have a paper ionophoretic mobility less than that of heparin but comparable with that of chondroitin sulphate (Lash and Whitehouse, 1960).

The metachromatic polysaccharide, which could be precipitated with Cetavlon, hexaminocobaltichloride and neomycin, exhibited marked anticoagulant activity. It showed a high sulphate content (35%) which must be bound as O-sulphate since the only sugar produced on acid hydrolysis was glucose (57%). Only a feeble ninhydrin reaction was given by the polysaccharide hydrolysate corresponding to a 0·08% α-amino content. Since both the polyglucose sulphate and a partially desulphated preparation gave no stain with iodine it is unlikely that α-1:4-glucosidic linkages are present, indeed its low optical rotation suggests β-glucosidic linkages. The glucose is almost certainly of the D-configuration since it was attacked by glucose oxidase. Phosphate, aminosugars and uronic acids were absent from the acid hydrolysate of the polysaccharide.

Polyribose Phosphate

Maki (1956b) has isolated a water soluble polyribose phosphate from the liver of a squid (*Ommastrephes sloani pacificus*). This polysaccharide was easily depolymerized by acid, alkali and ribonuclease. Another polysaccharide isolated from the liver contained hexosamine, hexuronic acid and sulphate.

Poly L-Fucose Sulphate

Aqueous extraction of ethanol-dried trepang tissue (*Stichopus japonicus*) and addition of benzidine was found to precipitate a poly L-fucose sulphate–protein complex. It contained 60·1% fucose, sulphur (hydrolysable) 10·9%, and N, 1·2% (Maki and Hiyama, 1956). The jelly coat substances of eggs of the sea urchin species *Strongulocentrotus droebachiensis*, *Paracentrotus lividus* and *Echincardium cordatum* are also probably poly L-fucose sulphates (Vasseur, 1948). About one sulphate group per sugar residue was present.

Polygalactose Sulphate

The jelly coat of the egg of the sea urchin (*Echinus esculentus*) is a polygalactose sulphate containing about one ester sulphate group per sugar residue (Vasseur, 1948). Isolation of the sugar after acid hydrolysis has shown that it has the unusual L-configuration. It showed $[\alpha]_D^{19} - 74 \cdot 5°$ in water. The low melting point of its methylphenylhydrazone was probably due to the presence of a small amount of the D-isomer. Periodate oxidation results indicated that the structure of the polygalactose sulphate was similar to that of carrhageenin, i.e. galactopyranose residues linked 1:3 and carrying a sulphate group on C_4.

Jelly coat substances have been shown to have a rather strong anticoagulating action (Immers, 1949). Runnström and Immers (1956) have concluded that the acid mucopolysaccharides in the cortical layer of unfertilized sea urchin eggs act as enzyme inhibitors of fertilization. The natural activation of the eggs probably causes a break up of the inhibitory substances and thus releases certain enzyme systems. Other sulphated polysaccharides which were found to act like the jelly coat were heparin, human blood group H substance, chitin disulphate, dextran sulphate and chondroitin sulphate.

Mucoitin Sulphate

Mucoitin sulphate was the name given by Levene (1925) to describe a polysaccharide isomeric with chondroitin sulphate in which chondrosamine was replaced with glucosamine. Mucoitin sulphate also appeared to have less stable sulphate groups than chondroitin sulphate. Following the procedures of Levene (1925) and Komarov (1938) mucoitin sulphate (I) was isolated by alkaline digestion from commercial pig gastric mucin (Meyer, Smyth and Palmer, 1937). Later the acidic polysaccharide (II) was isolated without alkaline digestion (Meyer and Smyth, 1938). These preparations had I, 4·0% N; 32·8% glucosamine; 39·1% uronic acid; acetyl, 8·8% and 4·7% S—II, 3·0% N; 30·6%, glucosamine; 27·6% uronic acid; acetyl 8·8% and 3·1%S. The acid salt of I had $[\alpha]_D{}^{24} - 20\cdot2°$, the neutral salt of I had $[\alpha]_D{}^{25} - 35\cdot7°$ and acid salt of II showed $[\alpha]_D{}^{25} - 22\cdot2°$. Mucoitin sulphate was found to exhibit little anticoagulant activity (1% that of heparin) (Meyer, 1938). The hexosamine in mucoitin sulphate was characterized by analysis and optical rotation of the crystalline sugar as D-glucosamine hydrochloride. Evidence as to the nature of the uronic acid was not presented.

Wolfrom et al. (1943) isolated sodium mucoitin sulphate (neutral salt) from commercial pig gastric mucin (40 g) using the method of Meyer, Smyth and Palmer (1937). It was further purified by filtration through activated charcoal and Super-Cel and by alcohol precipitation to yield 1·6 g of the neutral sodium salt having $[\alpha]_D - 15°$ and C, 31·8; H, 5·05; N, 2·51; S, 6·06; acetyl, 7·8; anhydroglucuronic acid, 29·0; anhydrohexosamine, 29·0. These analyses correspond to a molar ratio of anhydrohexosamine; anhydrohexuronic acid; N-acetyl: ester sulphate of 1:1·1:1·0:1·0.

Wolfrom and Rice (1947) re-examined their preparation of mucoitin sulphuric acid in a Longsworth and MacInnes (1939) electrophoresis apparatus. In 1% phosphate buffer (μ 0·2; pH neutral) two moving components comprising 41% and 19% respectively together with a stationary component (40%) were detected. Neither of the mobile components moved as fast as heparin.

At this stage Masamune (1949) reported that he had searched in vain for mucoitin monosulphate in the animal body. However, in their study of the virulence enhancing factor in hog gastric mucin Smith, Gallop and Stanley (1952) obtained an impure polysaccharide fraction which was predominantly the mucoitin monosulphuric ester of Meyer, Smyth and Palmer (1937). The fraction ($[\alpha]_D{}^{24} - 35\cdot7°$) contained equal amounts of hexosamine, 25·1% (16 hr at 100° with 3N-HCl) and hexuronic acid, 27·6% (Lefèvre and Tollens, 1907); 5·2% S as hydrolysable sulphate was also present. The amino groups in the hexosamine residues carried N-acetyl groups (5·2%). Most of the virulence enhancing activity of the polysaccharide fraction was attributed to a heparin-like impurity.

A polysaccharide has been isolated from the viscera of trepangs (Stichopus japonicus) and found to be composed of glucosamine, glucuronic acid and ester sulphate. It was considered to be a mucoitin sulphate (Maki, 1956a).

Limacoitin Sulphate

A polysaccharide designated limacoitin sulphate was first isolated from the mucus mucin of the snail (Masamune, Yasuoka, Takahashi and Asagi, 1947) using a procedure which involved treatment with formalin (Masamune and Osaki, 1943). This polysaccharide was believed to be composed of acetyl hexosamine, galacturonic acid and sulphate residues.

Pneumogalactan

During the commercial preparation of heparin from beef lung a polysaccharide which has been characterized as a galactan is often encountered (Wolfrom, Weisblat, Karabinos and Keller, 1947). Purification can be effected by treatment with decolourizing charcoal, repeated precipitation with ethanol and finally by two passages down a column of mono-bed MB-3 ion exchange resin (Rohm and Hass Co.). Polysaccharide isolated in this way (Wolfrom, Sutherland and Schlamowitz, 1952) showed, $[\alpha]_D^{29} + 19°$ (H$_2$O) and contained C,44·3 H,6·3% corresponding to a formula of $[C_6H_{10}O_5]_n$. Titration revealed that one acidic function, probably uronic acid, was present for every 35–40 hexose units. That this acidic function was an integral part of the molecule was demonstrated by its electrophoretic mobility ($-2·35 \times 10^{-5}$ cm^2 sec^{-1} in phosphate buffer, pH 8·0; μ 0·20, 0°, 4·15 v/cm). The nature of the hexose units was confirmed as D-galactose by acidic hydrolysis and crystallization; no L-galactose residues were present.

The galactan yields a tri-O-acetate and a tri-O-methyl ether. Preparation of the latter required care because of the sensitivity of the polysaccharide to alkali. This was overcome by preparing the thallous salt of the galactan and then reacting it with methyl iodide. The final stages of methylation were effected with silver oxide/methyl iodide. Methanolysis and hydrolysis of the resulting methyl ether ($[\alpha]_D - 54°$) yielded methyl sugars characterized as the crystalline anilides of 2:4-di-O-methyl D-galactose, 2:3:4-tri-O-methyl-D-galactose and 2:3:4:6-tetra-O-methyl-D-galactose. Since these methyl sugars were present in equal amounts the structure shown (Fig. 5.2) was postulated.

Confirmation of the arrangement shown was obtained from the results of periodate oxidation. Each anhydrotrisaccharide unit consumed 4 moles of periodate and liberated 2 moles of formic acid. The anomeric character of the glycosidic linkages was favoured as β- on the basis of rotational evidence.

Further evidence for the presence of β-1:3 and β-1:3:6 linkages accrues from the strong cross-reaction exhibited by the galactan with anti-Type XIV *Pneumococcus* serum (Heidelberger, 1955). The galactan also precipitated antiserum to Type II *Pneumococcus* immediately suggesting that the unknown acidic function in the galactan was glucuronic acid

(Heidelberger, Dische, Brock Neely and Wolfrom, 1955) since it was known that Type II *Pneumococcus* polysaccharide contained glucose, rhamnose and glucuronic acid.

This supposition was confirmed by methanolysis of the lung galactan, treatment of the products with sodium borohydride and the chromatographic identification of glucose resulting from the reduction of some of the glucuronic acid residues. D-Glucurono-γ-lactone and the free acid were also detected. Analyses were carried out to determine the ratio of glucuronic acid (μg)/150 μg galactose in the polysaccharide. In the intact

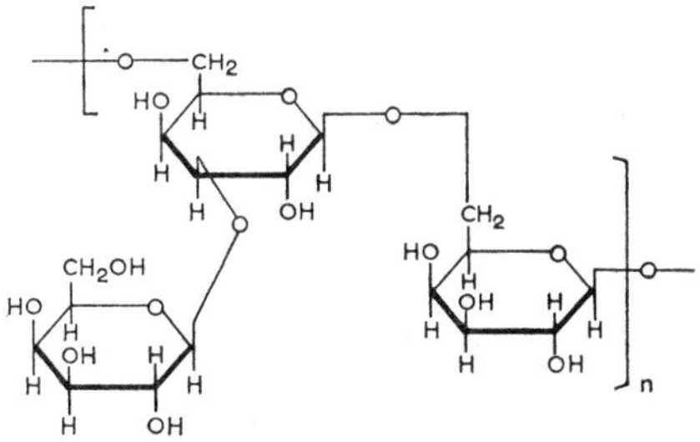

Fig. 5.2

polysaccharide this ratio was 2·8, but the polysaccharides precipitated with anti-Type XIV and anti-Type II *Pneumococcus* sera exhibited ratios of 1·2 and 6·0 respectively. It was therefore suggested that pneumogalactan was a mixture of molecular species containing different galactose:glucuronic acid ratios. Precipitation with Type XIV serum, which was dependent on the presence of galactose non-reducing end groups and galactose residues linked β-1:3, selectively separated the molecular species richer in these moieties. Conversely, precipitation with Type II serum selectively separated the species richer in uronic acid groups.

Helix Pomatia Galactan

The snail *Helix pomatia* has long been known (Hammarsten, 1885) to contain a polysaccharide in its albumin glands which has been characterized by May (1931, 1932, 1934) as a polygalactan. Purified polysaccharide was isolated by alkaline digestion (30% aqueous potassium hydroxide) followed by precipitation of the galactan as a copper complex. Such a galactan showed $[\alpha]_D - 16 \cdot 1°$ (water) (Baldwin and Bell, 1938). Acidic hydrolysis yielded crystalline D-galactose but rotational evidence suggested that some L-galactose might also be present. Methylation of the galactan tri-*O*-acetate yielded a methyl ether having OMe, 43·1% and $[\alpha]_D - 20°$. Hydrolysis of the methyl ether afforded 2:3:4:6-tetra-*O*-methyl galactose and 2:4-di-*O*-methyl galactose.

Subsequent work (Bell and Baldwin, 1941) established that L-galactose was present in snail galactan. The tetra-O-methyl galactose isolated above as its anilide was found to be a DL-mixture but the di-O-methyl galactose appeared only to contain the D-isomer. Hence the galactan could be pictured as having only D-galactose residues linked β-1:3 in the back-bone of the polymer to which were attached single side chains of galactose residues linked β-1:6. Three out of every four of these side chains were D-galactose residues while the other one was L-galactose.

During the acid hydrolysis of *Helix pomatia* galactan, L-galactose was found to be split off more rapidly than D-galactose (May and Weinland, 1956). Separation of a partial acid hydrolysate of the galactan yielded 3-O-β-D-galactosyl D-galactose, 6-O-β-D-galactosyl D-galactose together with traces of 6-O-α-L-galactosyl D-galactose (Weinland, 1956).

The galactan is not attacked readily by enzymes present in the snail and when injected intravenously into pregnant rabbits is degraded only slowly (33% in 42 days) (Weinland, 1953).

Galactans have been isolated from common South Indian gastropods, e.g. the uterus of fully mature *Pila*, the albumin gland of *Viviparus* and *Ariophanta* and the albuminous fluid of *Pila* eggs (Meenakshi, 1954). In the uterus of *Pila* they declined during the sexually active period from 28% to 14–15% after oviposition. This percentage increased within a few weeks after egg laying to 24–5% but declined again during aestivation. Horstmann (1956) in a study of the galactan content of the eggs of *Lymnala stagnalis* found that of the 36% present in the freshly laid egg the embryos used 46–78% while the rest was used as nutriment by the young snails.

REFERENCES

Bacila, M. and Ronkin, R. R. *Biol. Bull. Wood's Hole* **103**, 296 (1952).
Baldwin, E. and Bell, D. J. *J. Chem. Soc.* 1461 (1938).
Bell, D. J. and Baldwin, E. *J. Chem. Soc.* 125 (1941).
Egami, F., Asahi, T., Takahashi, N., Suzuki, S., Shikata, S. and Nishizawa, K. *Bull. Chem. Soc. Japan* **28**, 695 (1955).
Gardell, S. *Acta Chem. Scand.* **11**, 668 (1957).
Gardell, S. and Rastgeldi, S. *Acta Chem. Scand.* **8**, 362 (1954).
Hallén, A. *Acta Chem. Scand.* **12**, 1869 (1958).
Hammarsten, *Pflügers Arch.* **36**, 873 (1885).
Heidelberger, M. *J. Amer. Chem. Soc.* **77**, 4308 (1955).
Heidelberger, M., Dische, Z., Brock Neely, W. and Wolfrom, M. L. *J. Amer. Chem. Soc.* **77**, 3511 (1955).
Hirano, G., Hoffman, P. and Meyer, K. *Fed. Proc.* **19**, 146 (1960).
Hoffman, P., Linker, A. and Meyer, K. *Biochim. Biophys. Acta* **30**, 184 (1958).
Horstmann, H. J. *Biochem. Z.* **328**, 342 (1956).
Immers, J. *Arkiv. Zool.* **42A**, No. 6 (1949).

Kaplan, D. and Meyer, K. *Nature* **183,** 1267 (1959).
Komarov. *J. Biol. Chem.* **123,** lxxxiv (1938).
Kuhn, R. and Leppelmann, H. J. *Liebigs Ann. Chem.* **611,** 254 (1958).
Kwart, H. and Shashoua, V. E. *J. Amer. Chem. Soc.* **80,** 2230 (1958).
Lash, J. W. *Science* **130,** 334 (1957).
Lash, J. W. and Whitehouse, M. W. *Biochem. J.* **74,** 351 (1960).
Lefèvre, K. U. and Tollens, B. *Ber.* **40,** 4513 (1907).
Levene, P. A. *Hexosamines and Mucoproteins.* Longmans, Green & Co. (1925).
Longsworth, L. G. and MacInnes, D. A. *Chem. Revs.* **24,** 271 (1939).
Maki, M. *Hirosaki Med. J.* **7,** 150 (1956a).
Maki, M. *Hirosaki Med. J.* **7,** 211 (1956b).
Maki, M. and Hiyama, N. *Hirosaki Med. J.* **7,** 142 (1956).
Malmgren, H. and Sylvén, B. *Biochim. Biophys. Acta* **9,** 706 (1952).
Masamune, H. *Chem. Researches (Japan) Biochem.* **4,** 1 (1949).
Masamune, H. and Osaki, S. *Tohuku J. Exp. Med.* **45,** 121 (1943).
Masamune, H., Yasuoka, T., Takahashi, M. and Asagi, Y. *Tohoku J. Exp. Med.* **49,** 177 (1947).
May, F. *Z. Biol.* **91,** 215 (1931); **92,** 319, 325 (1932); **95,** 277, 401, 606, 614 (1934).
May, F. and Weinland, H. *Z. physiol. Chem.* **305,** 75 (1956).
Meenakshi, V. R. *Current Sci.* (India) **23,** 301 (1954).
Meyer, K. *Cold Spring Harb. Sym. quart. Biol.* **6,** 91 (1938).
Meyer, K., Davidson, E., Linker, A. and Hoffman, P. *Biochim. Biophys. Acta* **21,** 506 (1956).
Meyer, K., Hoffman, P. and Linker, A. *Science* **128,** 896 (1958).
Meyer, K., Linker, A., Davidson, E. A. and Weissman, B. *J. Biol. Chem.* **205,** 611 (1953).
Meyer, K. and Smyth, E. M. *J. Biol. Chem.* **123,** lxxxiv (1938).
Meyer, K., Smyth, E. M. and Palmer, J. W. *J. Biol. Chem.* **119,** 73 (1937).
Nakanishi, K., Takahashi, N. and Egami, F. *Bull. Chem. Soc. Japan* **29,** 434 (1956).
Roden, L. *Arkiv för Kemi.* **10,** 383 (1956).
Rosen, O., Hoffman, P. and Meyer, K. *Fed. Proc.* **19,** 147 (1960).
Runnström, J. and Immers, J. *Exp. Cell Res.* **10,** 354 (1956).
Shashoua, V. and Kwart, H. *J. Amer. Chem. Soc.* **81,** 2899 (1959).
Shetlar, M. R. and Masters, Y. F. *Proc. Soc. Exp. Biol. Med.* **90,** 31 (1955).
Smith, H., Gallop, R. C. and Stanley, J. L. *Biochem. J.* **52,** 15 (1952).
Soda, T. and Terayama, H. *J. Chem. Soc. Japan* Pure Chem. Sect. **69,** 65 (1948).
Suzuki, S. and Ogi, K. *J. Biochem. (Japan)* **43,** 697 (1956).
Suzuki, S., Takahashi, N. and Egami, F. *Biochim. Biophys. Acta* **24,** 444 (1957).
Vasseur, E. *Acta Chem. Scand.* **2,** 900 (1948).
Weinland, H. *Biochem. Z.* **324,** 19 (1953).
Weinland, H. *Z. physiol. Chem.* **305,** 87 (1956).
Wolfrom, M. L., Weisblat, D. I., McNeely, W. H., McLean, J. and Karabinos, J. V. *J. Amer. Chem. Soc.* **65,** 2077 (1943).
Wolfrom, M. L. and Rice, F. A. H. *J. Amer. Chem. Soc.* **69,** 2918 (1947).
Wolfrom, M. L., Sutherland, G. and Schlamowitz, M. *J. Amer. Chem. Soc.* **74,** 4883 (1952).
Wolfrom, M. L., Weisblat, D. I., Karabinos, J. V. and Keller, O. *Arch. Biochem.* **14,** 1 (1947).

Chapter 6

MILK OLIGOSACCHARIDES

Oligosaccharides of Human Milk

INTEREST in the oligosaccharides of human milk was stimulated by the discovery of the prevalance of the micro-organism *Lactobacillus bifidus* in the intestinal flora of the normal breast-fed infant in contrast to the mixed flora of infants fed on cow's milk (Moro, 1900). Strains of *Lact. bifidus* requiring human milk for prolific growth (György, Kuhn, Norris, Rose and Zilliken, 1952, 1953) were isolated from the stools of breast-fed and bottle-fed infants and from the vaginal secretions of pregnant women (Harrison, Stahl, Magavran, Sanders, Norris and György, 1953). A search for an essential growth-promoting factor in human milk (the Bifidus factor) was therefore commenced. Such a factor was organic in origin since activity was destroyed by ashing (György, Norris and Rose, 1954). Comparison showed that the highest activity was in human colostrum followed by rat colostrum, human milk, rat milk and cow's colostrum (György, Kuhn, Rose and Zilliken, 1954). Cow's milk and the milk of goats and ewes showed only very slight activity. Human saliva, semen, amniotic fluid, meconium and tears contained high concentrations of the bifidus growth factor. The bifidus active components of human milk could be fractionated by dialysis (György, Hoover, Kuhn and Rose, 1954). The dialysable fraction represented 40–75% of the overall activity, the residual components possessing activity being non-dialysable. Removal of the cream, proteins and salts from human milk caused little loss in bifidus activity (Gauhe, György, Hoover, Kuhn, Rose, Ruelius and Zilliken, 1954). The residual material was concentrated and then freed from lactose and found to contain at least four different active components all of which contained N-acetyl glucosamine residues. Other sugars characterized in the hydrolysate of the lactose-free concentrate were L-fucose, D-glucose and D-galactose. The chemistry of the oligosaccharides discussed below is mainly due to the work of Kuhn and co-workers in Germany. Montreuil (1957) has also reported the occurrence of lacto-N-tetraose and a series of fucose containing oligosaccharides in human milk. These include a second fucosyl-lactose and at least five other substances in which fucose is present.

This trisaccharide (Fig. 6.1) occurs to the extent of 150–300 mg/litre in human breast milk and has been obtained in the crystalline α-form (Kuhn, Baer and Gauhe, 1956a).

Hydrolysis of the trisaccharide $[\alpha]_D - 57°$ (H_2O) gave equimolar amounts of D-glucose, D-galactose and L-fucose. Partial hydrolysis yielded L-fucose and lactose; the latter was isolated as its crystalline α-hydrate (m.p. 201°) (Kuhn, Baer and Gauhe, 1955). Oxidation of the reducing group present in the trisaccharide with hypoiodite followed by acid hydrolysis gave fucose and galactose but no glucose. The glucose component must therefore carry the reducing group. Methylation of the trisaccharide was effected with $NaOH/Me_2SO_4$ followed by the Purdie reagents. Methanolysis of the methyl ether yielded methyl 2:3:4-tri-O-methyl α-L-fucopyranoside. Subsequent aqueous acidic hydrolysis of the glycosides yielded 2:3:4-tri-O-methyl L-fucose (characterized as its crystalline anilide), 2:3:6-tri-O-methyl D-glucose and 3:4:6-tri-O-methyl D-galactose (characterized as its phenylosazone and by oxidation to 3:4:6-tri-O-methyl D-galactonic acid). The above evidence established the structure shown. The assignment of an α-glycosidic linkage to the fucosyl residue was made on the basis of a comparison of the rates of hydrolysis of the fucosyl-lactose and ethyl α-L-fucopyranoside together with data from the optical rotation of the

Fig. 6.1

trisaccharide and its component moieties. The fucosyl-lactose forms a phenylosazone and a tosylhydrazone. If the fucosyl residue had been attached to C_2 of the glucose residue the products with phenyl hydrazine would have been a mixture of lactosazone and fucosazone.

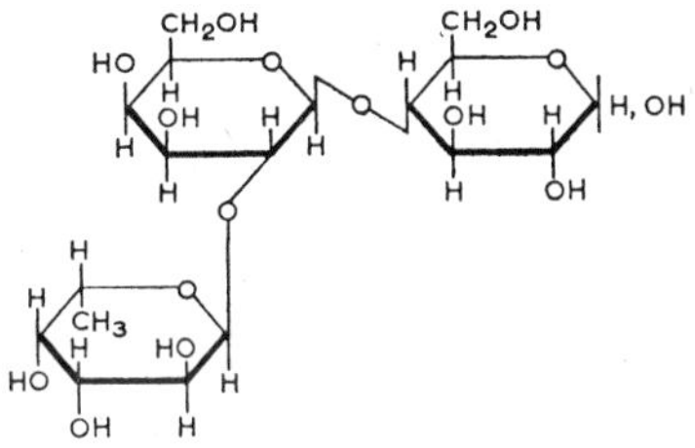

Montreuil (1954, 1956) has confirmed the presence of the α-L-fucopyranosyl lactose in human milk and has claimed the detection of an isomeric trisaccharide containing galactose, glucose and fucose. On the basis of the products of hydrolysis of the alkali-treated trisaccharide he has postulated that in the latter case the fucosyl residue is attached to the glucosyl moiety of lactose.

Lactose-lactaminic acid

This trisaccharide has been detected in human breast milk and human colostrum (Kuhn and Brossmer, 1956a). Only the structural details of the same (or similar) trisaccharide in cow's milk have been elucidated.

Lacto-difuco-tetraose

The structure of this tetrasaccharide, which is probably identical with oligosaccharide 5 of Montreuil (1956) has been determined by Kuhn and

Gauhe (1958). Complete acidic hydrolysis yields two moles of L-fucose, one mole of D-glucose and one mole of D-galactose. Partial acid hydrolysis liberates fucosidolactose, lactose and fucose. It thus appears to be a fucosyl homologue of the trisaccharide fucosidolactose (see above) which was isolated in the crystalline form from the hydrolysate. Alkaline hydrolysis gives *inter alia* 2-O-fucosyl galactose and 2-O-fucosyl talose together with free fucose. Hence the additional fucosyl residue was probably attached to the C_3 of the glucose residue which had been shown to carry the reducing group. The formula shown (Fig. 6.2) has been confirmed by periodate oxidation of the tetrasaccharide and acidic hydrolysis of the residual skeleton. The arabinose detected in the hydrolysate must have come from the glucose residue by oxidation between C_1 and C_2. The anomeric character of the second fucosyl linkage was α because of the higher negative rotation ($[\alpha]_D - 106°$) of the tetrasaccharide compared with that of fucosidolactose.

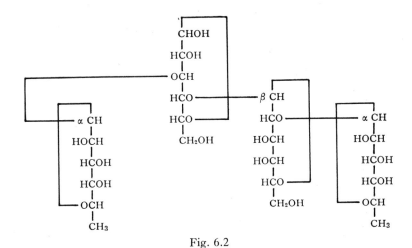

Fig. 6.2

Lacto N-triose I and lacto N-triose II

Both these trisaccharides are produced by acid hydrolysis of lacto N-tetraose (Kuhn, Gauhe and Baer, 1956). Triose I gave galactose and glucosamine on acid hydrolysis. Infrared spectra of its phenylosazone showed N-acetamido groupings hence glucosamine was not the reducing end group. Alkaline degradation products established that it was galactose-N-acetyl-glucosamine-galactose. Triose II gave glucose, galactose and glucosamine on acid hydrolysis. Treatment with $0.05 \text{N-Na}_2\text{CO}_3$ gave products which showed that lacto N-triose II was N-acetyl glucosamine-galactose-glucose. The points of linkage in these two trisaccharides follows from the methylation studies of lacto N-tetraose discussed below.

Kuhn, Gauhe and Baer (1954) have partially acid hydrolysed this tetrasaccharide (Fig. 6.3) and obtained two nitrogen containing trisaccharides (lacto N-trioses I and II), two nitrogen containing disaccharides (lacto N-bioses I and II) and lactose (identified as its α-hydrate). The nitrogen was present in D-glucosamine residues and this sugar was isolated as its crystalline hydrochloride. In order to determine which of the three

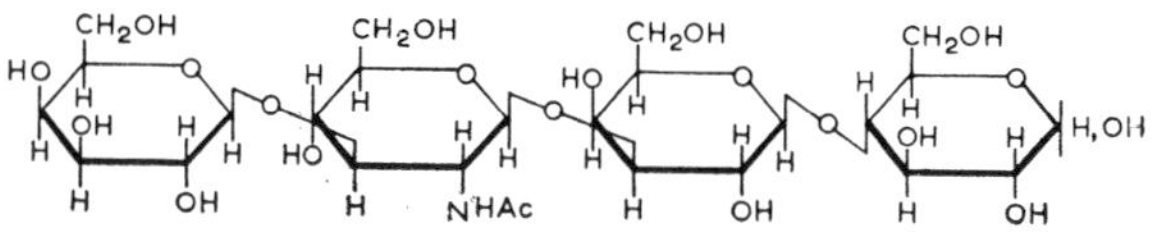

Fig. 6.3

constituent sugars present in the tetrasaccharide carried a reducing group the phenylosazone of the oligosaccharide was hydrolysed. Galactose and glucosamine were detected but no glucose; hence this sugar was the reducing moiety. Comparison of the absorption spectra of the oligosaccharide osazone and glucosazone confirmed that it was a tetrasaccharide. From the structures of the two trisaccharides (see above) the sequence in the tetrasaccharide was probably galactose-glucosamine-galactose-glucose. This was confirmed by reduction of the tetrasaccharide, methylation of the alcohol obtained and identification of the products of hydrolysis (Kuhn and Baer, 1956). Isolation of 2:3:4:6-tetra-O-methyl D-galactose showed that galactose was a non-reducing end group. Detection of 1:2:3:5:6-penta-O-methyl sorbitol confirmed that glucose was on the reducing end of the tetrasaccharide and was linked through the 4 position. Finally characterization of 4:6-di-O-methyl D-glucosamine and 2:4:6-tri-O-methyl D-galactose showed that these residues were both linked through the 3-position in the manner shown. Further confirmation was obtained by periodate oxidation studies.

Lacto N-biose I

This disaccharide is one of the acid hydrolysis products of lacto N-tetraose. Its structure has apparently been established (Kuhn, Baer and Gauhe, 1954) by its conversion to 3-O-β-D-galactosyl-D-glucosazone with phenylhydrazine. This osazone was identical with that produced from synthetic 3-O-β-D-galactosyl-D-glucose (Kuhn and Baer, 1954). Hence lacto N-biose I is 3-O-β-D-galactosyl-N-acetyl D-glucosamine.

Lacto N-fucopentaose I

α-Fuc 1—2 β-Gal 1—3 β-GNAc 1—3 β-Gal 1—4G

One of the pentasaccharides present in human milk is Morgan–Elson positive and can be partially hydrolysed to yield lacto N-tetraose which has been isolated crystalline. The other component present in the penta-saccharide is L-fucose (Kuhn, Baer and Gauhe, 1956b). Reduction of the pentasaccharide to its alcohol, methylation and hydrolysis yields 1:2:3:5:6-penta-O-methyl D-sorbitol, 2:4:6-tri-O-methyl D-galactose, 4:6-di-O-methyl D-glucosamine, 3:4:6-tri-O-methyl D-galactose and 2:3:4-tri-O-methyl L-fucose. Hence the fucosyl residue is a non-reducing end group and the pentasaccharide has the structure shown. The linkage joining the fucosyl residue is designated α from a comparison of the rotations of the tetrasaccharide $+25°$ (lacto N-tetraose) and pentasaccharide $-16°$.

Lacto N-fucopentaose II

β-Gal 1—3 β-GNAc 1—3 β-Gal 1—4G
4
|
1
α-Fuc

This isomeric pentasaccharide present in human milk gives one mole each of glucose, N-acetyl D-glucosamine and L-fucose and two moles of D-galactose (Kuhn, Baer and Gauhe, 1955). Partial hydrolysis with oxalic acid yielded fucose and lacto N-tetraose. Methylation of the alcohol of lacto N-fucopentaose gave an ether which on hydrolysis yielded 1:2:3:5:6-penta-O-methyl D-sorbitol, 2:4:6-tri-O-methyl D-galactose, 6-O-methyl D-glucosamine, 2:3:4:6-tetra-O-methyl D-galactose and 2:3:4-tri-O-methyl L-fucose (Kuhn, Baer and Gauhe, 1958a). Hence the non-reducing end group is this time attached through the 4 position of the glucosamine moiety. Again this linkage is designated α since lacto N-fucopentaose II shows $[α]_D -28·1°$ (equil.).

Lacto N-difucohexaose I

α-Fuc 1—2 β-Gal 1—3 β-GNAc 1—3 β-Gal 1—4G
4
|
1
α-Fuc

This hexasaccharide is the higher fucosyl homologue of lacto N-fuco-pentaose I. Kuhn, Baer and Gauhe (1958a) postulated the structure shown from the evidence provided by the nature of the alkaline degradation products of the hexasaccharide. These included 2-O-α-L-fucopyranosyl D-galactose characterized as its benzylphenylhydrazone.

Lacto N-difucohexaose II

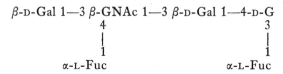

The crystalline tetrahydrate shows $[\alpha]_D^{25} - 68 \cdot 8°$ (Kuhn and Gauhe, 1960). Total hydrolysis gave fucose, glucose, galactose and glucosamine in the same quantities as present in hexoase I. Partial hydrolyses of varying severity showed that its structure included lacto *N*-fucopentaose II, lacto *N*-tetraose, lacto *N*-biose I, etc. Hence the main problem was the location of the second fucosyl residue. This followed from the detection of arabinose in the acid hydrolysate of the periodate-oxidized hexasaccharide. Galactose and glucosamine were also present.

Malpress and Hytten (1958) have independently isolated the fucose containing oligosaccharides of human milk. Their technique for separation was based on successive chromatography on charcoal-Celite eluted with aqueous ethanol, cellulose columns eluted with butanol–pyridine–water (6:1:1) and final purification by band chromatography on Whatman No. 3 MM paper. In this final step two mixed solvents were used, ethyl acetate:pyridine:water (2:1:2) and ethyl acetate–pyridine–water–acetone (10:5:10:2); the latter was particularly useful for separation of oligosaccharides containing more than five or six sugar units. Crystalline lacto *N*-tetraose was isolated together with pure amorphous samples of fucosyl-lactose, a monofuco-lacto *N*-tetraose which could be Kuhn's lacto *N*-pentaose I or II, and a difuco-lacto *N*-tetraose ≡ Kuhn's lacto *N*-difuco-hexaose. Five new compounds were detected having the following properties and all containing one or more lacto *N*-tetraose moieties.

Di(lacto N-tetraose)

This fucose-free oligosaccharide gave lacto *N*-tetraose as its major product on treatment with 0·005N-HCl for 2 hr at 100° indicating that it might be a dimer or trimer of this pentasaccharide. It was tentatively assigned the structure of a di(lacto *N*-tetraose) on the basis that it gave almost exactly 50% of the colour intensity of the same weight of lacto *N*-tetraose when determined by the modified method of Dische and Shettles (1948). The chromogens from both compounds also showed similar absorption curves.

Monofuco-di(lacto N-tetraose)

Delicate acid hydrolysis with 0·01N-HCl liberated di(lacto *N*-tetraose) and fucose from this oligosaccharide together with a trace compound also noted in a similar hydrolysate of di(lacto N-tetraose). Stronger hydrolysis ($0\cdot1N$-HCl) caused a further breakdown to include lacto N-tetraose among its products. The fucose content found for this oligosaccharide supported its tentative identification as a monofuco-di(lacto N-tetraose).

Difuco-di(lacto N-tetraose)

This oligosaccharide appeared to be the fucosyl homologue of monofuco-di(lacto N-tetraose) since the latter oligosaccharide was liberated on hydrolysis with $0\cdot01N$-HCl together with fucose, di(lacto N-tetraose) and a trace of lacto N-tetraose. More vigorous hydrolysis ($0\cdot1N$-HCl) gave fucose, di(lacto N-tetraose) and lacto N-tetraose only. The fucose content ($17\cdot0\%$) of this oligosaccharide was in fair agreement with that ($19\cdot4\%$) calculated for a difuco-di-(lacto N-tetraose).

Monofuco-tri(lacto N-tetraose)

Again the major evidence for the structure was obtained by acid hydrolysis: $0\cdot01N$-HCl gave fucose and a new compound [tri(lacto N-tetraose?)]; $0\cdot1N$-HCl gave fucose, monofuco-di(lacto-N-tetraose), a trace of di(lacto N-tetraose) and lacto N-tetraose. Since no difuco-di(lacto N-tetraose) was ever detected a new 'core' structure was probably present. The fucose content ($8\cdot5\%$) was more in agreement with that ($7\cdot4\%$) calculated for a monofuco-tri(lacto N-tetraose) than that ($5\cdot6\%$) for a monofuco-tetra(lacto N-tetraose). Supporting evidence from its reaction in the Dische and Shettles (1948) reaction enabled the compound to be assigned the probable structure of a monofuco-tri(lacto N-tetraose).

Difuco-tri(lacto-N-tetraose)

This oligosaccharide, which contained 10% fucose, had a fucose:tri (lacto N-tetraose) ratio of $0\cdot13$ to 1 compared with the proportion of $0\cdot16$ calculated for a difuco-tri(lacto-N-tetraose). The products obtained on acid hydrolysis [fucose, monofuco-tri(lacto N-tetraose), tri(lacto N-tetraose)?, difuco-di(lacto N-tetraose), monofuco-di(lacto-N-tetraose), lacto N-tetraose] suggested that it was indeed a difuco-tri(lacto-N-tetraose).

In their study of the various oligosaccharides, Malpress and Hytten (1958) noted that the smaller oligosaccharides, in particular fucosyl-lactose, lacto N-tetraose and monofuco-lacto-N-tetraose, were present in the largest amount. They estimated that the total oligosaccharide content of human milk was $0\cdot6$ g/100 ml. The total fucose content of human milk samples obtained from 3 to 43 days *post partum* remained fairly constant with a mean value of 128 mg/100 ml.

Oligosaccharides of Cows' Milk

Besides the common milk sugar lactose, cow's milk contains small amounts of other oligosaccharides. Trucco, Verdier and Rega (1954) removed the lactose from milk by fermentation with *Saccharomyces fragilis* or by fractionation on charcoal. After chromatography on Whatman No. 1 paper the series of carbohydrates were eluted and found to yield the following sugars on acidic hydrolysis; compound 1 gave galactose, glucose, mannose, acetylglucosamine; compound 2 gave the same sugars; compounds 3 and 4 both gave neuraminic acid and lactose while compounds 5, 6 and 7 all gave lactose, galactose and glucose.

Lactaminic acid (N-acetyl neuraminic acid)

The methoxy derivative of lactaminic acid is conveniently isolated from skimmed cow colostrum (Kuhn, Brossmer and Schulz, 1954). After dialysis the protein present within the dialysis bag is precipitated with acid and the product hydrolysed at pH 1 and 70–80° for 40 min. After

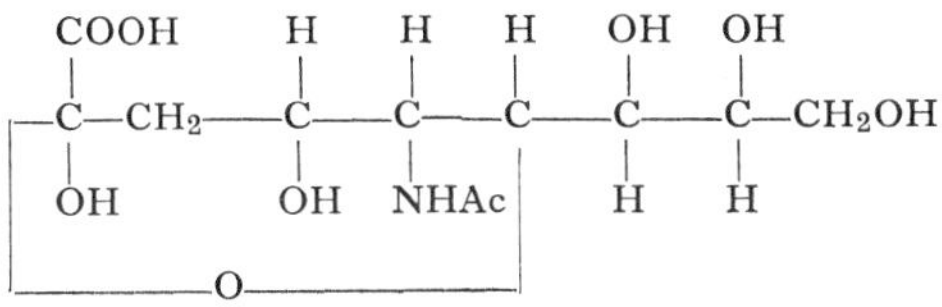

Fig. 6.4

removal of salts and passage through alumina the concentrated solution yields crystals of the methoxy derivative of lactaminic acid (m.p. 183–5°; $[\alpha]_D^{20} - 35°$ (methanol)). This had the tentative formula $C_{11}H_{19}O_9N$ (8·96% OMe; 13·7% acetyl). Treatment with pyridine and nickel (II) acetate at 100° afforded N-acetyl D-glucosamine (Kuhn and Brossmer, 1956). Later work (Kuhn and Brossmer, 1958) showed that this product arose by epimerization of N-acetyl D-mannosamine; only 10–20% N-acetyl D-mannosamine was present in the epimerization mixture.

Crystalline lactaminic acid was converted to N-acetylmannosamine by *Clostridium perfringens* suspension (Kuhn and Brossmer, 1958). Since the same suspension had no effect on N-acetylglucosamine, the lower 6 carbon atoms of the nine carbon chain in lactaminic acid probably has the *manno*-configuration shown in Fig. 6·4.

Further evidence for the structure of lactaminic acid has been obtained by the following degradation scheme (Kuhn and Brossmer, 1959). Chromatographically homogeneous lactaminic acid was treated with ethyl mercaptan to yield the diethylmercaptal of 5-acetamido 3,5-dideoxy

D-glycero D-talo 2-oxononoic acid γ-lactone (m.p. 124–5°; $[\alpha]_D^{23} - 83°$ in methanol). This product did not reduce Fehling's solution and gave negative reactions to the Bial and Ehrlich tests. When treated with methanolic potassium hydroxide the observed rotation was $[\alpha]_D^{22} - 69°$ (2 min) → 9·5° (12 hr). Regeneration of lactaminic acid could be effected in aqueous acetone with mercuric chloride or cadmium carbonate followed by treatment with hydrogen sulphide. The diethylmercaptal was reduced with Raney nickel to 5-acetamido-2,3,5-trideoxy D-glycero D-talononoic acid γ-lactone (m.p. 148–9; $[\alpha]_D^{23} - 35°$ in methanol). This product was oxidized with nitric acid at 120° for 5 hr to yield succinic acid (CH_2 . $COOH)_2$ characterized by conversion to succinic anhydride m.p. 117–18°.

O-Acetyl-lactaminic acid-lactose

Kuhn and Brossmer (1956a) isolated chromatographically pure lactaminic acid-lactose having $[\alpha]_D^{20} + 20°$ (H_2O) from cow colostrum (3·6 g per 16 l). Treatment with dilute acid gave one mole of lactose, one mole of acetic acid and one mole of lactaminic acid (syn. N-acetyl neuraminic acid). Reaction of the trisaccharide with diazomethane followed by methylation with silver oxide/methyl iodide in dimethylformamide gave a methyl ether (OMe, 37·6%). Further methylation using barium oxide instead of silver oxide sufficed to raise the methoxyl content to OMe, 43·8%. Only a very weak OH band was then observed in its infrared spectrum. Hydrolysis of the ether and fractionation of the products yielded crystalline 2:3:6-tri-O-methyl D-glucose and 2:4:6-tri-O-methyl D-galactose. A smaller amount of 2:3:4:6-tetra-O-methyl D-galactose was also isolated. The lactaminic acid was therefore attached to the C_3 of the galactose residue as shown in Fig. 6.5.

The following optical rotations in dimethylsulphoxide were observed β-lactaminic acid $[\alpha]_D^{23} - 115°$ (7 min) → − 24° (equil.); lactose hydrate $[\alpha]_D^{80} + 85°$ (6 min) → + 53° (equil.); lactaminic acid lactose $[\alpha]_D^{23} + 6°$. It was therefore suggested that the lactaminic acid is bound α-ketosidically to the lactose. O-Acetyl lactaminic acid lactose is hydrolysed by the receptor destroying enzyme of *Vibrio cholera* (Kuhn and Brossmer, 1956b).

The trisaccharide is present in the milk of other mammalian species. Trucco and Caputto (1954) isolated a so-called neuramin-lactose from the mammary gland of rats. A similar compound was observed in the mammary glands of guinea-pigs (Malpress and Morrison, 1952). Kuhn and Brossmer (1956b) report that the following quantities of O-acetyl lactaminic acid lactose (mg/100 cm^3) are present; human milk, 50–60; cow's milk, 3–6; sheep's milk, 28–35; human colostrum, 55–70; cow's colostrum, 30–90; sheep's colostrum, 60–85; pig's colostrum, 65–85.

A rapid method for the isolation of neuramin-lactose from bovine colostrum has been described by Mayron and Tokes (1960). The dialysate of fresh colostrum was passed down a column of Dowex-1(Cl⁻). Washing with water eluted sugars but none contained neuraminic acid. The fraction eluted with 0·1M-NaCl contained the neuramin-lactose as evinced from the hexose:sialic acid ratio of 2:1. For purification this fraction

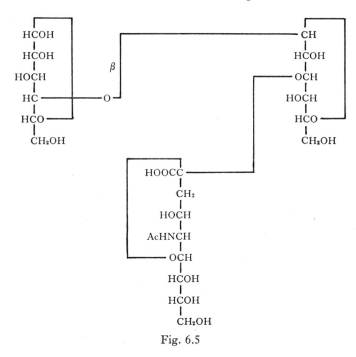

Fig. 6.5

was passed through a column of charcoal (Darco-60) and the salt eluted with water. The neuramin-lactose was eluted in a 60% ethanol eluate and recovered by *in vacuo* evaporation and freeze-drying. Viral neuraminidase liberated neuraminic acid and lactose from the neuramin-lactose.

Biological Activity of Milk Oligosaccharides

It is now realized that *Lactobacillus bifidus* var. *pennsylvanicus* has a specific growth requirement for N-acetyl D-glucosamine which should either be in the form of its β-glycosides (e.g. alkyl N-acetyl β-D-glucosaminides rather than the corresponding alkyl N-acetyl α-D-glucosaminides) or incorporated as the terminal reducing sugar in 4-O-β-substituted disaccharides, etc. (e.g. N-acetyl lactosamine) (Zilliken, Rose, Braun and György, 1955; Tomarelli, Hassinen, Eckhardt, Clark and Bernhart, 1954). The reason for both these types of derivatives exhibiting such growth promoting activity is probably due to their conversion to a common metabolic precursor of muramic acid (3-O-D-lactyl-D-glucosamine)

(O'Brien, Glick and Zilliken, 1960) which is an important constituent of the cell walls of certain bacteria. This precursor could be uridinediphosphate N-acetyl D-glucosamine since Strominger (1958) has demonstrated a pyruvic acid transfer from phosphoenol pyruvate to this sugar nucleotide using extracts of S. *aureus*, *E. coli* and *Aerobacter aerogenes*. Glick, Sall, Zilliken and Mudd (1960) have been able to show that bizarre forms of *L. bifidus* var. *pennysylvanicus* result from the deficiency of an N-acetyl amino sugar.

Those oligosaccharides found in human milk which exhibit growth promoting activity for *Lactobacillus bifidus* var. *pennsylvanicus* include lacto N-tetraose, lacto N-fucopentaose I, lacto N-fucopentaose II and lacto N-difucohexaose. No activity is exhibited by fucosyl-lactose. Of the oligosaccharides reported as present in cow's milk by Trucco, Verdier and Rega (1954) only compounds containing acetylglucosamine (i.e. compounds 1 and 2) were active.

Inhibition reactions

The range of human milk oligosaccharides have been tested for their ability to inhibit the reaction between Le (a+) red cells and human anti-Le^a serum (Watkins and Morgan, 1957). The minimum amount of each substance giving inhibition (μgm/0·1 ml) varied considerably. Following human Le^a substance (0·04 μg) in activity were lacto N-fucopentaose II and its alcohol lacto N-fucopentaitol II both active at the 1 μg level. Except for lacto N-difucohexaose (60 μg) the levels of all the other milk oligosaccharides tested (fucosido-lactose, lacto N-tetraose, lacto difucotetraose, lacto N-fucopentaose I) were over 1000 μg. The same large amounts were required of L-fucose, D-fucose, 2-O-α-fucosyl-fucose and 2-O-α-fucosyl galactose. Similar results were obtained in haemolysis inhibition tests with human or rabbit anti-Le^a serum and in precipitin inhibition tests in which a precipitating rabbit anti-Le^a serum was used. These results suggest that L-fucose is an important part of the determinant specificity of Le^a substance probably when joined α-glycosidically as a branching unit via a 1 → 4 linkage to N-acetyl D-glucosamine.

When the oligosaccharides were tested for inhibition of the agglutination of Le (b+) cells by human anti-Le^b serum only lacto N-difucohexaose and lacto-difucotetraose gave weak but definite inhibition. The ability of the oligosaccharides to inhibit the agglutination of O cells by eel serum has also been tested (Kuhn and Osman, 1956). Only the fucosyl-lactose showed slight activity.

Errors in Galactose Metabolism

Holzel, Schwarz and Sutcliffe (1959) have reported two cases of defective lactose absorption causing malnutrition in two siblings. Whereas both glucose and galactose were readily absorbed in the intestine the ingestion of lactose did not lead to a significant increase in the blood level of mono- saccharides. The enzyme defect therefore appears to be the inability to hydrolyse lactose. Another more general defect in galactose metabolism gives rise to galactosemia in children. Here the enzyme defect appears in the conver- sion of galactose 1-phosphate to glucose 1-phosphate since the former was found to accumulate in the red blood cells of galactosemic infants following administration of galactose (Schwarz, Golberg, Komrower and Holzel, 1956). In actual fact the enzyme lesion is galactose 1-phosphate uridyl transferase (Kalckar, 1960). This enzyme catalyses the conversion

α-Galactose 1-phosphate + Uridinediphosphoglucose $\rightleftharpoons$ α-Glucose 1-phosphate + Uridinediphosphogalactose

The enzymes galactokinase, uridinediphosphogalactose 4-epimerase, and glucose 1-phosphate/PP uridyl transferase were not affected.

REFERENCES

Dische, Z. and Shettles, L. B. *J. Biol. Chem.* **175**, 595 (1948).
Gauhe, A., György, P., Hoover, J. R. E., Kuhn, R., Rose, C. S., Ruelius, H. W. and Zilliken, F. *Arch. Biochem. Biophys.* **48**, 214 (1954).
Glick, M. C., Sall, T., Zilliken, F. and Mudd, S. *Biochim. Biophys. Acta* **37**, 361 (1960).
György, P., Hoover, J. R. E., Kuhn, R. and Rose, C. S. *Arch. Biochem.* **48**, 209 (1954).
György, P., Kuhn, R., Norris, R. F., Rose, C. S. and Zilliken, F. *Amer. J. Diseases Children* **84**, 484 (1952); **85**, 632 (1953).
György, P., Kuhn, R., Rose, C. S. and Zilliken, F. *Arch. Biochem. Biophys.* **48**, 202 (1954).
György, P., Norris, R. F. and Rose, C. S. *Arch. Biochem. Biophys.* **48**, 193 (1954).
Harrison, W., Stahl, R. C., Magavran, J., Sanders, M., Norris, R. F. and Györgv. P. *Amer. J. Obstet. Gynecol.* **65**, 352 (1953).
Holzel, A., Schwarz, V. and Sutcliffe, K. W. *Lancet* **1**, 1126 (1959)
Kalckar, H. M. *Fed. Proc.* **19**, 984 (1960).
Kuhn, R. and Baer, H. H. *Chem. Ber.* **87**, 1560 (1954).
Kuhn, R. and Baer, H. H. *Chem. Ber.* **89**, 504 (1956).
Kuhn, R., Baer, H. H. and Gauhe, A. *Chem. Ber.* **87**, 1553 (1954).
Kuhn, R., Baer, H. H. and Gauhe, A. *Chem. Ber.* **88**, 1135 (1955).
Kuhn, R., Baer, H. H. and Gauhe, A. *Chem. Ber.* **89**, 2513 (1956a).
Kuhn, R., Baer, H. H. and Gauhe, A. *Chem. Ber.* **89**, 2514 (1956b).
Kuhn, R., Baer, H. H. and Gauhe, A. *Chem. Ber.* **91**, 364 (1958a).
Kuhn, R., Baer, H. H. and Gauhe, A. *Annalen*, **611**, 242 (1958b).
Kuhn, R. and Brossmer, R. *Ang. Chem.* **68**, 211 (1956a).
Kuhn, R. and Brossmer, R. *Chem. Ber.* **89**, 2471 (1956); *Annalen* **616**, 221 (1958).

Kuhn, R. and Brossmer, R. *Chem. Ber.* **89,** 2013 (1956b); *Annalen* **624,** 137 (1959).
Kuhn, R., Brossmer, R. and Schulz, W. *Chem. Ber.* **87,** 123 (1954).
Kuhn, R. and Gauhe, A. *Annalen* **611,** 249 (1958).
Kuhn, R. and Gauhe, A. *Chem. Ber.* **93,** 647 (1960).
Kuhn, R., Gauhe, A. and Baer, H. H. *Chem. Ber.* **87,** 289 (1954).
Kuhn, R., Gauhe, A. and Baer, H. H. *Chem. Ber.* **89,** 1027 (1956).
Kuhn, R. and Osman, H. G. *Z. Physiol. Chem.* **303,** 1 (1956).
Malpress, F. H. and Hytten, F. E. *Biochem. J.* **68,** 708 (1958).
Malpress, F. H. and Morrison, A. B. *Nature* **169,** 1103 (1952).
Mayron, L. W. and Tokes, Z. A. *Biochim. Biophys. Acta* **45,** 601 (1960).
Montreuil, J. *Compt. rend.* **239,** 510 (1954); **242,** 192 (1956).
Montreuil, J. *Compt. rend.* **242,** 828 (1956).
Montreuil, J. *Bull. soc. chim. biol. Paris* **39,** 395 (1957).
Moro, E. *Wein. Klin. Wochschr.* **13,** 114 (1900).
O'Brien, P. J., Glick, M. C. and Zilliken, F. *Biochim. Biophys. Acta* **37,** 359 (1960).
Schwarz, V., Golberg, L., Komrower, G. M. and Holzel, A. *Biochem. J.* **62,** 34 (1956).
Strominger, J. L. *Biochim. Biophys. Acta* **30,** 645 (1958).
Tomarelli, R. M., Hassinen, J. B., Eckhardt, E. R., Clark, R. H. and Bernhart, F. W. *Arch. Biochem. Biophys.* **48,** 225 (1954).
Trucco, R. E. and Caputto, R. *J. Biol. Chem.* **206,** 901 (1954).
Trucco, R. E., Verdier, P. and Rega, A. *Biochim. Biophys. Acta* **15,** 582 (1954).
Watkins, W. M. and Morgan, W. T. J. *Nature* **180,** 1038 (1957).
Zilliken, F., Rose, C. S., Braun, G. A. and György, P. *Arch. Biochem. Biophys.* **54,** 392 (1955).

Chapter 7

BLOOD GROUP POLYSACCHARIDES

Introduction

BLOOD proteins of an animal can be sharply differentiated ('grouped'), by quantitative immunochemical methods. Human blood of a particular group contains antigens (agglutinogens) associated with the erythrocytes and antibodies (agglutinins) in the plasma, each of which can react (by 'isoagglutination') with the antigens or antibodies as appropriate of persons belonging to other groups.

There are four main groups—humans O, A, B and AB together with many subgroups A_1, A_2, A_1 B, etc. with other unrelated blood groups Rh, M, N, MN, etc. Persons of blood group A have A substance in their erythrocytes and the anti-B specific isoagglutinin in their serum. Persons of blood group B have B substance in their erythrocytes and the anti-A specific iso-agglutinin in their serum. Both these iso-agglutinins are absent from sera of people belonging to blood group AB but both are present in sera of persons of blood group O.

It is possible to obtain substances (haptenes) from a variety of sources, particularly animal tissues, which in very high dilution will inhibit the isoagglutination reaction. These haptenes are termed 'blood group substances'.

Early workers demonstrated that blood group substances could be extracted with ethanol from erythrocytes where they appeared in a water-insoluble lipid-bound form. Later workers, somewhat deterred by the exceedingly small amounts of these substances present in the erythrocyte stroma, seized upon the discovery that human blood-group substances occurred in a water-soluble form in the tissue fluids and secretions of certain individuals. Blood group substances of a mucoid nature were isolated from saliva (Landsteiner and Harte, 1941), human urine (Freudenberg and Eichel, 1934, 1935) and gastric juice (Witebsky and Klendshoj, 1940, 1941). Blood group substances having group A activity were also prepared from pig gastric mucin (Meyer, Smyth and Palmer, 1937), commercial peptone (Goebel, 1938; Freudenberg and Westphal, 1938) and hog stomach linings (Bendich, Kabat and Bezer, 1946). A major step forward came with the discovery that pseudomucinous ovarian cyst fluids were potent sources of the blood group substances (Morgan and van Heyningen, 1944). Recently Klenk and Uhlenbruck (1960) have isolated

135

N-acetyl neuraminic acid containing mucoids from the stroma of human erythrocytes. These inhibited the virus haemagglutination reaction and showed marked properties specific for the M and N blood groups.

Meconium

About 60–200 g of meconium are excreted by infants after birth. If the infant is a secretor then it contains the blood group substance corresponding to the blood type of the infant (Rapoport and Buchanan, 1950). This blood group activity could be assessed by its ability to inhibit isoagglutination (Morgan and King, 1943). Crude blood group substance was obtained by deproteinization with barium hydroxide and zinc sulphate or chloroform-amyl alcohol and recovery from the aqueous supernatant by precipitation

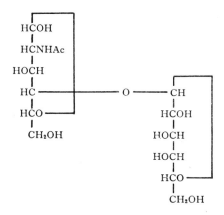

Fig. 7.1

with alcohol (Buchanan and Rapoport, 1951). Such materials gave negative tests for pentoses, uronic acids and sulphate. Acidic hydrolysis released galactose, hexosamine and fucose. Of the total reducing sugar produced from various meconiums those exhibiting blood group A and B activity contained the highest proportions of fucose. Blood group activity was reported in calf meconium and dog meconium.

Blood group substance from human meconium (40–50 g from 1 kg) was submitted to partial acid hydrolysis and after removal of high molecular weight material separated on a charcoal-Celite column (Kuhn and Kirschenlohr, 1954). A crystalline disaccharide $[\alpha]_D + 49°$ (3 min) → $+28·5°$ (1000 min) was obtained containing one methanol of crystallization. Acid hydrolysis of the disaccharide liberated galactose and N-acetyl glucosamine. The sequence was established as galactosyl-N-acetyl glucosamine by oxidation with hypoiodite and the disappearance of glucosamine from the hydrolysate. Treatment of the disaccharide with phenylhydrazine hydrochloride/sodium acetate yielded an osazone identical with lactosazone. Hence the dissaccharide (Fig. 7.1) was 4-O-β-D-galactosyl-N-acetyl-D-glucosamine.

Coutelle and Rapoport (1956) have examined blood group activity in the stools from infants of various ages. They report that between 70–120 days of age such activity disappears and is accompanied by a considerable decrease in amino sugar content.

Human Blood Group A Substance

For the isolation of group A substance, the cyst fluid from a patient with blood group A_1 was made 5% with respect to trichloracetic acid to precipitate most of the protein accompanying the A substance (Aminoff, Morgan and Watkins, 1950). The crude A substance was then precipitated from the neutralized supernatant by addition of three volumes of ethanol. The dried precipitate was extracted three times with 90% (wt/vol) phenol and the extract fractionally precipitated with ethanol; the serologically active fraction was obtained between 4·4–8·5% ethanol (vol/vol). Further purification yielded pure A substance, electrophoretically homogeneous between pH 4 and 8. It showed $[\alpha]_{5461} + 15 \pm 5°(H_2O)$ and no absorption between 220 mμ and 260 mμ. It was not precipitated by the normal protein precipitants. Elementary analysis gave C, 44·2; H, 6·96; N, 5·72%; acetyl 8·8–9·1%. The hexosamine content of A substance was 37%. Galactose (about 17%) and fucose (18%) were also present, the remainder being aminoacids (lysine, arginine, aspartic acid, glutamic acid, glycine, serine, alanine, threonine, proline, valine, leucine) of which threonine represented the largest component. Intact A substance did not show any reaction with horse anti-Type XIV pneumococcal serum but did so after mild treatment with acetic acid. Blood group A substance showed weak antigenicity in rabbits but has been converted into a powerful antigen by combination with the conjugated protein component of the O antigen of *Shigella shigae*. The A substance contained no detectable amounts of material able to neutralize the agglutinins B, M, N and Rh.

Some structural details of blood group A substance have been revealed by partial hydrolysis and identification of certain oligosaccharide fragments (Côte and Morgan, 1956). After heating with 0·1N-HCl at 100° for 3 hr followed by N-HCl at 100° for 30 min, the acid was removed on a 'Deacidite E' column and the oligosaccharide fragments fractionated on a charcoal-Celite column. Further purification on cellulose columns irrigated with amyl alcohol:dioxan:water (15:3:2) gave the following disaccharides—

(1) 3-O-β-D-galactopyranosyl N-acetyl D-glucosamine.

(2) 4-O-β-D-galactopyranosyl N-acetyl D-glucosamine.

(3) A component which was probably lacto-N-biose II, i.e. 3-O-β-N-acetyl D-glucosaminyl-D-galactose, and

(4) A dextrorotatory disaccharide ($[\alpha]_D + 150°$) containing galactosamine and galactose. The sequence in this disaccharide must be galactosamine-galactose since reduction with sodium borohydride and subsequent acid hydrolysis afforded galactosamine and dulcitol.

(5) An acid-labile disaccharide containing fucose and glucosamine.

Since disaccharide (4) reacts with alkaline triphenyltetrazolium chloride the glycosidic linkage is not through the 2-position. Alkali treatment gave some free N-acetyl amino sugar and the corresponding free chromogen. Hence this evidence and its chromatographic behaviour prompted the authors to suggest that (4) was 3-O-α-N-acetyl D-galactosaminyl-D-galactose.

Disaccharide (5) did not react with alkaline triphenyltetrazolium chloride indicating that the 2-position was substituted (by an N-acetamido group?).

Fig. 7.2

Like 6-O-α-D-galactosyl N-acetylglucosamine it yielded a brownish-red spot with benzidine-trichloracetic acid and on treatment with alkali formed a chromogen without being decomposed into its component sugars. It is therefore probably 6-O-L-fucosyl-N-acetyl D-glucosamine.

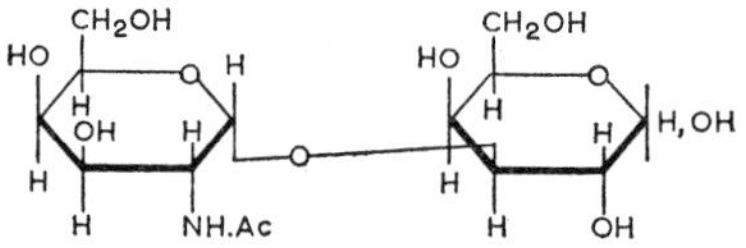

Earlier Morgan and Watkins (1953) had found that N-acetylgalactosamine played a definite part in A specificity since the agglutination of group A cells by extracts of *Vicia cracca* seeds and Lima beans was inhibited by N-acetylgalactosamine and to an even greater extent by its α-methyl glycoside. Partial inhibition of the precipitation of A substance by human anti-A serum using N-acetylgalactosamine has also been demonstrated by Kabat and Leskowitz (1954). The ability of *Trichomonas foetus* extracts to destroy A substance is also specifically inhibited by both N-acetylgalactosamine and its methylglycoside (Watkins and Morgan, 1955). The fact that disaccharide 4 shows considerably more activity than either N-acetylgalactosamine or its methylglycoside in similar inhibition tests indicates that a considerable part of the determinant immunological specificity of group A substance is associated with the structure shown in Fig. 7.2.

Aminoff and Morgan (1951) have carried out an extensive study of the periodate oxidation of group A substance. When oxidized at pH 5 one mole of periodate was consumed by 427 g of A substance. Such oxidation rapidly caused loss of the power of the A substance to inhibit isoagglutination. Chromatographic analyses were performed on acid hydrolysates of the oxidized group A substance. These revealed that fucose, galactose and half of the total N-acetylgalactosamine residues were oxidized. During the oxidation formaldehyde (1 g mol HCHO per 1964 g of A substance) and formic acid (1 g mol per 2000 g of A substance) were liberated but no acetaldehyde or ammonia. About 34% of the maximum amino acid nitrogen in blood group A substance is in the form of hydroxy-amino-N (as serine or threonine). Under certain conditions these could be oxidized by periodate, but the fact that no ammonia was liberated ruled out the possibilities that such amino acid residues were at the end of a peptide chain or attached as single molecules to sugar residues via ester linkages involving the carboxyl group of the amino acid and the primary or secondary alcohol groups of the sugar residues.

Baer and Naylor (1955) claim to have devised a less drastic method of isolation of blood group A substance from human ovarian cyst fluids than that involving the use of phenol. After dialysis of the fluids they were separated in an electroconvection apparatus and a single substance isolated which appeared to be a protein-blood group A substance complex. This, complex was homogeneous at pH 2·5, 4·9, 6·9 and 8·3. It was more active as determined by the test for inhibition of haemagglutination than substances isolated by the phenol extraction method. More striking was the fact that such products were antigenic for the rabbit in contrast to the phenol extracted material which required coupling with *Shiga* protein.

Investigation of the action of ficin (an enzyme from fig latex) on blood group A substances gives strong indications that the non-reducing end residues of certain oligosaccharides are mainly responsible for the serological character on which group specificity depends (Pusztai and Morgan, 1958). This enzyme degrades A substance by rupture of a limited number of peptide bonds and sets free relatively large carbohydrate/amino acid units without concomitant liberation of simple monosaccharides or diffusible oligosaccharides.

A potent group A substance from human red cells has been isolated by Koscielak and Zakrzewski (1960) and shown to be a water-soluble muco-polysaccharide containing 50% carbohydrate and having a glucosamine: galactosamine ratio of c. 1:1.

Human Blood Group B Substance

Baer, Kabat and Knaub (1950) have isolated purified B substance from human group B saliva. A more convenient source is ovarian cysts from secretors belonging to group B. Gibbons and Morgan (1954) have isolated both B and B′ substances from this source using the conventional method of extraction with 90% phenol. The B substance inhibited the agglutinating action of natural human β-agglutinin or immune anti-B agglutinin on group B red cells with about equal facility. By contrast the B′ substance had a considerably smaller power to neutralize the β-agglutinin but showed a greater capacity to prevent haemagglutination with immune B antibody. Both B and B' substance failed to form a specific precipitate with anti-Type XIV *Pneumococcus* serum. B substance shows $[\alpha]_{5461}^{20}\ 0° \pm 5°$, B' substance exhibits $[\alpha]_{5461}^{20} - 20° \pm 5°$ in water. Neither shows any absorption peaks in the region 220–320 mμ. Neither could be precipitated by conventional protein precipitants (e.g. 10% trichloracetic acid, 2% phosphotungstic acid, etc.). Elementary analysis showed B substance contained C, 41; H, 6·6; N, 5·7%; fucose, 17·9%; acetyl, 7·0% while B' substance contained C, 43; H, 7·0; N, 4·9; fucose, 20·0; acetyl 7·1%. The constituent sugars of both B substances were the same, namely L-fucose, D-glucosamine, D-galactosamine and D-galactose. The same eleven amino acids (total about 30%) were found in both. Quantitatively, however, both B and B' substances contained much lower (20 and 22% hexosamine respectively) amounts of hexosamine than the other blood group substances A, H and Le^a (33–37%). Crystalline D-galactosamine hydrochloride and D-glucosamine hydrochloride were isolated from hydrolysates of B substance. In addition D-galactose was isolated as its crystalline O-tolylhydrazone and L-fucose as its diphenylhydrazone.

The cyst fluids from two 'secretors' belonging to group A$_1$ B were treated in the usual way for the isolation of blood group substances. The mucoid obtained showed a negligible capacity to inhibit natural β-agglutinin but was fully active when assayed against immune rabbit anti-B sera.

Watkins and Morgan (1955) have studied the effects of various sugars on the inhibition of *Trichomonas foetus* extracts which normally destroy B substance. This destruction was found to be inhibited by D-galactose, α- and β-methyl D-galactopyranosides, lactose and melibiose but not by L-fucose, N-acetyl glucosamine or N-acetyl D-galactosamine. Kabat and Leskowitz (1955) have also shown that an α-D-galactoside structure inhibits the B-anti B system.

Zarnitz and Kabat (1960) have demonstrated that coffee bean α-galactosidase splits off galactose from blood group B and BP1 substances. Further evidence thus accrues that terminal non-reducing α-linked galactoses are responsible for the specificity of each of these materials. Both enzyme-treated substances exhibited increased cross reactivity with Type XIV antipneumococcus sera. The precipitating power of the B substance for human anti-B was reduced but its capacity to inhibit haemagglutination of B cells by anti-B was completely destroyed.

Human Blood Group H Substance

Schiff and Sasaki (1932) demonstrated that individuals belonging to blood group A$_1$ B secrete a substance which is probably identical with that found to a variable extent on the surface of the erythrocytes of the majority of human subjects. Early literature designated this as the O substance, but since it is now recognized that anti-O sera detect a substance which is not a specific product of the activity of Bernstein's O gene, Morgan and Watkins (1948) have renamed this the H substance. Annison and Morgan (1952b) isolated purified H substance by phenol extraction of ovarian cysts. The average rotation of the most active preparations was $-30 \pm 3°$ (H_2O). H substance showed no absorption between 220–330 mμ and was not precipitated by the usual protein precipitants. Elementary analysis showed C, 41·4; H, 6·9; N, 5·3; acetyl, 8·7%. Acetic acid was identified as its crystalline S-benzylthiouronium acetate (m.p. 136°). H substance contained 14% fucose (characterized by isolation of L-fucose diphenylhydrazone), D-galactose (characterized as the α-methylphenylhydrazone pentaacetate), together with D-glucosamine and D-galactosamine both identified via their N-2:4-dinitrophenyl derivatives. The total hexosamine content was 31%. The α-amino acid nitrogen was equivalent to about 41% and the α-amino nitrogen to 88% of the total nitrogen. The same eleven amino acids encountered in other blood group substances were also present in H substance. Periodate oxidation of H substance consumed one mole of oxidant per 362 g of H substance. Such oxidation resulted in the loss of serological activity.

H substance was not antigenic in rabbits but could be made so by coupling it with the conjugated protein component of *Shigella shigae*. H substance did not give a precipitate with anti-pneumococcal type XIV serum and did not inhibit the agglutination of fowl cells by the heated Lee (type B) influenza virus. However, acid treatment of H substance produces a product which possesses the property of reacting with horse anti-pneumococcal type XIV serum.

Watkins and Morgan (1952) have investigated the reaction whereby H substance when mixed with the H-agglutinin in eel serum neutralizes completely its power to agglutinate group O cells. Certain simple sugars at high dilution could also bring about this inhibition. Whereas H substance was active at a dilution of 1:819,200, methyl α-L-fucopyranoside was active at 1:51,200, L-fucose at 1:12,800, 2-deoxy L-fucose at 1:6,400, methyl β-L-fucopyranoside at 1:3,200 while N-acetyl D-glucosamine, N-acetyl D-galactosamine and D-galactose were inactive at 2% concentration. However, since H-antibodies of different origin are probably different, L-fucose failed to inhibit the agglutination of O cells by other anti-H sera (cattle sera, rabbit sera, chicken sera, etc.). A specific role for an α-L-fucopyranosyl structure in H specificity has also been indicated by experiments with an anti-H reagent of plant origin (*Lotus tetragonolobus* seed extract) (Morgan and Watkins, 1953). Similar confirmation was obtained from studies with *Trichomonas foetus* extracts (Watkins, 1953).

Human Blood Group Le[a] Substance

In 1946, Mourant discovered a new human blood group antigen which was independent serologically of the ABO, MN, Rh, P and Lutheran systems. The name Lewis was proposed for this antigen. Twenty-five per cent (24 out of 96) group O bloods of English people were agglutinated by anti-Lewis sera. Subsequently a further Lewis antigen was discovered (Andresen, 1948) and so the two genes responsible were designated Le[a] and Le[b] respectively (Andresen, Callender, Fisher, Grubb, Morgan, Mourant, Pickles and Race, 1949). An interesting relationship was discovered between Le positive individuals and non-secretors. Those individuals whose erythrocytes were agglutinated by anti-Le[a] serum were found to secrete Le[a] substance in their tissue fluids, but not the A, B or H substances which would be expected from their ABO blood group designation (Grubb, 1948; Grubb and Morgan, 1949). The secretions of this class of individuals are therefore the most convenient source of Le[a] substance.

Using methods similar to those applied for the isolation of other blood group substances, Annison and Morgan (1952a) obtained a supply of Le[a] substance from the ovarian cyst fluids of Lewis-positive persons (83 g from 2·5 l). Le[a] showed $[\alpha]_{5461} - 41 \pm 4°$ in water but did not exhibit any significant absorption between 260–300 mμ. It was not precipitated by the usual protein precipitants like 10% trichloracetic acid, 20% salicylsulphonic acid, tannic acid or picric acid. Elementary analysis showed that it contained C, 41·5; H, 7·1, N, 5·3% and acetyl, 10%. The sugars present were L-fucose, D-glucosamine, D-galactose and D-galactosamine which were isolated as crystalline derivatives. Aminoacid analysis of the acid hydrolysate of Le[a] substance revealed the presence of lysine, arginine, aspartic acid, glutamic acid, glycine, serine, alanine, theonine, proline, valine and leucine of which threonine was the most abundant. Quantitative analysis showed that Le[a] substance contained 12% fucose and that of the total hexosamines (equivalent to 9% of N-acetyl glucosamine) there was about two to three times more glucosamine than galactosamine. 1 mg of Le[a] substance reduced $0·273 \times 10^{-5}$ g mole of HIO_4 (1 g mole periodate per 365 g of Le[a] substance). Such oxidation resulted in complete loss of serological activity.

Our meagre knowledge of the arrangement of the sugars in Le[a] substance accrues mainly from immunological reactions. Le[a] substance gives a precipitate with horse antipneumococcal type XIV serum in contrast to human A, B and H substances which failed to precipitate with the type XIV reagent. This reaction suggests a similar arrangement of either galactose or N-acetylglucosamine residues in both Type XIV polysaccharide and Le[a] substance. In the former it is known that the galactose residues occur as non-reducing end-groups and linked β-1:3 while the N-acetylglucosamine residues occur mainly in β-1:4:6-branchpoints.

The inhibition studies made on the Le (a+) red cells–anti-Le^a serum system using human milk oligosaccharides has already been mentioned elsewhere. It showed that L-fucose was an important part of the determinant specificity of Le^a substance since lacto N-tetraose (containing no fucose) showed a low order of activity compared to the highly active lacto-N-fucopentaose II which contains an α-L-fucosyl residue, linked $1 \rightarrow 4$ to a β-N-acetylglucosaminyl residue. The corresponding isomeric lacto-N-fucopentaose I in which the α-L-fucosyl residue is linked to a β-galactosyl residue was only weakly active. The drop in activity observed in proceeding from lacto N-fucopentaose II to lacto N-difucohexaose could only indicate that non-reducing end groups of galactose play some role in the immunological specificity since this feature is absent in lacto N-difucohexaose. Watkins and Morgan (1957) suggested that one of the specific determinant groupings in Le^a substance could be a branched trisaccharide unit as shown in Fig. 7.3.

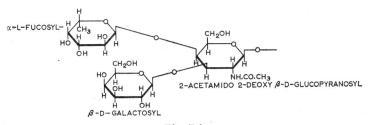

Fig. 7.3

Further evidence as to the importance of L-fucose comes from the observation that *Trichomonas foetus* extracts which will destroy the serological activity of the Lewis Le^a substance are prevented from doing so by L-fucose. However, the α-L-fucosyl alone is unable to neutralize Le^a antibody since it was demonstrated that methyl α-L-fucopyranoside, 2-O-α-fucosyl fucose, etc. did not inhibit the Le (α+) red cells–anti-Le^a serum system.

Pusztai and Morgan (1961) have isolated a sialo-mucopolysaccharide from a pseudomucinous ovarian cystadenoma. The patient's blood phenotype was A_1Le (a+). The mucopolysaccharide, which was an active Le^a-specific substance, contained 18% sialic acid (as N-acetylneuraminic acid) in addition to the fucose, galactose, glucosamine, galactosamine and aminoacids usually found in Le^a substance. After incubation of the sialomucopolysaccharide with neuraminidase the original ability to act as a potent inhibitor of haemagglutination by heated type A and B influenza viruses is lost but activity as a Le^a substance is retained. By contrast the destruction of Le^a specificity by *Trichomonas foetus* extracts leaves a mucopolysaccharide which contains sialic acid and is an inhibitor of viral haemagglutination. The sialomucopolysaccharide precipitates with anti-Type XIV pneumococcus serum.

Other Blood Group Substances

Although many other blood-group characters are known including the important group of Rhesus factors, M, N and P, etc. (Race and Sanger, 1958) these are not found to occur in appreciable quantities in the body secretions and tissue fluids. However, a mucoid material from human erythrocytes possessing both M and N group specificity has been isolated by Klenk and Uhlenbruch (1960). Romanowska (1960) reports that a similar mucoid prepared from erythrocytes contained 40% carbohydrate including 20% sialic acid. The presence of sialic acid probably accounts for the destruction of M and N group specificity by the receptor destroying enzyme and its inactivation by the Lee strain of influenza virus.

Other Mammalian Blood Group Substances

Work on horse and bovine blood group substances suggests that in many cases they show behaviour more characteristic of the species than of ABO specificity (Leskowitz and Kabat, 1954b). Thus horse blood group A substance reacts only weakly with anti-hog A and anti-human A sera (Kabat, Baer, Day and Knaub, 1950). An exception to this generalization is horse blood group B substance which is almost as active as human blood group B substance in its reaction with human anti-sera (Leskowitz and Kabat, 1954b). Bovine blood group substances, which contain the J factor of cattle (Stormont, 1949), give only weak precipitin reactions with anti-hog A and anti-human A and B sera (Beiser and Kabat, 1952). Cow B substance has the ability to precipitate human antibody to horse B substance. The above behaviour suggests that the designation of ABO in horse and bovine blood group substances is based on cross-reactions in which only a small portion of the total structure of the blood group substance is effective.

Hog Blood Group Substances

Acidic treatment of hog blood group substances results in a gradual destruction of blood group activity and a concomitant increase in ability to react with anti-Type XIV *Pneumococcus* sera (Kabat, Baer, Bezer, and Knaub, 1948). The major constituent (60–80%) of the dialysable fragments from acid degraded hog A and O(H) substances is L-fucose. Only small amounts of hexosamine, galactose and amino acids were liberated under the mild hydrolysis conditions. Accompanying this removal of fucose there was an alteration in the ratio of glucosamine:galactosamine present in the non-dialysable fractions from 1·8 to 0·8 (Leskowitz and Kabat, 1954b). Quantitative assays of the glucosamine:galactosamine ratio in blood group substances can be performed by micro-separation of the 2:4-dinitrophenyl aminohexitols (Leskowitz and Kabat, 1954a). Close similarity in these ratios were found in hog and human blood group substances, e.g. hog A substance, 1·5; human A substance 1·6; hog O(H) substance, 2·2; human O(H) substance 2·5. In such preparations from both species the amount of hexosamine rendered dialysable after acid hydrolysis at pH 1·6 was very similar and ranged from 15–29%.

Two strains (Iseki and McClung) of *Clostridium tertium* enzymes have been incubated with hog blood group substances (Howe, Schiffman, Bezer and Kabat, 1958). The Iseki strain inactivated both hog A substance and human A substance. B or O(H) substances, however, retained their capacity to react with the corresponding haemagglutinin. By contrast the McClung enzyme did not effect any change in A substance shown by haem-agglutination inhibition. Both enzymes, however, destroyed the ability of all blood group substances tested to react with horse anti-Type XIV *Pneumococcus* serum. This property of cross reactivity with anti-XIV has been shown to bear an inverse relationship to the fucose content (Baer, Dische and Kabat, 1948) of hog substances. Treatment of hog A and O(H) substances with snail enzymes results in an increase in this cross-reaction (Kabat, Baer, Bezer and Knaub, 1948). Schiffman, Howe and Kabat (1958) have postulated that the ability of blood group substances to cross-react with anti-S XIV is in part attributable to a terminal non-reducing β-linked galactose residue probably attached to C_4 of N-acetylglucosamine.

A series of structural studies have been made on blood group substances from pig stomach mucus-mucin. A group A substance treated with periodate, dialysed and then oxidized with bromine gave on acid hydrolysis tartronic acid, D-glyceric acid and glucosamine (Yoshizawa, 1951). One of the disaccharide units in group A substance was believed to be 'N-acetylglucosamine-4-β-D-galactoside', i.e. 4-O-β-D-galactopyranosyl N-acetylglucosamine (Yoshizawa, 1950a). The synthesis of this disaccharide was described (Yoshizawa, 1950b). Acetolysis of the group mucopoly-saccharides from pig gastric mucus, deacetylation and chromatography yielded *inter alia* 'acetyglucosamine-4-galactoside-4-acetylgalactosaminide'. This trisaccharide gave glucosamine, galactosamine and galactose on acid hydrolysis (Masamune, Yoshizawa and Haga, 1956). Further studies suggested that aspartic acid was linked by its COOH group to the NH_2 group of the glutamic acid and by its NH_2 group to the C-1 of a terminal acetylglucosamine (Masamune, Hakomori and Masamune, 1956). A tri-saccharide composed of two moles of galactose and one mole of L-fucose has also been isolated by acetolysis (Masamune and Shinohara, 1958).

Bovine Blood Group Substances

These blood group factors have been isolated by Beiser and Kabat (1952) from bovine stomachs and have been found to exhibit A, B and O activities, combinations of these activities or no activity. Glucosamine: galactosamine ratios in the various preparations varied from 1·4 to 3·0 (Leskowitz and Kabat, 1954a). When six typical preparations were subjected to mild acid hydrolysis all showed some decrease in the glucosamine–galactosamine ratio (Leskowitz and Kabat, 1954b).

Horse Blood Group Substances

Blood group substances isolated from horses' stomachs (Baer, Kabat and Knaub, 1950) have been found to have glucosamine:galactosamine ratios of 1·0 to 2·3 (Leskowitz and Kabat, 1954a). The non-dialysable residues remaining after mild acid hydrolysis of the blood group substances had decreased glucosamine–galactosamine ratios (Leskowitz and Kabat, 1954b).

REFERENCES

Aminoff, D. and Morgan, W. T. J. *Biochem. J.* **48**, 74 (1951).
Aminoff, D., Morgan, W. T. J. and Watkins, M. *Biochem. J.* **46**, 426 (1950).
Andresen, P. H. *Acta path. microbiol. scand.* **25**, 728 (1948).
Andresen, P. H., Callender, S. T., Fischer, R. A., Grubb, R., Morgan, W. T. J., Mourant, A. E., Pickles, M. M. and Race, R. R. *Nature* **163**, 580 (1949).
Annison, E. F. and Morgan, W. T. J. *Biochem. J.* **50**, 460 (1952a).
Annison, E. F. and Morgan, W. T. J. *Biochem. J.* **52**, 247 (1952b).
Baer, H., Dische, A. and Kabat, E. A. *J. Exp. Med.* **88**, 59 (1948).
Baer, H., Kabat, E. A. and Knaub, V. *J. Exp. Med.* **91**, 105 (1950).
Baer, H. and Naylor, I. *J. Amer. Chem. Soc.* **77**, 3514 (1955).
Beiser, S. M. and Kabat, E. A. *J. Immunol.* **68**, 19 (1952).
Bendich, A., Kabat, E. A. and Bezer, A. E. *J. Exp. Med.* **83**, 485 (1946).
Buchanan, D. J. and Rapoport, S. *J. Biol. Chem.* **192**, 251 (1951).
Côte, R. H. and Morgan, W. T. J. *Nature* **178**, 1171 (1956).
Coutelle, R. and Rapoport, S. *Klin. Wochschr.* **34**, 103 (1956).
Freudenberg, K. and Eichel, H. *Liebigs Ann.* **510**, 240 (1934); **518**, 97 (1935).
Freudenberg, K. and Westphal, O. *S.B. Heidelberg Akad. Wiss. Math nat.* 1Abh. (1938).
Gibbons, R. A. and Morgan, W. T. J. *Biochem. J.* **57**, 283 (1954).
Goebel, W. F. *J. Exp. Med.* **68**, 221 (1938).
Grubb, R. *Nature* **162**, 933 (1948).
Grubb, R. and Morgan, W. T. J. *Brit. J. Exp. Path.* **30**, 198 (1949).
Howe, C., Schiffman, G., Bezer, A. E. and Kabat, E. A. *J. Amer. Chem. Soc.* **80**, 6656 (1958).
Kabat, E. A., Baer, H., Bezer, A. E. and Knaub, V. *J. Exp. Med.* **88**, 43 (1948).
Kabat, E. A., Baer, H., Day, R. L. and Knaub, V. *J. Exp. Med.* **91**, 433 (1950).
Kabat, E. A. *J. Amer. Chem. Soc.* **76**, 3709 (1954).

Kabat, E. A. and Leskowitz, S. *J. Amer. Chem. Soc.* **77,** 5159 (1955).

Klenk, E. and Uhlenbruch, G. *Z. Physiol. Chem.* **319,** 151 (1960).

Koscielak, J. and Zakrzewski, K. 'Biologically Active Mucoids' Warsaw Symp. (1960).

Kuhn, R. and Kirschenlohr, W. *Chem. Ber.* **87,** 560 (1954).

Landsteiner, K. and Harte, R. A. *J. Biol. Chem.* **140,** 673 (1941).

Leskowitz, S. and Kabat, E. A. *J. Amer. Chem. Soc.* **76,** 4887 (1954a).

Leskowitz, S. and Kabat, E. A. *J. Amer. Chem. Soc.* **76,** 5060 (1954b).

Masamune, H., Hakomori, S. and Masamune, O. *Tohoku J. Exp. Med.* **64,** 281 (1956).

Masamune, H. and Shinohara, H. *Tohoku J. Exp. Med.* **69,** 53 (1958).

Masamune, H., Yoshizawa, Z. and Haga, M. *Tohoku J. Exp. Med.* **64,** 267 (1956).

Meyer, K., Smyth, E. M. and Palmer, J. W. *J. Biol. Chem.* **119,** 73 (1937).

Morgan, W. T. J. and Watkins, W. M. *Brit. J. Exp. Path.* **29,** 159 (1948).

Morgan, W. T. J. and King, H. *Biochem. J.* **37,** 640 (1943).

Morgan, W. T. J. and Watkins, W. M. *Brit. J. Exp. Path.* **29,** 159 (1948).

Morgan, W. T. J. and Watkins, W. M. *Brit. J. Exp. Path.* **34,** 94 (1953).

Morgan, W. T. J. and van Heyningen, C. R. *Brit. J. Exp. Path.* **25,** 5 (1944).

Mourant, A. E., *Nature* **158,** 237 (1946).

Pusztai, A. and Morgan, W. T. J. *Biochem. J.* **78,** 135 (1961).

Pusztai, A. and Morgan, W. T. J. *Nature* **182,** 648 (1958).

Race, R. R. and Sanger, R. *Blood Groups in Man.* Oxford. Blackwell Scientific Publications (1958).

Rapoport, S. and Buchanan, D. J. *Science* **112,** 150 (1950).

Romanowska, E. *Naturwiss.* **47,** 66 (1960).

Schiff, F. and Sasaki, H. *Z. Immunforsch.* **77,** 129 (1932).

Schiffman, G., Howe, C. and Kabat, E. A. *J. Amer. Chem. Soc.* **80,** 6662 (1958).

Stormont, C. *Proc. Nat. Acad. Sci.* **35,** 232 (1949).

Watkins, W. M. *Biochem. J.* **54,** xxxiii (1953).

Watkins, W. M. and Morgan, W. T. J. *Nature* **169,** 825 (1952).

Watkins, W. M. and Morgan, W. T. J. *Nature* **175,** 676 (1955).

Watkins, W. M. and Morgan, W. T. J. *Nature* **180,** 1038 (1957).

Witebsky, E. and Klendshoj, N. C. *J. Exp. Med.* **72,** 663 (1940); **73,** 655 (1941).

Yoshizawa, Z. *Tohoku J. Exp. Med.* **52,** 111 (1950a).

Yoshizawa, Z. *Tohoku J. Exp. Med.* **52,** 145 (1950b).

Yoshizawa, Z. *Tohoku J. Exp. Med.* **54,** 115 (1951).

Zarnitz, M. L. and Kabat, E. A. *J. Amer. Chem. Soc.* **82,** 3953 (1960).

Chapter 8

MUCOPROTEINS IN HEALTH AND DISEASE

Protein Bound Carbohydrates in Normal Human Serum

THE presence of carbohydrates in acid hydrolysates of normal human serum was first established by Mörner (1893). At least six carbohydrates have been identified as constituents of serum proteins namely D-mannose (Dische, 1928), D-galactose (Bierry, 1930), D-glucosamine (Rimington, 1931), D-galactosamine (Goa, 1955), fucose (Dische and Shettles, 1948) and neuraminic acid (Odin, 1955). In the glycoproteins the last three mentioned sugars occur as N-acetylglucosamine, N-acetylgalactosamine and N-acetylneuraminic acid respectively.

The nature of the neuraminic acids occurring in various sera has been investigated by Mårtensson, Raal and Svennerholm (1958). Only N-acetylneuraminic acid was found in human serum but N-glycolylneuraminic acid was detected additionally in sheep serum (13–14% of the total neuraminic acid), horse serum (14–18%), hog serum (15–16%) and ox serum (64–65%). Böhm, Ross and Baumeister (1957) have also isolated crystalline N-acetylneuraminic acid from human serum by enzymic cleavage with influenza virus B (Lee) neuraminidase and with the A-toxin of *Cl. welchii*.

The total amount of protein-bound hexose in normal human serum has been variously reported as: 73–131 mg/100 ml (Seibert and Atno, 1946), 93–127 mg/100 ml (Shetlar, Foster, Kelly, Shetlar, Bryan and Everett, 1949), and 93–140 mg/100 ml (Stary, Bursa, Kaleoglu and Bilen, 1950) using carbazole, tryptophane and orcinol reagents respectively. By the anthrone method ranges of 119–160 (Berkman, Rifkin and Ross, 1953), 103–146 (Björnesjo, 1955) and 138–192 (Goa, 1955) were obtained. The total amount of protein-bound hexosamine in normal human serum has been determined as 63–88 mg/100 ml (Nilsson, 1937), 76–110 mg/100 ml (West and Clarke, 1938), 77–113 mg/100 ml (Rosenberg and Schloss, 1949), 61–78 mg/100 ml (Shetlar *et al.*, 1952), 84–116 mg/100 ml (Berkman, Rifkin and Ross, 1953) and 74–118 mg/100 ml (Goa, 1955). Chatagnon and Chatagnon (1954) reported that the neuraminic acid content of normal human serum varied between 40–65 mg/100 ml serum. Blix, Tiselius and Svensson (1941) isolated fractions of two normal human sera by boundary electrophoresis and reported their percentage hexose contents as albumin

148

1·1, 1·2; α-globulin, 6·0; β-globulin, 8·3, 6·2; γ-globulin, 3·6, 3·0. Seibert, Pfaff and Seibert (1948) reported the percentage hexose contents of human plasma fractions isolated according to Cohn et al. (1940; 1943) as γ-globulin, 1·55% (fraction II-2); β_1-globulin, 2·65% (fract. III); α_1-globulin, 1·64% (fract. IV-1); α_2-globulin, 5·83% (fract. IV-6) and albumin, 0·13% (fract. V). In a more recent study Goa (1955) reported the distribution of protein-bound hexosamines among components of human serum separated by paper electrophoresis in barbiturate buffer, pH 8·6 (see Table 8.I).

Table 8.I. *Hexosamine contents of serum proteins*

	Albumin	α_1-	α_2-	β-	γ-
Total hexosamine content (%)	0·17, 0·50	5·4, 3·5	3·8, 3·7	2·2, 2·5	1·5, 1·5
Glucosamine/ Galactosamine ratio	16·5, 17·3	16·2, 17·6	15·6, 16·1	13·6, 11·1	18·1, 18·5

Further details of the protein-bound carbohydrate of more highly purified serum fractions are given below.

Pre-Albumin

Under certain conditions of electrophoresis, such as that on strips of cellulose acetate and using a buffer containing TRIS, EDTA and boric acid (Aronsson, Grönwall and Lausing, 1959), albumin separates into prealbumin and the main albumin fraction. Prealbumin, which is the tryptophan rich fraction, has been reported to contain 1·1% hexoses and 0·15% N-acetyl hexosamine (Schultze and Schwick, 1959).

Albumin

Goa (1955) made a special investigation into the carbohydrate content of normal human serum albumin. By repeated zone electrophoresis at pH 8·6 an albumin of constant carbohydrate composition was obtained having only 0·05% hexosamine and 0·6% hexose. Previous higher values were probably due to admixture with α_1-globulin. Schultze and Schwick (1959) report only 0·05% hexoses and 0·03% N-acetylhexosamine.

α_1-Globulin Fraction

A homogeneous mucoprotein, which migrated with the α_1-globulin in barbiturate buffer, pH 8·6, was isolated from normal human plasma by Weimer, Mehl and Winzler (1950).

The method employed required the successive removal of precipitates from the plasma (mixed with 1 volume of $0 \cdot 1M$ sodium acetate) obtained on addition of ammonium sulphate to $2 \cdot 73M$ and adjustment of the pH first to $4 \cdot 9$ and then to $3 \cdot 7$. Final addition of ammonium sulphate to saturation precipitated the mucoprotein. After a further reprecipitation at pH $3 \cdot 7$ with saturated ammonium sulphate the electrophoretically homogeneous mucoprotein was obtained in a yield of 500 mg/l plasma.

Analysis revealed the presence of $16 \cdot 4\%$ hexoses, $11 \cdot 9\%$ hexosamine and the absence of hexuronic acid. It had a molecular weight of 44,100 and an average sedimentation constant* (S) of $3 \cdot 11$ (Smith, Brown, Weimer and Winzler, 1950). The mucoprotein had the remarkably low isoelectric point of pH $1 \cdot 8$ (this is probably of the trichloracetate complex; Bettelheim-Jevons, 1958).

Schmid (1950) prepared a similar mucoprotein by a different method starting from Cohn *et al.* (1940, 1943) fractions VI and VII and purifying them by precipitations with ethanol at pH $5 \cdot 8$ and $-5°C$ in the presence of zinc and barium ions. This mucoprotein again had a low isoelectric point (pH $2 \cdot 9$–$3 \cdot 0$) and contained 17% hexose and 12% hexosamine. The mucoprotein was later crystallized (Schmid, 1953). Like Winzler's mucoprotein it had a molecular weight of 44,000 and a sedimentation constant of $3 \cdot 5$.

Studies by Odin and Werner (1952) established that Winzler's mucoprotein contained about 10% neuraminic acid in addition to hexosamine ($11 \cdot 5\%$) and hexoses ($14 \cdot 1\%$). It was the presence of neuraminic acid which conferred the low isoelectric point upon the mucoprotein. The hexosamines were identified as glucosamine and galactosamine and the hexoses as galactose and mannose. Other recent analyses of the mucoprotein are $9 \cdot 8\%$ galactose, $4 \cdot 9\%$ mannose, $0 \cdot 7\%$ fucose, $11 \cdot 2\%$ hexosamine and 11% neuraminic acid (Schultze, 1958); $6 \cdot 5\%$ galactose, $4 \cdot 8\%$ mannose, $12 \cdot 3\%$ glucosamine, $0 \cdot 9$–$1 \cdot 1\%$ fucose and $10 \cdot 8\%$ neuraminic acid (Yamashina, 1956).

Components similar to Winzler's mucoprotein (called orosomucoid or α_1-glycoprotein by some authors) have been isolated from the serum of five other mammalian species (Weimer and Winzler, 1955) and have the per-centage composition shown in Table 8.II.

A related mucoprotein (fetuin) has been isolated from foetal calf serum (Deutsch, 1954) and contained 8% glucosamine and $9 \cdot 5\%$ mannose. Its reaction with Dische's diphenylamine reagent suggested the presence of neuraminic acid. Fetuin has now been obtained which is homogeneous both in the ultracentrifuge and by electrophoresis in the pH range $1 \cdot 1$–$11 \cdot 5$

---

* The sedimentation constant is related to the molecular weight M of a homogeneous polymer by the expression $M = RTS/D (1 - V\rho)$, where D is the diffusion constant, V is the partial specific volume of the solute and ρ the density of the solution.

Table 8.II. *Mucoproteins of the α₁-glycoprotein type*

Species	Hexoses	Hexosamine	Neuraminic acid
Human	16·5	12·0	11·2
Beef	13·9	7·9	10·9
Rabbit	12·3	9·1	6·9
Horse	12·3	7·0	6·8
Guinea-pig	11·1	6·6	6·2
Rat	9·9	6·4	5·1

(Spiro, 1959). Its isoelectric point was pH 3·3 and contained 8·3% neutral sugars, 5·6% hexosamine (mainly glucosamine with a small amount of galactosamine) and 8·7% neuraminic acid. Klenk and Faillard (1957) isolated N-acetylneuraminic acid ($[\alpha]_D - 30 \cdot 1°$ in H_2O) in crystalline form from a hydrolysate of fetuin.

The metabolism of the α₁-glycoprotein of guinea-pig serum has been studied by Boström, Roden and Yamashina (1958) who reported a short half-life for the glycoprotein of between 1–2 days compared to the longer half-life of the bulk of remainder of the plasma proteins.

α₂-Globulin Fraction

Schmid (1954) reported the isolation of a fraction from normal human plasma which contained essentially all the α₂-globulins. Isolation had been achieved by fractional precipitation with ethanol in the presence of barium and zinc acetates at $-5°$. The fraction contained 4% α₁-, 91% α₂- and 5% β-globulins when analysed by electrophoresis in barbiturate buffer, pH 8·6. It consisted of three major α₂-components separable in acetate buffer pH 3·5–4·5 and having their isoelectric points within this pH range. Analysis revealed c. 6% hexoses and c. 4% hexosamines.

The complete purification of one of the three α₂-glycoproteins was achieved by discarding the precipitate obtained on suspension in 19% ethanol containing 0·02M-barium acetate at $-5°$ and recovering the α₂-glycoprotein from the centrifuged solution by addition of 0·02M zinc acetate (Schmid, 1956). Solution in cold neutralized EDTA, dialysis and application on Amberlite IRC-50 in 0·05M sodium citrate buffer, pH 5·0 and elution with 0·10M sodium citrate buffer, pH 5·7 gave an α₂-glycoprotein electrophoretically homogeneous between pH 4 and 10. Analysis showed the presence of 5% hexose, 3·5% hexosamine and 7% neuraminic acid. Its isoelectric point was 3·8–3·9 and sedimentation constant $S_{20,w}$ 2·6.

Studies on human haptoglobin were started by Polonovski and Jayle as early as 1937. It belongs to the α₂-globulins and is precipitated by 70% ethanol or 0·5M-trichloracetic acid but not by 0·6M-perchloric acid or

0.2M-sulphosalicylic acid. Human serum haptoglobin contains 4.5% neuraminic acid, 5.7% glucosamine and 11.3% galactose-mannose (Jayle and Boussier, 1954). Its isoelectric point is pH 4.13 and the sedimentation constants (S_{20}) of haptoglobin and its haemoglobin complex are 4.3 and 5.2 respectively. Ultracentrifugal studies indicate a molecular weight of 85,000.

A mucoprotein with the electrophoretic mobility of an α_2-globulin has been crystallized from fraction III-0 of pooled normal human plasma (Brown, Baker, Peterkofsky and Kauffman, 1954). It had a high sedimentation constant (14.6) and contained 5.3% hexose and 3.8% hexosamine. Except for the lower sedimentation constant it bears a certain resemblance to the high molecular weight α_2-mucoprotein of Müller-Eberhard, Kunkel and Franklin (1956). Their α_2-mucoprotein, isolated during a study of the $S_{20,w} = 19S$ fraction of human serum, contained 4.55% hexose, 2.68% hexosamine and 2.3% neuraminic acid.

Prothrombin–Thrombin

Bovine prothrombin is a glycoprotein present in serum which has an electrophoretic mobility approximately equivalent to that of α_1-globulin (Seegers, McClaughry and Fahey, 1950) while that of thrombin to which it is converted is less. The isoelectric points of prothrombin and thrombin are pH 4.2 and 4.8 respectively. Laki, Kominz, Symonds, Lorand and Seegers (1954) reported that bovine prothrombin contained 6.5% hexoses and $1.57-1.68\%$ hexosamine. Schultze (1958) obtained the following results, prothrombin: 3.06% galactose; 1.53% mannose; 0.09% fucose; 2.3% hexosamine and 4.2% neuraminic acid. Thrombin: 2.34% galactose; 1.17% mannose; 0.07% fucose; 2.2% hexosamine and 3.9% neuraminic acid. The conversion of prothrombin to thrombin is influenced by two other factors proaccelerin and proconvertin; the latter migrates between β- and γ-globulin. Normal blood plasma contains the enzyme prothrombin at a concentration of about 70 mg/l (Hughes, 1955). Thrombin is not present in normal circulating blood.

The coagulation process consists of the conversion of prothrombin to thrombin and of the subsequent action of thrombin on fibrinogen to produce fibrin.

Fibrinogen–Fibrin

Fibrinogen is present in blood plasma to the extent of about 2 g/l. Consden and Stanier (1952) detected hexosamine, mannose and galactose in hydrolysates of human fibrin. Analyses showed the presence of glucosamine, mannose and galactose in the hydrolysates of fibrin and fibrinogen of other species (Szára and Bagdy, 1953). Some results quoted were:

bovine fibrinogen 1·64% hexoses, 0·56% glucosamine; bovine fibrin 1·33% hexoses, 0·54% glucosamine; rabbit fibrinogen 1·98% hexoses, 0·59% glucosamine; rabbit fibrin 1·66% hexoses, 0·60% glucosamine. Stenhagen (1938) reported that human fibrinogen migrated at a velocity intermediate between that of γ- and β-globulins.

Plasma Cholinesterase

Surgenor and Ellis (1954) have reported an 11·1% hexose content for a plasma cholinesterase fraction.

Ceruloplasmin

Ceruloplasmin, the blue copper-containing protein of serum (Holmberg and Laurell, 1948) is an α_2-globulin with a molecular weight of about 151,000. Schulze (1958) has reported that his preparation, with a sedimentation constant of 7·1S, contained 2·0% galactose, 1·0% mannose, 0·18% fucose, 1·9% hexosamine and 2% neuraminic acid.

Transferrin

The iron-combining component of plasma is variously known as transferrin, siderophilin, and the β_1-metal-combining (pseudo) globulin. The distribution of carbohydrates (expressed as a percentage of the total carbohydrate present) has been reported as 27·2% galactose, 13·6% mannose, 1·2% fucose, 34·1% acetylglucosamine and 23·9% acetylneuraminic acid (Sonnet, Louis and Heremans, 1955).

Serum Gonadotropin

The carbohydrate content of pregnant mare serum gonadotropin, which has an isoelectric point of pH 2·6–2·65, has been studied by a number of workers. Hexose contents ranging from 14·1 to 17·6% have been reported (Li, Evans and Wonder, 1940; Gurin, 1942; Rimington and Rowlands, 1944) and the hexose has been identified as galactose (Gurin, 1942). The hexosamine content is 8·4%.

β-Globulin Fraction

Goa (1955) diluted normal human plasma with 0·9% NaCl (1:1) and removed the bulk of the protein by adding an equal volume of 1M-perchloric acid. The mucoprotein present in the supernatant was precipitated by phosphotungstic acid and after further reprecipitation from aqueous ethanol separated by zone electrophoresis at pH 8·6. One component (MP-2) migrated with the mobility of a β-globulin. Electrophoretically prepared β-globulin was further fractionated into β-1 (precipitable with perchloric acid) and β-2 (precipitable from the supernatant with phosphotungstic acid). Analysis of MP-2, β-1 and β-2 showed hexosamine contents of 6·0, 1·9 and 3·7% and glucosamine/galactosamine ratios of 1·8, 16·2 and 4·5 respectively. In normal human β-globulin about 85% is β-1 and about 15% is β-2. MP-2 and β-2 probably contain the same mucoprotein which is rather unique in serum because of its high relative galactosamine content.

Heremans, Heremans and Schultze (1959) have isolated β_{2A}-globulin from normal human serum and plasma by a combination of zinc sulphate precipitation, ammonium sulphate precipitation and starch block preparative electrophoresis. It contained 4·9% hexoses and 3·74% hexosamines and had a sedimentation constant of $S_{20} = 7$. The β-globulin fraction together with the α_1-globulin contains the largest amounts of bound lipid of the various serum proteins.

γ-Globulins

Normal human γ-globulin isolated electrophoretically is composed of two major ultracentrifugal components with sedimentation coefficients of 7S and 19S.

Weimer, Redlich-Moshin, Salkin and Boak (1954) reported that γ-globulin fraction isolated from normal human plasma contained 13 mg% carbohydrate. Müller-Eberhard and Kunkel (1956) found that γ-globulin isolated directly from normal serum by zone electrophoresis in a starch- or polyvinyl-supporting medium contained about 5–10% of a heavy component ($S_{20,w}$ – 19S) in addition to the usual 7S material. Müller-Eberhard, Kunkel and Franklin (1956) employing repeated preparative ultracentrifugation obtained the 19S fraction and found that it separated into two peaks when submitted to starch zone electrophoresis. One of the peaks moved in the α_2-region and the other in the γ_1-region (see section on α_2-globulin fraction). Analysis showed that the heavy γ-globulin fraction (19S) which contained 5·2% hexose, 0·62% fucose, 2·9% hexosamine and 1·7% neuraminic acid was much richer in bound carbohydrate than the lighter γ-globulin fraction (7S) which contained 1·2% hexose, 0·29% fucose, 1·14% hexosamine and 0·22% neuraminic acid.

Human γ-globulins prepared by electrophoresis have been fractionated on columns of DEAE cellulose anion exchanger. Fractions 1 to 4 were proteins with sedimentation coefficients of 6·6S and progressively increasing hexose contents from 1·1 to 2·3% (Fahey, 1959). Fraction 5, comprising all the 18S γ-globulins and only a small amount of 6·6S protein, contained 5% hexose.

Protein Bound Carbohydrates in Pathological Human Sera

Two of the numerous reports of elevated levels of protein bound hexosamine in sera from patients suffering from a wide range of conditions are summarized below. These and many other later investigations revealed an apparent non-specific rise in the total hexosamine level following many common diseases. By contrast normal hexosamine levels have been reported in cases of cirrhosis of the liver, γ-globulinemia and chronic colitis (Goa, 1955).

Elevated Serum Hexosamine Levels

These are encountered in patients suffering from: Carcinoma of the stomach, cervical lymph gland, caecum, bronchus, colon, ovary and lung; reticulum cell sarcoma; lymphatic leukemia; multiple myeloma; Hodgkin's disease.

Pneumonia, influenza, rheumatic fever, tuberculosis, meningococcus bacteremia, bacterial endocarditis, rheumatoid arthritis, hemolytic streptococcal pharyngitis, lymphogranuloma inguinale, acute psoas abscess, gonococcal arthritis, myocardial infarction.

See West and Clarke (1938); Rosenberg and Schloss (1949).

Goa (1955) has investigated the distribution of hexosamine among various electrophoretically separated fractions of pathological sera. Of 17 cases studied the hexosamine content of the γ-globulin deviated from normal in only a case of multiple myeloma and a case of cirrhosis of the liver. In the latter there was a pathological protein fraction moving between β- and γ-globulin which was included in the γ-globulin fraction. Again in most of the cases the hexosamine content of the β-globulin fraction was normal but was low in two cases where cirrhosis of the liver (posthepatitic) and acute hepatitis had been diagnosed. The main increases occurred in most cases in the albumin + α_1-globulin and α_2-globulin fractions. These increases were in general paralleled by high mucoprotein contents as determined by the method of Winzler, Devor, Mehl and Smyth (1948). In multiple myeloma, abnormal production of usually only a single type of protein occurs. Smith, Brown, McFadden, Buettner-Janusch and Jager (1955) selected four patients having myeloma globulins of very different electrophoretic mobilities. Three of these (myeloma γ-globulins) had low carbohydrate contents viz. A, $1 \cdot 95\%$ hexose; $0 \cdot 30\%$ hexosamine; B, $0 \cdot 83\%$ hexose, $0 \cdot 81\%$ hexosamine; C, $1 \cdot 11\%$ hexose, $1 \cdot 32\%$ hexosamine while the fourth D (a β-myeloma globulin) contained $3 \cdot 99\%$ hexose and $3 \cdot 10\%$ hexosamine. The isoelectric points of A, B, C and D were $7 \cdot 2$, $7 \cdot 05$, $6 \cdot 4$ and $4 \cdot 7$ respectively and it was suggested that D contained an acidic carbohydrate component.

Laurell, Laurell and Waldenström (1957) reported that analyses of sera from eighteen cases of myeloma fell in the ranges 138–357 mg hexose/100 ml (normal 106–132), 86–226 mg hexosamine/100 ml (normal 80–100), 10–35 mg fucose/100 ml (normal 6·0–11·2) and 41–150 mg neuraminic acid/100 ml (normal 50–65). The degree of increase in carbohydrate content depended generally on the concentration of the abnormal component which varied between 0·8–7·7%. This abnormal component had varying mobilities in the β–γ-globulin range. Abnormal components with the mobility of γ_1–γ_2-globulins had hexose contents in the range 0·5–1·2% while those of lower mobility contained 0·7–4·2% hexose. Müller-Eberhard and Kunkel (1956) have reported that hydrolysates of myeloma proteins contain mannose and galactose. Twelve purified myeloma proteins isolated electrophoretically were analysed and these analyses expressed as approximate molar ratios. The mean values moles/mole of protein for group 1 myeloma proteins were hexose, 8·5; hexosamine, 8·5 and for group 2 myeloma proteins, hexose 24·30; hexosamine, 20·80. Group 1, those with the mobility of γ-globulins, thus contained much less carbohydrate than those in group 2 which had mobilities of β-globulins.

Owen, Got and Silberman (1958) have reported that in certain cases the abnormal myeloma globulin can be resolved. Thus seven sera gave evidence of containing five closely grouped abnormal components, six sera showed two abnormal components while in three sera only single abnormal bands were present.

Ultracentrifugal studies and carbohydrate analyses have been carried out by Müller-Eberhard and Kunkel (1959) on four macroglobulinemia patients. In two of these the *relative* concentration of neutral hexose sugars were approximately 15% fucose, 20% galactose and 65% mannose. All four macroglobulins showed similar analyses for hexoses, hexosamine, fucose and neuraminic acid which closely resembled that of the normal 19S γ-globulin.

Deutsch and Morton (1957) and Glenchur, Zinneman and Briggs (1958) reported that mercaptoethanol depolymerizes γ_1-macroglobulins to monomers with sedimentation constants of 7S. These monomers are antigenically different from the 7S γ-globulins usually found in human serum (Putman, 1959; Korngold and van Leeuwen, 1959).

Macroglobulinemia sera, like those of multiple myeloma, contain high concentrations of an abnormal globulin component which migrates with the β- or γ-fractions or intermediate between these two. This protein has a high sedimentation constant (17 to 20S) indicating a molecular weight of about 1 million. Laurell, Laurell and Waldenström (1957) found that this abnormal component occurred in a concentration range of 2·6–5·4% and had hexose contents from 3·5 to 6·0% (6 patients studied). Müller-Eberhard, Kunkel and Franklin (1956) reported a similar hexose content

(4·85%) for the abnormal component obtained from a case of Waldenström's macroglobulinemia. The other sugars present were fucose (0·62%) hexosamine (2·66%) and neuraminic acid (1·71%). These workers commented that immunological evidence suggested a close relationship between the normal heavy component of γ-globulin and the pathological macroglobulins. The normal concentration of this 19S component of γ-globulin was found to be markedly reduced in the sera of four patients with agammaglobulinemia.

Flynn (1954) concluded that much useful diagnostic information could be obtained from the changes in the paper electrophoresis patterns of serum in health and disease. In nearly all cases of malignant disease the α-globulins were notably increased and the albumin often diminished. In agammaglobulinemia there was no γ-globulin detectable by this technique. The pattern observed in non-bacterial tissue injury (coronary thrombosis, fractured femur, etc.) was that of increased α-globulins. α-Globulins were characteristically increased in acute infections during the acute stage. In the late stage and during convalescence the γ-globulin increased. In chronic infections the most notable finding was an increase of γ-globulin, α-globulins also being increased in the more active infections. The characteristic features of liver diseases (infective hepatitis, acute hepatic necrosis, cirrhosis) was a large increase of γ-globulin and diminution of the serum albumin. In cases of the nephrotic syndrome the pattern was quite diagnostic with marked diminution of the albumin, tremendous increase of the α_2-globulin and in the vast majority of cases diminution of the γ-globulin. A considerable increase of the γ-globulin component was the most notable and consistent feature in collagen diseases. It was accompanied by an increase of the α_2-globulin in almost all cases while an increase of α_1-globulin and diminution of albumin was also often found.

Dagnall (1957) postulated that an increase, or relative increase (with respect to α_2) of α_1-mucoprotein was often compatible with a poor prognosis and tissue degeneration and that an increase in α_2-mucoprotein was mainly associated with growth processes. In many cases examined, a stronger α_1-mucoprotein band was demonstrated as death approached. An α_2-mucoprotein band was usually predominant in normal adults, normal children, during pregnancy, after an operation, and in neoplasia.

Lawrence, Weimer and Salkin (1959) have investigated the effects of pulmonary tuberculosis on the concentration and distribution of the protein-bound carbohydrates in serum. They reported that statistically significant increases in total serum glycoprotein and the protein-bound carbohydrates of the α_2- and β-globulin fractions occurred in patients with extensive exudative disease. Only in the most acutely ill patients did significant elevations occur in the α_1-globulin fraction.

Nyman (1959) has carried out extensive investigations of the hapto-globin levels in human serum. She found a somewhat higher haptoglobin level in women at times of menstruation which she believed to be due to the destruction of tissue during this phase of the cycle. Haptoglobin was demonstrated in only 11 of 79 samples of umbilical blood from new-born children but the haptoglobin level in full term new-born children appeared to rise fairly fast. Haptoglobin constitutes about 24% of the α_2-globulin fraction of normal serum. Comparison between the values found for the haptoglobin level and the total α_2-globulin fraction has shown that in most diseases with the exception of nephrosis and rheumatic fever the variation in the α_2-globulin fraction only reflects the variation in haptoglobin level in that the concentration of the other α_2-globulins is essentially constant (Jayle and Boussier, 1955). In pulmonary tuberculosis the haptoglobin level varies closely with the extent of the lesions and activity of the disease (Trosier, Polonovski, Jayle and Brissaud, 1940). In cases of pneumonia, Nyman (1959) found increased haptoglobin levels within the first two days of the onset of symptoms and within a week these had risen to a level between 4–7 times that of normal serum. Even local inflammations such as tonsillitis caused a 3–4-fold rise. Determination of the haptoglobin con-centration is of little value in the diagnosis of cancer and even in very wide spread cancer the haptoglobin level in the blood may be normal. In chronic hepato-cellular failure the haptoglobin level is generally decreased, while in acute hepato-cellular failure (infectious or toxic) the level is normal or decreased.

Markowitz, Gubler, Mahoney, Cartwright and Wintrobe (1955) found serum ceruloplasmin levels of 34 ± 4 mg/100 ml in normal subjects, 84 ± 15 mg/100 ml in sera from pregnant women in their last trimester of pregnancy, 68 mg/100 ml in sera from patients with certain chronic infec-tions, and 2–19 mg/100 ml in sera from patients with hepatolenticular degeneration.

Biological Activity of Serum Components

Enzymic activity

Although haemoglobin is itself an alkyl peroxidase the formation of a complex with haptoglobin causes a four-fold increase in peroxidase activity and, within certain limits, produces a linear relationship between activity and haemoglobin concentration. This peroxidase activity of the complex has been utilized by Jayle (1940) to determine the haptoglobin content of serum. The complex is generally used to catalyse the reaction $C_2H_5OOH + 2I' + 2H^+ \rightarrow C_2H_5OH + I_2 + H_2O$ and the amount of iodine released determined by titration with thiosulphate.

The 'pseudo' cholinesterase present in serum can hydrolyse acetyl choline and certain non-choline esters such as ethyl acetate and phenyl benzoate. Its determination has proved of value in the detection of poisoning by organic phosphorus insecticides such as Parathion since a lowering of the pseudocholinesterase level precedes the onset of symptoms (Galley, Davies and Bidstrup, 1952; Gage, 1955). Numerous other authors (e.g. McArdle, 1940; Wescoe, Hunt, Riker and Litt, 1947) have demonstrated that a low 'pseudo' cholinesterase level may be indicative of liver malfunction.

Two serum deoxyribonucleases have been distinguished, DNase I with pH optimum 7·2 and requiring Mg^{++} as an activator and DNase II with pH optimum 5·6 and not requiring Mg^{++} as an activator. Kowlessar and McEvoy (1956) reported that a marked and protracted elevation of DNase I occurred in acute hemorrhagic pancreatitis during which tissue breakdown is a major pathological feature. Significantly low values of both DNase I and II were reported in a large number of patients with malignant disease (Gavosto, Buffa and Maraini, 1959).

Very small amounts of lipoprotein lipase have been found in human plasma (Engelberg, 1956; Gates and Gordon, 1958). Korn (1959) has summarized the reaction catalysed by the enzyme as: Triglyceride + lipoprotein $\rightarrow$ ' triglyceride-lipoprotein' $\xrightarrow[\text{lipoprotein lipase}]{}$ 'triglyceride-lipoprotein-lipoprotein lipase' $\rightarrow$ glycerol + fatty acids + (lipoprotein) + (lipoprotein lipase).

This reaction requires a fatty acid acceptor such as serum albumin (Gordon, 1955). Injection of heparin induces the appearance of lipoprotein lipase in the blood and this has been used in the treatment of certain normal and pathological hyperlipemias. Lipoprotein lipase migrates in starch electrophoresis with either the α_1–globulins (Brown, Boyle and Anfinsen, 1953) or β-globulins (Nikkila, 1953).

Other serum enzymes having important applications in medicine are serum amylase in pancreatic disease, acid phosphatase in carcinoma of the prostate, alkaline phosphatase in diseases of bone and liver and transaminase in coronary heart disease (Fishman and Davidson, 1957).

γ-Globulin antibody activity

It is now well established that human antibodies are sited in the 7S and 19S fractions of γ-globulins. Pedersen (1945) found that anti-A and anti-B isoagglutinins had sedimentation constants of about 19–20S. Deutsch, Alberty, Gosting and Williams (1947) reported that the anti-B had a sedimentation constant of 18S and that its electrophoretic mobility was that of a γ_1-globulin. The human Wasserman antibody obtained from human syphilitic sera was also found to have a high sedimentation constant (S_{20} = 18·4) and an electrophoretic mobility similar to that of γ_1-globulin.

The antibodies of various animal species immunized to different antigens have also been shown to possess electrophoretic mobilities in the range of the two human γ-globulins. Among these are horse diphtheria antitoxin (Pappenheimer, Lundgren and Williams, 1940; Kekwick and Record, 1941), rabbit anti-egg albumin (Tiselius, 1937), horse anti-pneumococcal component (Tiselius and Kabat, 1939) and horse tetanus antitoxin (van der Scheer and Wyckoff, 1940). Human γ-globulins have been shown to contain antibodies reacting with diphtheria toxin, streptococcal erythrogenic toxin, influenza A virus, mumps virus and the H antigen of *E. typhosa* (Enders, 1944).

Gordon (1953) found that a purified preparation of cold agglutinins obtained from the serum of a patient with the cold haemagglutination syndrome had a sedimentation coefficient of 18S. Fudenberg and Kunkel (1957) analysed the sera of 12 patients with acquired hemolytic anaemia. The high titre cold agglutinins from eight of these were 'fast' γ-globulins having sedimentation constants in the 19S range. By contrast the warm variety of hemolytic anaemia antibodies had sedimentation coefficients of approximately 7S and the mobilities of γ_2-globulins.

Franklin, Holman, Müller-Eberhard and Kunkel (1957) found that in 14 out of 31 sera from patients with rheumatoid arthritis a component could be detected in the ultracentrifuge which sedimented more rapidly than the 19S component from which it eventually separated. In one case this higher molecular weight component was present in a concentration of 340 mg% (i.e. in greater concentration than the normal 19S component). In six others this concentration was between 75 and 175 mg% while in seven of the patients it was less than 75 mg%. Some of the sera containing the unusual component were separated by starch electrophoresis. The high molecular weight component was detected in the γ-globulin fraction and was found to have a sedimentation constant of approximately 22S. In urea it dissociated to 19S and 7S components and may therefore be a complex of two types of protein. Sera from patients with rheumatoid arthritis are known to potentiate certain immunological reactions such as the sensitized sheep cell agglutination (Rose, Ragan, Pearce and Lipman, 1949) and also react with Cohn Fraction II γ-globulin to give a precipitate (Epstein, Johnson and Ragan, 1956). Franklin *et al.* (1957) obtained evidence for a direct relationship between the 22S component and the γ-globulin precipitation test. Absorption of serum with altered aggregated γ-globulin removed the 22S component. The 22S fraction was also always observed in sera giving the most positive sheep cell agglutination reactions.

α-Globulin fraction

Francis (1947) discovered that all normal sera contained a substance capable of inhibiting influenza virus haemagglutination. An electrophoretically homogeneous mucoprotein isolated from human plasma by the method of Winzler, Devor, Mehl and Smyth (1948) was found to consistently inhibit haemagglutination by influenza virus in dilutions which contained 0·15 to 0·3 μg of mucoprotein (Stulberg, Schapira, Robinson, Basinski and Freund, 1951). The electrophoretic mobility of this mucoprotein was $4·3 \times 10^{-5}$ cm²/sec/volt in 0·1M acetate buffer pH 4·5. Klenk and Lempfrid (1957) have reported that incubation of human erythrocytes with a cholera vibrio filtrate, which contained the cell-receptor destroying enzyme, liberated N-acetylneuraminic acid which was obtained in crystalline form. Support was thus given to the view that cell receptors for the influenza virus contain N-acetylneuraminic acid.

Fetuin, the mucoprotein of foetal calf serum markedly inhibits trypsin (Deutsch, 1954), Schmid's (1953) crystalline human serum α_1-glycoprotein displayed about 10% of the antitryptic activity of fetuin.

Markowitz, Gubler, Mahoney, Cartwright and Wintrobe (1955) have reported a high degree of correlation between the serum oxidase level [as measured by the method of Holmberg and Laurell (1951) employing paraphenylenediamine as a substrate] and the serum ceruloplasmin levels in pregnant women during their last trimester of pregnancy and patients with certain chronic infections.

Normal Human Urinary Mucoprotein

Tamm and Horsfall (1950) found that normal human urine contained a highly active inhibitor of viral haemagglutination active against influenza virus (PR8), swine virus, Newcastle disease virus and mumps virus. This inhibitory action could be destroyed by incubation of the urine with influenza virus or a cholera vibrio filtrate at 37° for 1–2 hr. The inhibitor could be recovered from urine by addition of 6 vol. of 95% ethanol and thereafter purified by partition with chloroform-octyl alcohol. Tamm and Horsfall (1952) later described a procedure involving precipitation of the inhibitor with sodium chloride (0·58M). The inhibitor proved to be a mucoprotein containing 33% reducing sugars and 9·2% hexosamine and having a molecular weight of the order of 7×10^6. A demonstrable inhibiting reaction with influenza virus could be obtained with 0·0003 μg of the mucoprotein.

Gottschalk (1952) reported that urinary mucoprotein contained 5·4% galactose, 2·7% mannose, 1% fucose and 7·6% hexosamine (glucosamine, galactosamine). Simultaneously Odin (1952) reported 6·8% hexose, 0·7% fucose, 6·4% hexosamine and 7·3% neuraminic acid for mucoprotein prepared by Tamm and Horsfall's (1950) method and 8·4% hexose, 9·4% hexosamine, 1·1% fucose, 9·1% neuraminic acid for mucoprotein obtained by their 1952 method.

Anderson (1954) devised an improved method for the isolation of urinary mucoproteins. He reported the following analyses. Mucoprotein A had N, 10·54%; acetyl, 3·67%; hexosamine, 14·41% and 17·5% reducing power expressed as glucose after acid hydrolysis. Mucoprotein B had N, 5·1%; acetyl, 9·03%; hexosamine, 18·29%; and 30·7% reducing power expressed as glucose after acid hydrolysis. Both mucoproteins contained amino acids, galactose, mannose, fucose, glucosamine and probably galactosamine. Klenk, Faillard and Lempfrid (1955) found that urinary mucoprotein A isolated by the method of Anderson (1954) contained 4·03–4·43% neuraminic acid. This was isolated as crystalline N-acetylneuraminic acid after incubation of the urinary mucoprotein with influenza virus (strain B Lee). They concluded that the cell receptor sites for influenza virus contained N-acetylneuraminic acid. Faillard (1957) later reported that N-acetyl neuraminic acid could also be cleaved from urinary mucoprotein by incubation with the receptor destroying enzyme from $V.$ cholerae.

Anderson and MacLagan (1955) reported that, on average, normal males excrete $146 \pm 7·5$ mg mucoprotein/24 hr while females excrete $106 \pm 6·4$ mg.

Berggård (1960) has used immunoelectrophoresis to identify the plasma proteins present in normal human urine. It was demonstrated with certainty that pre-albumin, albumin, α_1-seromucoid, haptoglobin, ceruloplasmin, transferrin, β_1A-globulin and γ-globulin were present. Indications were also obtained of two or three α_1-globulins, sometimes one additional α_2-globulin, one more β_1-globulin and a precipitation line with the same shape and electrophoretic mobility as the β_2A-globulin in plasma. Lack of reaction with specific antisera seemed to indicate the absence of α_2- and β-lipoproteins in normal urine.

A fraction of the nondialysable solids of human urine has been found to exhibit specific inhibitory activity on erythrocyte clumping and to contain similar constituents to the blood group substances (King, Fielden and Boyce, 1960). One such fraction, further purified by passage through DEAE-cellulose, had $[\alpha]_D^{20} - 13·3°$ and a number average particle weight of 1800. Preparations obtained from urine collected during the summer months had a sialic content higher than those collected during the winter months. The carbohydrate in one preparation comprised 23·5% hexosamine, 37% hexose (orcinol determination), 14·2% fucose and 13·1% sialic acid. Galactose, fucose and mannose were present together with the same amino acids reported for blood group substances of salivary origin.

Mucoproteins from Pathological Urine

Popenoe (1955) has isolated a glycoprotein from the urine of children with nephrotic syndrome which he has shown is identical with the plasma α_1-acid glycoprotein of Weimer, Mehl and Winzler (1950) and Schmid

(1953). It contained glucosamine, mannose and galactose and was distinct from the normal urinary mucoprotein of Tamm and Horsfall (1950). Popenoe and Drew (1957) later reported that the glycoprotein contained 11·4% neuraminic acid which could be cleaved from it by incubation with a culture filtrate of *Clostridium perfringens*. After such treatment the iso-electric point of the glycoprotein shifted from pH 2·7 to 5·0. Squire (1955) reported that all the normal constituents of serum can be detected by electrophoresis of nephrotic urine although in greatly different proportions. In particular the α_2-globulin is only just detectable. He suggested that this supported the classical theory that urinary proteins were derived from normal serum proteins by a malfunctioning kidney.

Markowitz, Gubler, Mahoney, Cartwright and Wintrobe (1955) reported that four patients with the nephrotic syndrome excreted between 46 and 75 mg of ceruloplasmin per 24 hr in their urine. Significant amounts of ceruloplasmin were not found in the urine of patients with hepatolenticular degeneration.

Browne and Venning (1936) showed that the human chorionic gonadotropin (HCG) excreted during pregnancy reached its highest level between the 60th and 80th days of pregnancy. The hormone, which has an iso-electric point between 3·2 and 3·3, has been found to contain 10·7% galactose and 5·2% hexosamine (Gurin, Bachman and Wilson, 1940; Li, 1949). HCG causes reactions ascribed to the interstitial cell-stimulating hormone of the pituitary gland.

After treatment with viral neuraminidase, chorionic and pituitary gonadotropins lose their biological activity. Got and Bourrillon (1961) found that incubation of human menopausal gonadotropin with neuraminidase (Behringwerke) caused the loss of 80% of gonadotropic activity and the liberation of N-glycolylneuraminic acid. For some reason this N-glycolylneuraminic acid was separable into two peaks on Dowex-2 formate. Confirmation of the presence of a glycolyl residue was obtained by hydrolysis with N-sulphuric acid and release of glycolic acid.

Human Saliva and Sputum

Kinersly (1953–4) carried out paper electrophoretic studies of saliva at varying pH's and detected the components with amido black or a modified periodic acid-Schiff staining technique. In veronal buffer pH 7·9 and in acetate buffer pH 4·5 three major components were detected. The position of amylase on the filter paper was located by the reduction in colour of the starch–iodine reaction. Human salivary amylase had previously been studied electrophoretically by Bernfeld, Staub and Fischer (1948).

Kinersly and Leite (1956–7) in further paper electrophoretic studies of saliva reported the presence of two sharp fractions and two diffuse fractions on the cathode side and two faint fractions on the anode side when separation was effected in phosphate buffer, pH 6·2. Using $Ca^{45}Cl_2$ and $Fe^{59}Cl_3$ it was demonstrated that some component of saliva could combine with calcium but not iron. The position of secreted blood group substance was also located. Gabl and Egger (1959) in similar studies reported the presence of 5–7 fractions in saliva separable by paper electrophoresis. Verschure (1959) found 9 components in saliva separated by paper electrophoresis at pH 8·6 in barbiturate buffer. Three of these components, including that associated with the amylase activity, could be detected with a carbohydrate stain. All the components could be located after labelling with [131]I.

Boundary electrophoresis of human parotid saliva (Zipkin, Adamik and Saroff, 1957) in veronal pH 8·6 has revealed the presence of seven components with mobilities of $+2·14$, $+0·77$, $+0·32$, $-0·77$, $-2·08$, $-3·02$ and $-4·18 \times 10^{-5}$ cm^2 sec^{-1} volt^{-1} respectively. Five of these components were detected in parotid saliva samples from all individuals examined. The two remaining components ($+0·77$ and $-0·77$) were only present occasionally. The major component was that with mobility $+0·32 \times 10^{-5}$ cm^2 sec^{-1} volt^{-1} which comprised 50% of the fractions. No fraction had the mobility of albumin but some may be globulins.

Rose (1950) reported the existence of three factors in mucoid secretions of the human respiratory tract (sputum). The first of these was destroyed by heating to 100° and was responsible for the ability of certain sputum specimens to inhibit viral (influenza virus) haemagglutination, to reduce infectivity of virus inoculated intranasally in mice and to restrict multiplication of the virus in chick embryos. A second factor was stable to heating at 100°, could inhibit viral haemagglutination but had no effect on the infectious properties of the virus. The third factor, like hog gastric mucin, markedly enhanced the infectivity of influenza virus (PR8 strain) injected intraperitoneally into mice.

Curtain, Marmion and Pye (1953) isolated an electrophoretically homogeneous mucoprotein from chronic bronchitis sputum.

Precipitation was effected by the addition of an equal volume of acetate buffer (pH 3·6, $\mu = 1·0$ containing 0·02N-calcium chloride) to sputum diluted with physiological saline (10 volumes) which had been previously centrifuged at 500 g (20 min) and 20,000 g (25 min).

This mucoprotein had a mobility of $6·7 \times 10^{-5}$ cm^2 sec^{-1} volt^{-1} in phosphate buffer (pH 7·0, $\mu = 0·1$) which was reduced to $4·9 \times 10^{-5}$ cm^2 sec^{-1} volt^{-1} after incubation with the receptor destroying enzyme of *Vibrio cholerae*. The mucoprotein could inhibit viral haemagglutination before but not after treatment with the enzyme. It was effective against both enzymically active and indicator influenza viruses *in vitro*.

Odin (1952) reported that neuraminic acid was present in human saliva. Werner (1953) crystallized galactosamine and glucosamine HCl from hydrolysates of acute bronchitis sputum and also reported the presence of galactose, fucose and mannose. White, Elmes and Whitley (1959) found that a mucoprotein isolated from chronic bronchitis sputum by the method of Curtain and Pye (1955) contained N, 8·6%; hexosamine, 6·1%; fucose, 5·1% and neuraminic acid, 4·2%. No gross heterogeneity was observed by boundary electrophoresis at pH 4·5 and 8·5. A mucoprotein isolated by Brogan (1959) from chronic bronchitis sputum contained N, 8·7%; total reducing sugars (including mannose, galactose and fucose), 26·3% and amino sugars (glucosamine and galactosamine), 14·3%. The presence or absence of neuraminic acid was not discussed.

Atassi, Barker and Stacey (1959) have reported that weak acidic hydrolysis of chronic bronchitis sputum liberated ribose and 2-deoxyribose (from the corresponding nucleic acids), fructose (probably from a levan elaborated by a member of the bacterial flora present in the throat) and a mixture of four nonulsoaminic acids including N-acetyl, N,O-diacetyl and N-glycolylneuraminic acid. N-acetylneuraminic acid was crystallized from the mixture and shown by X-ray powder photography, infrared spectra, decomposition point and chromatographic behaviour to be identical with an authentic specimen. Stronger hydrolysis liberated galactose, mannose, fucose and hexosamines. One of the latter was crystallized and characterized as D-glucosamine hydrochloride. A mucoprotein fraction obtained from chronic bronchitis sputum by isoelectric precipitation contained neuraminic acid (5·4%), glucosamine (12·8%), galactosamine (2·0%) and 13·4% total hexoses (galactose, mannose and fucose).

Neuraminic acid determination has proved a valuable indicator of the mucoprotein content of chronic bronchitis sputum (Anzai, Barker and Stacey, 1957) since little neuraminic acid is present in saliva. With bronchitics and normal controls the neuraminic acid content of the bronchial mucus was on average 30 and 8 times greater respectively on a dry weight basis than that of their salivas (Atassi, Barker, Houghton and Stacey, 1959). Although there was little difference in the neuraminic acid content of saliva from chronic bronchitics and healthy subjects there was a definite trend to higher values in the bronchial mucus of bronchitics than in that of controls. These findings enabled the progress of chronic bronchitis to be followed chemically since as the patient improved the proportion of bronchial mucus in the sputum became progressively less. One patient followed thus gave sputum whose neuraminic acid content (percentage dry weight) decreased from 2·94% to 1·04% over 26 days. Another patient showed a similar decrease from 3·99% to 2·39% over 31 days. Warfringe (1955) and Bukantz and Berns (1957) have both carried out paper electrophoretic analyses of sputa from patients with a wide range of pulmonary and bronchial diseases. Warfringe (1955) found a greatly increased amount of albumin in a case of bronchiolar carcinoma while Bukantz and Berns (1957) detected large amounts of albumin in 11 cases of 58 studied. Of these cases, 5 were proven pulmonary carcinomas and the other six while not allowing a positive diagnosis all showed pulmonary densities.

Animal Salivary Mucoproteins

Bovine submaxillary mucoprotein

Blix (1936) isolated a crystalline neuraminic acid (called by him B-sialic acid) from bovine submaxillary gland mucoprotein by hot aqueous auto-hydrolysis. Blix, Svennerholm and Werner (1952) identified galactosamine as another constituent of the mucoprotein. Klenk and Lauenstein (1952) isolated crystalline methyl neuraminosidic acid from submaxillary mucin by treatment with methanolic hydrogen chloride. Later, Klenk and Faillard (1954) isolated N-acetylneuraminic acid as a partial degradation product of bovine submaxillary mucin.

Curtain and Pye (1955) utilized methanol precipitation at low temperature in the presence of barium ions to isolate an electrophoretically homogeneous mucoprotein from bovine submaxillary gland. This mucoprotein had an electrophoretic mobility of $-5 \cdot 4 \times 10^{-5}$ cm^2 sec^{-1} volt^{-1} in phosphate buffer (pH 6·9, $\mu = 0 \cdot 1$) (Pye, 1955). Gottschalk and Ada (1956) reported that it contained 0·7% galactose, 0·2% mannose, 0·7% fucose, 0·8% glucosamine and 9·2% galactosamine.

Heimer and Meyer (1956) described the isolation of a homogeneous mucoprotein obtained by extraction at 0° of acetone powders of bovine submaxillary gland with aqueous 6N-urea adjusted to pH 9. The mucoprotein was recovered from such extracts by acidification to pH 3·5 and removal of extraneous proteins from the precipitate so obtained by partition with chloroform-amyl alcohol. The mucoprotein precipitated from the aqueous phase on addition of alcohol to 54% concentration. The mucoprotein was homogeneous both after ultracentrifugation and after electrophoresis at pH 4·5 and pH 8·6. It contained 24·8–31·6% neuraminic acid, 18·6% hexosamine and 9·1% N. The acetyl content 9·8% was indicative that the neuraminic acid residues contained two acetyl groups. Blix, Lindberg, Odin and Werner (1955; 1956) established that some, at least, of the neuraminic acid in the mucoprotein was N,O-diacetylneuraminic acid. Klenk and Uhlenbruck (1957) concluded that in addition the amino group in some of the neuraminic acid residues was also substituted by glycolic acid.

Gottschalk and Graham (1959) submitted bovine salivary mucoprotein to alkaline hydrolysis at 80° and passed a concentrated dialysate of the products down a column of Dowex-50 (H$^+$). The effluent was then fractionated on a Dowex-1-formate column by washing first with water and then by gradient elution with formic acid (0·05 to 0·4N). One of the fractions had C, 44·57; H, 6·06; N, 5·32. $C_{19}H_{32}O_{14}N_2$ requires C, 44·52; H, 6·29 and N, 5·49. Analysis showed that the ratio of hexosamine/neuraminic acid present was 0·84. Neuraminidase split the fraction into N-acetylneuraminic acid and N-acetylgalactosamine; a small percentage (14·5%) of the total neuraminic acid was N-glycolylneuraminic acid. The two major components of the disaccharide were further characterized by the nature of their alkaline degradation products and conversion of the N-acetylhexosamine to the free galactosamine. The results of periodate oxidation (4 moles consumed per mole of compound) and the formation of a chromogen with the neuraminic acid still attached to it indicated that the compound was 6-α-D-sialyl-N-acetylgalactosamine.

Ovine submaxillary gland mucoprotein

This sheep mucoprotein is the most potent virus haemaglutinin inhibitor so far obtained being active against a whole spectrum of indicator viruses (McCrea, 1953). Its carbohydrate moiety, which consisted of equimolecular amounts of N-acetylneuraminic acid and N-acetylgalactosamine, comprised some 42% of the mucoprotein (Graham and Gottschalk, 1960). Only traces of other sugars (galactose, 0·3%; mannose, 0·15% fucose, 0·40%) were detected. Treatment of the mucoprotein with barium hydroxide afforded *inter alia* a disaccharide containing equimolar amounts of N-acetylgalactosamine and N-acetylneuraminic acid. This was susceptible to the α-neuraminidase isolated from *Vibrio cholerae* and consumed four moles of periodate per mole of disaccharide. Further gentle alkaline treatment of the disaccharide gave N-acetylneuraminyl-chromogen I which reacted in the cold with Ehrlich reagent. A structural study of this product revealed that it was in fact 6-O-α-D-N-acetylneuraminyl-anhydro-N-acetylgalactosamine. Hence the prosthetic group of the mucoprotein was considered to be the disaccharide 6-O-α-D-N-acetylneuraminyl-N-acetylgalactosamine. Further support for this belief accrues from the observation that 93% of the N-acetylgalactosamine residues in the mucoprotein are susceptible to periodate oxidation. About 85% of the total N-acetylneuraminic acid in the mucoprotein was released by α-neuraminidase with a concomitant loss of almost all its biological activity.

The amino acids in the mucoprotein (g/100 g mucoprotein) consist of alanine (5·08), arginine (3·31), aspartic acid (3·04), cystine (1·61), glutamic acid (4·58), glycine (5·97), histidine (0·30), isoleucine (1·9), leucine (2·92), lysine (1·50), phenylalanine (1·96), proline (5·6), serine (7·57), threonine (7·00), tyrosine (0·68) and valine (4·20). Little or no tryptophan or methionine were present. By another procedure the total dicarboxylic acids were found to be 10·7% (aspartic, 4·1; glutamic, 6·17) (Gottschalk and

Simmonds, 1960). These amino acids are believed to be attached mainly via the free carboxyl groups of glutamic and aspartic acid residues to the reducing groups of the disaccharide prosthetic groups to form a glycosidic ester linkage. The first indication of this came from the observation that on alkaline treatment of the mucoprotein the number of prosthetic groups released was in full agreement with the number of carboxyl groups unmasked. That these carboxyl groups were those of the dicarboxylic amino acids was shown in the following manner. The mucoprotein was first treated with the proteolytic enzyme trypsin and then with phenyl *iso*-thiocyanate to block the N-terminal residues. The product was dissolved in anhydrous tetrahydrofuran and reacted with lithium borohydride, a reagent which effects a reductive cleavage of ester linkages without appreciable action on amide or peptide bonds (Chibnall and Rees, 1958). The low recovery (12%) of the dicarboxylic acids after such treatment indicated esterification of one of the carboxyl groups of the missing 88% dicarboxylic acids (Gottschalk, 1960). It was estimated that in all c. 84% of the prosthetic disaccharide units were linked to dicarboxylic acids and that about 16% were linked through an alkali-stable O-glycosidic linkage probably to serine and/or threonine.

Trypsin is specific for the carboxylic acid groups of the basic amino acids except where sterically hindered. In the mucoprotein one out of 6·4 amino acid residues carries a prosthetic group, and one out of 16 amino acid residues is a lysyl or arginyl residue. The steric hindrance caused by the prosthetic groups in the mucoprotein is illustrated by the fact that after neuraminidase treatment the number of peptide bonds split by trypsin increased by 45%.

Mucoproteins of Gastric Juice

Glass and Boyd (1949) distinguished the components of total gastric mucin as follows. The jelly-like mucus adhering closely to the mucosa which could be separated from gastric juice by centrifugation was termed the visible mucus. This was believed to originate from the columnar surface of epithelial cells. The dissolved mucin was composed of (a) the soluble mucus derived by physical dissolution of the visible mucus (b) the products of degradation (dissolved mucoproteose) of this soluble mucus and (c) glandular mucoprotein secreted by the mucoid neck cells of gastric glands.

Subsequent studies by Glass and Wolf (1952) and Mack, Wolf and Stern (1953) revealed that dialysed gastric juice could be separated into at least five electrophoretically distinct protein-containing components. The technique employed was free electrophoresis in a Tiselius apparatus using buffers between pH 5·1 and 8·5. Richmond, Caputto and Wolf (1955) achieved a much better fractionation using the adsorptive properties of

Amberlite IRC-50 (120–150 mesh) a cation exchange resin (Richmond and Caputto, 1954).

About 1 g of freeze-dried dialysed gastric juice could be separated on a column ($1\cdot4 \times 68$ cm) which was eluted with citrate or phosphate buffer of varying pH. When buffers of pH $3\cdot15$–pH 10 were used and the fractions analysed at least 12 components could be detected with varying hexose, hexosamine and protein content. The first carbohydrate-rich fraction (eluted with buffer pH $3\cdot12$) was found to contain blood group substance A. The fractions eluted between pH $3\cdot5$ to $4\cdot3$ contained intrinsic factor activity. The peptic activity was sited in a fraction eluted between $3\cdot8$ and $4\cdot3$.

Analyses revealed that not all the carbohydrate existed as mucoprotein but that independent polysaccharide and protein fractions were also present. Richmond, Caputto and Wolf (1955) also carried out analyses for total hexoses, hexosamine, fucose, sialic acid, glucuronic acid and proteins in gastric juice from various groups of patients and these are reproduced in Table 8.III (results quoted as mg% and number of patients examined in parentheses).

Table 8.III. *Carbohydrate contents of gastric juice from different groups of patients*

	Normal stomachs	Duodenal ulcers	Gastric ulcers	Cancer	Pernicious Anaemia
Total hexoses	$32\cdot1$ (16)	$34\cdot7$ (26)	36 (12)	$81\cdot2$ (11)	$60\cdot0$ (6)
Hexosamines	$32\cdot7$ (10)	$30\cdot2$ (21)	$45\cdot9$ (9)	$52\cdot4$ (9)	$74\cdot3$ (6)
Fucose	$13\cdot8$ (15)	$9\cdot65$ (20)	$16\cdot7$ (7)	$30\cdot7$ (9)	$33\cdot3$ (6)
Sialic acid	$7\cdot31$ (13)	$8\cdot1$ (20)	$9\cdot8$ (8)	$20\cdot8$ (9)	$18\cdot2$ (5)
Glucuronic acid	$2\cdot0$ (12)	$1\cdot76$ (22)	$1\cdot89$ (9)	$2\cdot1$ (8)	$2\cdot1$ (5)
Proteins	330 (11)	212 (19)	288 (10)	482 (10)	242 (5)

It reveals that the gastric juice of patients with cancer or pernicious anaemia can be sharply differentiated from those of normal controls and patients with ulcers by their much higher hexose and sialic acid (neuraminic acid) contents.

Glass, Stephenson and Rich (1956) have carried out extensive studies of gastric juice components in health and disease. The analytical technique used consisted of electrophoresis on Whatman No. 1 paper dampened with borate buffer, pH $9\cdot0$ ($\mu = 0\cdot12$) followed by staining either with Amido Black 10B or periodic acid–Schiff reagent (PAS). The resulting electrophoretogram was examined with an automatic scanner and integrator. Normal gastric juice examined in this way showed at least eight components consisting of P (pepsin activity), M_1, M_2, M_3, M_4 (all carbohydrate containing mucoproteins) and X, Y, Z (all proteins free of carbohydrates). Of the mucoproteins M_3 is the richest in carbohydrate and M_1 contains least. M_1 corresponds in mobility to the glandular mucoprotein which is probably secreted by the neck cells of fundic glands. Examination of the gastric juice obtained after stimulation by holding a gastric tube in the stomach for half an hour showed that X and Y peaks increased greatly whereas after histamine injection there was a sharp rise in pepsin. After insulin injection both peaks M_1 and P increased. The gastric juice from patients with the ulcer syndrome showed high pepsin, M_1, X and Y peaks patients with pernicious anaemia and gastric atrophy yield a gastric juice devoid of pepsin, M_1, Y and Z and in which X is either absent or in very low concentration. Glass and his co-workers (1956) interpreted these results as indicative of the atrophy of the glandular elements which secrete P and M_1 since M_2, M_3 and M_4 were considered to be mucous substances of surface epithelial origin. X, Y and Z were believed to represent products of digestion of the protein moieties of gastric mucoproteins by peptic enzymes and therefore they were absent in the gastric juice of patients with pernicious anaemia who lack the mechanism of peptic digestion. The pattern in a case of histamine refractory anacidity closely resembled that of pernicious anaemia except that in the former the M_1 peak was retained and intrinsic factor was present in the stomach.

Katzka (1959) has studied the macromolecular components of gastric juice by starch zone electrophoresis using $0 \cdot 1$M-veronal buffer (pH $8 \cdot 6$). The fasting gastric juice from normal subjects was separated into four major protein components A, B, C and D; two of the components A and C sometimes separated into A_1, A_2 and C_1, C_2, C_3 respectively. Whereas A and C were always present in similar proportions the amounts of B and D were variable. Gastric juice obtained from normal subjects after subcutaneous injection of histamine phosphate contained increased amounts of C as did the gastric juice from patients with duodenal and gastric ulcers. In gastric juice from four patients with pernicious anaemia B was by far the major component; D was absent in all and small amounts of A and C were only found in one of the four patients. Gastric juice from patients with histamine anacidity resembled those of pernicious anaemia. It was suggested that B may come from swallowed saliva as well as directly from gastric mucosa.

Gräsbeck (1956) in earlier starch zone electrophoresis studies of normal human gastric juice detected six protein components (1–6) after a 30 hour separation in a veronal-acetate–HCl buffer (pH $6 \cdot 1$, $\mu = 0 \cdot 1$). Katzka (1959) believed that these corresponded to four subpeaks in the C area plus B and D; the cathodic migration reported by Gräsbeck in some studies was probably A. Gräsbeck (1956) found that the B_{12}-binding capacity was distributed in two peaks in the areas of component 4 and component 5. Pepsin activity was found almost exclusively in component 6 which contained the least amount of carbohydrate. Most glucosamine was found in the slowest components. From parallel studies on saliva, Gräsbeck (1956) did not consider that saliva, which contained only one vitamin B_{12}-binding component, was an important source of B_{12}-binding components in gastric juice. Saliva only had about one-quarter of the B_{12}-binding power of gastric juice. Further studies indicated that there is originally only one B_{12}-binding fraction in gastric juice and that the faster migrating binder peak arises from other components by an autodigestive process. The B_{12}-binding component of gastric juice was found to be stable to alkali, non-dialysable, heat-labile and slowly digestible with pepsin. It was concluded that the intrinsic factor (the factor promoting the intestinal absorption of vitamin B_{12} in a specific manner) and the vitamin B_{12}-binding component are identical.

Mucoproteins of Cervical Mucin

Marked physical changes occur in bovine cervical mucin during the oestrus cycle (Scott-Blair, Folley, Malpress and Coppen, 1941). During pregnancy a thick plasto-elastic gel is secreted, while at oestrus a thinner visco-elastic 'spinnbar' material is produced. Gibbons (1959) has obtained mucoproteins from the gel phase of ultracentrifuged oestrus and pregnancy mucins by dissolving the gels in aqueous saturated calcium chloride solution–ethanol (9:1 vol/vol) and fractionating with alcohol. The purified mucoprotein from oestrus mucin contained galactose, 27·5%; fucose, 5·1%; glucosamine, 15·3%; galactosamine, 11·4%; sialic acid, 13·8%; acetyl, 10·0%, together with amino acids. The pregnancy muco-protein contained galactose, 28·1%; fucose, 5·0%; glucosamine, 12·6%; galactosamine, 15·7%; sialic acid, 17·5%; acetyl, 11·1%, and similar amino acids. The major amino acid component in each case was threonine (oestrus mucoprotein, 6·28%; pregnancy mucoprotein, 5·45%), which was accompanied by aspartic acid, glutamic acid, glycine, serine, alanine, proline, valine, isoleucine, leucine, phenylalanine, lysine and arginine in smaller amounts. Both mucoproteins were precipitable with cetyltri-methylammonium chloride and 0·01M-flavianic acid, and appeared to sediment as one component. Their molecular weights were of the order of 4×10^6 and the molecules appeared to be of the random-coil form (Gibbons and Glover, 1959). It was noteworthy that the amount of acetyl groups present was considerably greater than that required for acetylation of the amino groups of the hexosamine and the sialic acid, but was approximately correct if the sialic acid was mono-O-acetylated. Support for this came from the positive ferric hydroxamate test given by both mucoproteins.

As yet, the composition of human cervical mucus has not been studied in so much detail. However, Shettles, Dische and Osnos (1951) and Bergman and Werner (1951) have reported the presence of a mucopolysaccharide containing galactose, fucose, hexosamine and sialic acid in mid-cycle mucus. The composition of the mucopolysaccharide did not appear to change significantly during the menstrual cycle (Bergman and Werner, 1951) or pregnancy (Viergiver and Pommeremke, 1947). Other carbohydrates detected in the mucus include mannose, which probably arose from a mucoprotein, and glucose from glycogen secreted by the glandular elements of the uterus (Werner, 1953; Viergiver and Pommeremke, 1947). Odin (1955b) has, in addition, isolated N-acetylneuraminic acid from human cervical mucin.

Spencer, Sunseri and Sunseri (1957) have analysed the cervical mucus from normal, pregnant and carcinomatous patients by paper electrophoretic separation in barbiturate buffer ($\mu = 0.075$, pH 8.6). When stained with bromophenol blue two main protein bands (A and B) were detected in normal and pregnancy cervical mucus. The stationary band (A) reacted with periodic acid-Schiff reagent, was strongly metachromatic towards toluidine blue and gave a strong positive Feulgen reaction for nucleic acid. The mobile-negatively charged band B was PAS positive but showed only faint metachromasia towards toluidine blue. B contained no nucleic acid. A very faint protein band (C) which moved towards the cathode was also sometimes detected. Investigation showed that A was actually insoluble and could be separated by centrifugation; it was also very much reduced or even totally absent from the clear limpid mid-cycle mucus. In eight out of 56 cases a further protein staining component with the same fast-moving electrophoretic mobility as serum albumin was detected in the mucus. It was PAS and Feulgen negative, non-metachromatic and had a 260/280 mμ ratio of 0.80. Its identity with serum albumin was established by immunological methods and in each case it was accompanied by serum globulins. The four samples with the highest albumin contents (22.9–33.3%) were from patients with carcinoma of the cervix, vagina and endometrium. The next highest albumin content (20.7%) was from a pregnant patient with uterine myomata. Three samples with an albumin content of 5.4–9.7% were from one patient with cervicitis and two pregnant patients. All the remainder of the cases which consisted largely of 12 normal patients and 25 pregnant patients showed no albumin in their cervical mucus. The mucus from two cases of leukoplakia of the cervix and two cases of carcinoma *in situ* of the cervix also did not contain any albumin. It was concluded that as far as carcinoma of the genital tract was concerned the albumin appeared in the mucus as a result of exudation from fairly well-advanced carcinomas.

Mucoproteins of Seminal Plasma

Ross, Moore and Miller (1942) examined the proteins of human seminal plasma using a Tiselius electrophoresis apparatus and phosphate buffer containing sodium chloride (pH $7\cdot85$, $\mu = 0\cdot1$). In typical separations four distinct peaks (P1, P2, P3 and P4) were detected with mobilities of ±0, $-2\cdot8$, $-4\cdot5$ and $-5\cdot6$ cm^2 volt^{-1} sec^{-1} × 10^{-5} when a potential of $6\cdot4$ volts per cm was used. A fifth component P5 (mobility $-6\cdot4$ cm^2 volt^{-1} sec^{-1} × 10^{-5}) was sometimes detected. P4 was a glycoprotein containing $9\cdot3\%$ N and yielding $26\cdot8\%$ reducing substances (as glucose) following treatment with N-HCl at 100°. It contained $10\cdot8\%$ hexosamine and no uronic acid. From electrophoretic evidence less than $0\cdot02\%$ albumin was present in seminal plasma. Fresh specimens of seminal plasma in which cell autolysis had not occurred appeared to contain only minute quantities of nucleoprotein. In a comparison of normal and abnormal plasmas from human semen, Ross, Miller, Moore and Sikorski (1943) detected no definitely significant deviation in protein contents although P5 was present in all abnormal specimens and P4 absent from all but one. Such abnormal specimens were either abnormally viscous or the sperm was poorly motile, non-motile or absent. Schneider, Nowakowski and Voigt (1954) have carried out paper electrophoretic separations of human seminal plasma using barbiturate buffer pH $8\cdot7$ ($\mu = 0\cdot047$) and compared the mobilities of the five mobile components with those of human serum. Components 1, 2 and 3 had similar mobilities to those of γ-, β- and α_2-globulins. Staining with the Schiff's reagent showed that the carbohydrate was localized mainly in component 2, but some was also present in 1 and 3.

Svennerholm (1958) reported that the average neuraminic acid content of four specimens of human semen was $105\cdot5$ mg/100 g. Warren (1959) in a more extensive investigation of twenty normal human semen samples found an average of $124\cdot2$ mg per 100 ml with a range of $64\cdot5$ to $219\cdot0$ mg per 100 ml. In subnormal semen samples (15 specimens) where the content of spermatozoa was low the value was $90\cdot1$ mg per cent with a range of $42\cdot4$ to $134\cdot9$ mg per cent. Determination of the neuraminic acid content of human prostatic fluid ($60\cdot6$ mg per cent average for eight samples) and human seminal vesicle secretion ($231\cdot4$ mg per cent average for four samples) enabled Warren (1959) to predict that the prostate accounts for approximately two-thirds the volume of semen while the semen vesicles provide one-third. The spermatozoa contained only $0\cdot53\%$ of the total seminal neuraminic acid content. The neuraminic acid present in the seminal mucoproteins can be mostly (79%) cleaved by *Clostridium perfringens* neuraminidase and occurs as the N-acetyl derivative exclusively. The ion-exchange resin method of Svennerholm (1958) was recommended for neuraminic acid assay of semen in preference to the direct Ehrlich method of Werner and Odin (1952), resorcinol method (Svennerholm, 1957) or diphenylamine procedure (Pigman, Hawkins, Blair and Holley, 1958).

Mucoproteins of Human Sweat

Shelley and Hurley (1953) have reported the presence of proteins in sweat from apocrine glands. Jirka and Kotas (1957) have detected polarographically proteins of a mucoprotein nature in both eccrine and apocrine human sweat. The polarographically active component had a catalytic effect in a cobalt solution (Co^{3+} ions) and was soluble in 20% sulphosalicylic acid. Hexosamine analysis of sweat samples before and after hydrolysis gave values of 10·4 and 13·7 μg/ml before and 23·0 and 30·2 μg/ml after.

Mucoproteins of Cerebrospinal Fluid

Roboz, Murphy, Hess and Forster (1955) outlined a method for the isolation of glycoproteins from spinal fluid obtained from pneumoencephalograms. To obtain the protein-bound carbohydrate fraction the freeze-dried fluid was extracted with an ether:alcohol mixture (1:3) and the residue dissolved in 1·2% sodium carbonate solution. After precipitation of the crude glycoprotein fraction with ethanol it was hydrolysed with Permutit Q. Mannose, galactose, fucose, and glucosamine were detected in the hydrolysate. The hexosamine content of the ethanol precipitated fraction corresponded to 4·2 ± 1·8 mg/l in 14 cases of non-demyelinating diseases. Neuraminic acid assay on a trichloracetic acid precipitated fraction of ten cerebrospinal fluid samples revealed 2·4 ± 0·9 mg/l. Later studies by Bohm and Baumeister (1956) suggested normal protein-bound neuraminic acid levels of 1·4 μg/ml although values as high as 122 μg/ml were observed in cases of meningitis where the cerebrospinal fluid protein levels were proportionately increased. Ross and Bohm (1957) subsequently reported a 'normal' value of 2·7 ± 0·55 μg/ml.

Uzman and Rumley (1956) discovered that the neuraminic acid in cerebrospinal fluid existed in two distinct forms. One of these was freely dialysable and accounted for 60–80% of the total neuraminic acid while the residue was protein-bound and non-dialysable. The importance of the former is that it could arise from the release of neuraminic acid from tissue glycolipids in the course of cerebral metabolism. In 49 samples examined the total neuraminic acid content was found to vary between 10·7 and 33·5 μg/ml. Uzman, Bering and Morris (1959) have investigated the significance of variations in neuraminic acid concentration in cerebrospinal fluid from patients with different neurological diseases. They divided adult patients who had severe cerebral diseases into two groups, A and B. Group A consisted of those cases characterized clinically by evidence of progressive increase in intracranial pressure and cerebral edema,* with

* Swelling due to watery fluid in the intracellular spaces of connective tissue.

stupor and coma of at least 48 hr duration. Here the total neuraminic acid content of the ventricular fluid was uniformly very low (average of 9·5 μg/ml). Group B included patients over the age of 40 with focal seizures of recent onset or with dementia and focal signs, suggesting the possibility of tumour. Here the average total neuraminic acid content (17·4 μg/ml) was high. In spite of this the ventricular fluid of Group B patients had a much lower protein-bound neuraminic acid content showing that the dialysable neuraminic acid was very much higher in group B than in Group A. In their study of younger subjects the average neuraminic acid content of six cases of noncommunicating hydrocephalus was 27·1 μg/ml and that of three cases of communicating hydrocephalus significantly lower (17·9 μg/ml). Another interesting discovery was that all cases with verified spinal subarachnoid* obstruction had total neuraminic acid contents below 10 μg/ml. By contrast patients with chronic degenerative disease exhibited no significant difference in either dialysable and non-dialysable neuraminic acid when compared with patients having no neurological disease. In conclusion it was found that the dialysable neuraminic acid concentration was highest in the ventricle and decreased sharply in the spinal subarachnoid fluid while the protein-bound neuraminic acid is in lowest concentration in the ventricle and increases with the protein concentration as the spinal subarachnoid space is reached.

Mucoproteins of Ascitic and Pleural Fluids

The mucoprotein levels in ascitic† fluid and pleural‡ fluid of a number of patients were studied by Taipale and Hokkanen (1956). Thirty per cent perchloric acid was added drop by drop to the continuously agitated fluid until the final concentration was 6%. The mucoproteins were then precipitated from the solution with phosphotungstic acid and determined as biuret protein. Values obtained are given in Table 8.IV.

These workers concluded that whereas the mucoprotein level of the ascitic fluid was of significance from the standpoint of differential diagnosis that of pleural fluid was of no significant diagnostic importance.

Spak (1958) has also investigated the clinical value of mucoprotein assay of ascitic fluid from various patients. All cases of portal cirrhosis had a very low content of mucoprotein (mean 18 mg/100 ml) and could be sharply differentiated from those with cancer (mean 173 mg/100 ml), congestive heart failure (mean 85 mg/100 ml) and tuberculosis (mean 258 mg/100 ml).

* The subarachnoid space is between two of the membranes (the arachnoid and the pia mater) covering the brain.

† The serous fluid in the peritoneal cavity.

‡ The pleura is one of the two serous membranes which line the thorax and envelope the lungs.

13

Table 8.IV. *Mucoproteins of ascitic and pleural fluids*

Diseases	No. of cases	mg mucoprotein/100 ml ascitic fluid
Malignant tumour	7	89–191 (mean 134·3 ± 10·1)
Congestive heart failure	8	38–107 (mean 61·1 ± 4·75)
Cirrhosis of the liver	11	7–37 (mean 21·9 ± 2·70)
Tuberculous peritonitis	1	187
Lupus erythematosus dis-seminating	1	49
Polyserositis	1	47
Nephrotic nephritis	1	26
Diseases	No. of cases	mg mucoprotein/100 ml pleural fluid
Exudative pleurisy	24	63–196 (mean 118·1 ± 6·8)
Pleural empyema	11	172–285 (mean 233·3 ± 9·46)
Malignant tumour	11	88–201 (mean 113·6 ± 7·78)
Thoracic operation	15	59–193 (mean 120·5 ± 9·10)
Congestive heart failure	8	17–78 (mean 48·0 ± 8·21)
Primary amyloidosis	1	87
Polyserositis	1	51
Hepatitis with lung infarct	1	17

REFERENCES

Anderson, A. J. *Biochem. J.* **56**, xxv (1954).
Anderson, A. J. and MacLagen, N. F. *Biochem. J.* **59**, 638 (1955).
Anzai, T., Barker, S. A. and Stacey, M. *Clin. Chim. Acta* **2**, 491 (1957).
Aronsson, T., Grönwall, A. and Lausing, E. *Clin. Chim. Acta* **4**, 124 (1959).
Atassi, M. Z., Barker, S. A., Houghton, L. E. and Stacey, M. *Clin. Chim. Acta* **4**, 741 (1959).
Atassi, M. Z., Barker, S. A. and Stacey, M. *Clin. Chim. Acta* **4**, 823 (1959).
Berggård, I. *Nature* **187**, 776 (1960).
Bergman, P. and Werner, I. *Acta Obstet. Gynecol. Scand.* **30**, 273 (1951).
Berkman, G., Rifkin, H. and Ross, G. *J. Clin. Inv.* **32**, 415 (1953).
Bernfeld, P., Staub, A. and Fischer, E. H. *Helv. chim. acta* **31**, 2165 (1948).
Bettelheim-Jevons, F. R. *Adv. Protein. Chem.* **13**, 35 (1958).
Bierry, H. *Ber. Ges. Physiol.* **52**, 607 (1930).
Björnesjo, K. B. *Scand. J. Clin. Lab. Invest.* **7**, 147 (1955).
Blix, G. *Hoppe-Seyl. Z.* **240**, 43 (1936).
Blix, G., Lindberg, E., Odin, L. and Werner, I. *Nature* **175**, 340 (1955).
Blix, G., Lindberg, E., Odin, L. and Werner, I. *Acta Soc. Med. Uppsal.* **61**, 1 (1956).
Blix, G., Svennerholm, L. and Werner, I. *Acta Chem. Scand.* **6**, 358 (1952).
Blix, G., Tiselius, A. and Svensson, H. *J. Biol. Chem.* **137**, 485 (1941).
Böhm, P. and Baumeister, L. *Hoppe-Seyl. Z. Physiol. Chem.* **305**, 42 (1956).
Böhm, P., Ross, J. and Baumeister, L. *Z. physiol. Chem.* **308**, 181 (1957).
Boström, H., Rodén, L. and Yamashina, I. *J. Biol. Chem.* **230**, 381 (1958).

Brogan, T. D. *Biochem. J.* **71,** 125 (1959).
Brown, R. K., Baker, W. H., Peterkofsky, A. and Kauffman, D. L. *J. Amer. Chem. Soc.* **76,** 4244 (1954).
Brown, R. K., Boyle, E. and Anfinsen, C. B. *J. Biol. Chem.* **204,** 423 (1953).
Browne, R. K. and Venning, E. M. *Lancet* **2,** 1507 (1936).
Bukantz, S. C. and Berns, A. W. *J. Clin. Invest.* **36,** 877 (1957).
Chatagnon, C. and Chatagnon, P. *Compt. rend. soc. biol.* **148,** 1226 (1954).
Chibnall, A. C. and Rees, M. W. *Biochem. J.* **68,** 105 (1958).
Cohn, E. J., Luetscher, J. A., Oncley, J. L., Armstrong, S. H. and Davis, B. D. *J. Amer. Chem. Soc.* **62,** 3396 (1940).
Cohn, E. J. and Edsall, J. T. *Proteins, Aminoacids and Peptides.* New York, 1943.
Consden, R. and Stanier, W. M. *Nature* **169,** 783 (1952).
Curtain, C. C., Marmion, B. P. and Pye, J. *Nature* **171,** 33 (1953).
Curtain, C. C. and Pye, J. *Aust. J. Exp. Biol. Med. Sci.* **33,** 315 (1955).
Dagnall, P. *Clin. Chim. Acta* **2,** 381 (1957).
Davidson, H. M. *Methods of Biochem. Analysis* **4,** 259 (1957).
Deutsch, H. F. *J. Biol. Chem.* **208,** 669 (1954).
Deutsch, H. F., Alberty, R. A., Gosting, L. J. and Williams, J. W. *J. Immunol.* **56,** 183 (1947).
Deutsch, H. F. and Morton, J. I. *Science* **125,** 600 (1957).
Dische, Z. *Biochem. Z.* **201,** 74 (1928).
Dische, Z. and Shettles, L. B. *J. Biol. Chem.* **175,** 595 (1948).
Enders, J. F. *J. Clin. Invest.* **23,** 510 (1944).
Engelberg, H. *J. Biol. Chem.* **222,** 601 (1956).
Epstein, W., Johnson, A. and Ragan, C. *Proc. Soc. Exp. Biol. Med.* **91,** 235 (1956).
Fahey, J. L. *Fed. Proc.* **18,** 43 (1959).
Faillard, H. *Z. Physiol. Chem.* **307,** 62 (1957).
Fishman, W. H. and Davidson, H. M. *Methods of Biochemical Analysis* **4,** 257 (1957).
Flynn, F. V. *Proc. Roy. Soc. Med.* **47,** 827 (1954).
Francis, T. *J. Exp. Med.* **85,** 1 (1947).
Franklin, E. C., Holman, H. R., Müller-Eberhard, H. J. and Kunkel, H. G. *J. Exp. Med.* **105,** 425 (1957).
Fudenberg, H. H. and Kunkel, H. G. *J. Exp. Med.* **106,** 689 (1957).
Gabl, F. and Egger, E. *Clin. Chim. Acta* **4,** 62 (1959).
Gage, J. C. *Brit. Med. J.* **1,** 1370 (1955).
Galley, R. A. E., Davies, D. R. and Bidstrup, P. L. *Proc. Roy. Soc. Med.* **45,** 567 (1952).
Gates, H. S. and Gordon, R. S. *Fed. Proc.* **17,** 437 (1958).
Gavosta, F., Buffa, F. and Maraini, G. *Clin. Chim. Acta* **4,** 192 (1959).
Gibbons, R. A. *Biochem. J.* **73,** 209 (1959).
Gibbons, R. A. and Glover, F. A. *Biochem. J.* **73,** 217 (1959).
Glass, G. B. J. and Boyd, L. J. *Gastroenterology* **12,** 821 (1949).
Glass, G. B. J., Stephanson, L. and Rich, M. *Gastroenterologia* **86,** 384 (1956).
Glass, G. B. J. and Wolf, S. *Proc. Soc. Exp. Biol. Med.* **79,** 674 (1952).
Glenchur, H., Zinneman, H. H. and Briggs, D. R. *Ann. Int. Med.* **48,** 1055 (1958).
Goa, J. *Scand. Clin. Lab. Invest.* **7,** supp. 22 (1955).
Gordon, R. S. *J. Immunol.* **71,** 220 (1953).
Gordon, R. S. *J. Clin. Invest.* **34,** 477 (1955).
Got, R. and Bourrillon, R. *Nature* **189,** 234 (1961).
Gottschalk, A. *Nature* **170,** 662 (1952).
Gottschalk, A. *Nature* **186,** 949 (1960).

Gottschalk, A. and Ada, G. L. *Biochem. J.* **62,** 681 (1956).
Gottschalk, A. and Graham, E. R. B. *Biochim. Biophys. Acta* **34,** 380 (1959).
Gottschalk, A. and Simmonds, D. H. *Biochim. Biophys. Acta* **42,** 141 (1960).
Graham, E. R. B. and Gottschalk, A. *Biochim. Biophys. Acta* **38,** 513 (1960).
Gräsbeck, R. *Acta med. Scand. suppl.* **314,** 1 (1956).
Gurin, S. *Proc. Soc. Exp. Biol. Med.* **49,** 48 (1942).
Gurin, S., Bachman, C. and Wilson, D. W. *J. Biol. Chem.* **133,** 467 (1940).
Heimer, R. and Meyer, K. *Proc. Nat. Acad. Sciences* **42,** 728 (1956).
Heremans, J. E., Heremans, M. T. H. and Schultze, H. E. *Clin. Chim. Acta* **4,** 96 (1959).
Holmberg, C. G. and Laurell, C. B. *Acta Chem. Scand.* **2,** 550 (1948).
Holmberg, C. G. and Laurell, C. B. *Acta Chem. Scand.* **5,** 476 (1951).
Hughes, W. L. *The Proteins* IIB, 663. Academic Press, New York (1954).
Jayle, M. F. *Compt. rend. Acad. Sci.* **211,** 574 (1940).
Jayle, M. F. and Boussier, G. *La Presse médicale* **62,** 1752 (1954).
Jayle, M. F. and Boussier, G. *Exp. ann. Biochim. med.* **17,** 157 (1955).
Jirka, M. and Kotas, J. *Clin. Chim. acta* **2,** 292 (1957).
Katzka, I. *Gastroenterology* **36,** 593 (1959).
Kekwick, R. A. and Record, B. R. *Brit. J. Exp. Path.* **22,** 29 (1941).
King, J. S., Fielden, M. L. and Boyce, W. H. *Arch. Biochem. Biophys.* **90,** 12 (1960).
Klenk, E. and Faillard, H. *Z. Physiol. Chem.* **298,** 230 (1954).
Klenk, E. and Faillard, H. *Deut. Zeit. f. Verd. u. Stoffwechsel.* **17,** 51 (1957).
Klenk, E., Faillard, H. and Lempfrid, H. *Z. Physiol. Chem.* **301,** 235 (1955).
Klenk, E. and Lauenstein, K. *Z. Physiol. Chem.* **291,** 147 (1952).
Klenk, E. and Lempfrid, H. *Z. Physiol. Chem.* **307,** 278 (1957).
Klenk, E. and Uhlenbruck, G. *Z. Physiol. Chem.* **307,** 266 (1957).
Kinersly, T. *Yale J. Biol. Med.* **26,** 211 (1953–4).
Kinersly, T. and Leite, H. B. *Yale J. Biol. Med.* **29,** 496 (1956–7).
Korn, E. D. *Methods of Biochem. Analysis* **7,** 145 (1959).
Korngold, L. and van Leeuwen, G. *J. Exp. Med.* **110,** 1 (1959).
Kowlessar, G. D. and McEvoy, R. K. *J. Clin. Invest.* **35,** 1325 (1956).
Laki, K., Kominz, D. R., Symonds, P., Lorand, L. and Seegers, W. H. *Arch. Biochem. Biophys.* **49,** 276 (1954).
Laurell, C. B., Laurell, H. and Waldenström, J. *Amer. J. Med.* **22,** 24 (1957).
Lawrence, S. H., Weimer, H. E. and Salkin, D. *Clin. Chim. Acta* **4,** 374 (1959).
Li, C. H. *Vitamins and Hormones* VII, 223 (1949).
Li, C. H., Evans, H. M. and Wonder, D. H. *J. Gen. Physiol.* **23,** 733 (1940).
Mack, M. H., Wolf, S. and Stern, K. G. *J. Clin. Invest.* **32,** 862 (1953).
Markowitz, H., Gubler, C. G., Mahoney, J. P., Cartwright, G. E. and Wintrobe, M. M. *J. Clin. Invest.* **34,** 1498 (1955).
Mårtensson, E., Raal, A. and Svennerholm, L. *Biochim. Biophys. Acta* **30,** 124 (1958).
McArdle, B. *Quart. J. Med.* **33,** 107 (1940).
McCrea, J. F. *Biochem. J.* **55,** 132 (1953).
Mörner, *Zeit. f. Physiol.* **7,** 581 (1893).
Müller-Eberhard, H. J. and Kunkel, H. G. *J. Exp. Med.* **104,** 253 (1956).
Müller-Eberhard, H. J. and Kunkel, H. G. *Clin. Chim. Acta* **4,** 252 (1959).
Müller-Eberhard, H. J., Kunkel, H. G. and Franklin, E. C. *Proc. Soc. Exp. Biol. Med.* **93,** 146 (1956).
Nikkila, E. A. *Scand. J. Clin. Lab. Invest.* **5,** Supp. 8 (1953).
Nilsson, I. *Biochem. Z.* **291,** 254 (1937).
Nyman, M. *Scand. J. Clin. Lab. Invest.* **11,** Supp. 39 (1959).

Odin, L. *Nature* **170,** 663 (1952).
Odin, L. *Acta Chem. Scand.* **9,** 714 (1955a).
Odin, L. *Acta Chem. Scand.* **9,** 1235 (1955b).
Odin, L. and Werner, I. *Acta Soc. Med. Upsal.* **57,** 227 (1952).
Owen, J. A., Got, C. and Silberman, H. J. *Clin. Chim. Acta* **3,** 605 (1958).
Pappenheimer, A. M., Lundgren, H. P. and Williams, J. W. *J. Exp. Med.* **71,** 247 (1940).
Pedersen, K. O. *Ultra-centrifuge Studies on Serum and Serum Fractions.* Almqvuist and Wiksells, Uppsala (1945).
Pigman, N., Hawkins, W. L., Blair, M. G. and Holley, H. L. *Arth. and Rheum.* **1,** 151 (1958).
Popenoe, E. A. *J. Biol. Chem.* **217,** 61 (1955).
Popenoe, E. A. and Drew, R. M. *J. Biol. Chem.* **228,** 673 (1957).
Putman, F. W. *Arch. Biochem. Biophys.* **79,** 67 (1959).
Pye, J. *Aust. J. Exp. Biol. Med. Sci.* **33,** 323 (1955).
Richmond, V. and Caputto, R. *Amer. J. Physiol.* **179,** 664 (1954).
Richmond, V., Caputto, R. and Wolf, S. *Gastroenterology* **29,** 1017 (1955).
Rimington, C. *Biochem. J.* **25,** 1062 (1931).
Rimington, C. and Rowlands, I. W. *Biochem. J.* **38,** 54 (1944).
Roboz, E., Murphy, J. B., Hess, W. C. and Forster, F. M. *Proc. Soc. Exp. Biol. Med.* **89,** 691 (1955).
Rosenberg, C. and Schloss, B. *Amer. Heart J.* **38,** 872 (1949).
Rose, H. M. *Fed. Proc.* **9,** 390 (1950).
Ross, J. and Böhm, P. *Klin. Wochs.* **35,** 351 (1957).
Ross, V., Miller, E. G., Moore, D. H. and Sikorski, H. *Proc. Soc. Exp. Biol. Med.* **54,** 179 (1943).
Ross, V., Moore, D. H. and Miller, E. G. *J. Biol. Chem.* **144,** 667 (1942).
Rose, H. M., Ragan, C., Pearce, E. and Lipman, M. D. *Proc. Soc. Exp. Biol. Med.* **68,** 1 (1949).
Schneider, W., Nowakowski, H. and Voigt, K. D. *Klin. Wochs.* **32,** 863 (1954).
Schmid, K. *J. Amer. Chem. Soc.* **72,** 2816 (1950).
Schmid, K. *J. Amer. Chem. Soc.* **75,** 60 (1953).
Schmid, K., *Fed. Proc.* **13,** 291 (1954).
Schmid, K. *Biochim. Biophys. Acta* **21,** 399 (1956).
van der Scheer, J. and Wyckoff, R. W. G. *Proc. Soc. Exp. Biol. Med.* **43,** 427 (1940).
Schultze, H. E. *Scand. J. Clin. Lab. Inv.* **10,** 135 (1958).
Schultze, H. E. and Schwick, B. *Clin. Chim. Acta* **4,** 15 (1959).
Scott-Blair, G. W., Folley, S. J., Malpress, F. H. and Coppen, F. M. V. *Biochem. J.* **35,** 1039 (1941).
Seegers, W. H., McClaughry, R. I. and Fahey, J. L. *Blood,* **5,** 421 (1950).
Seibert, F. B. and Atno, J. *J. Biol. Chem.* **163,** 511 (1946).
Seibert, F. B., Pfaff, M. L. and Seibert, M. V. *Arch. Biochem.* **18,** 279 (1948).
Shelley, W. B. and Hurley, H. J. *J. Invest. Dermatol.* **20,** 285 (1953).
Shetlar, M. R., Hellbaum, A. A., Devore, J. K., Bullock, J. A., Schmidt, H. L. and Lincoln, R. B. *J. Lab. Clin. Med.* **39,** 372 (1952).
Shetlar, M. R., Foster, J. V., Kelly, K. H., Shetlar, C. L., Bryan, R. S. and Everett, M. R. *Canc. Res.* **9,** 515 (1949).
Shettles, L. B., Dische, Z. and Osnos, M. *J. Biol. Chem.* **192,** 589 (1951).
Smith, E. L., Brown, D. M., McFadden, M. L., Buettner-Janusch, V. and Jager, B. V. *J. Biol. Chem.* **216,** 601 (1955).
Smith, E. L., Brown, D. M., Weimer, H. E. and Winzler, R. J. *J. Biol. Chem.* **185,** 569 (1950).

Spak, I. *Scand. J. Clin. Lab. Invest.* **10**, 34 (1958).
Spencer, B., Sunseri, L. Z. and Sunseri, S. G. *Clin. Chim. Acta* **2**, 485 (1957).
Spiro, R. G. *Fed. Proc.* **18**, 328 (1959).
Sonnet, J., Louis, L. and Heremans, J., *Acta Haemat.* **14**, 193 (1955).
Squire, J. R. *Adv. Int. Med. VII*, 201 (1955).
Stary, Z., Bursa, F., Kaleöglu, O. and Bilen, M. *Bull. Fac. Med. d'Istanbul* **13**, 243 (1950).
Stenhagen, E. *Biochem. J.* **32**, 714 (1938).
Stulberg, C. S., Schapira, R., Robinson, A. R., Basinski, D. H. and Freund, H. A. *Proc. Soc. Exp. Biol. Med.* **76**, 704 (1951).
Surgenor, D. M. and Ellis, D. *J. Amer. Chem. Soc.* **76**, 6049 (1954).
Svennerholm, L., *Biochim. Biophys. Acta* **24**, 604 (1957).
Svennerholm, L. *Acta Chem. Scand.* **12**, 547 (1958).
Szára, St. and Bagdy, D. *Biochim. Biophys. Acta* **11**, 313 (1953).
Taipale, E. and Hokkanen, E. *Acta Med. Scand.* **155**, 113 (1956).
Tamm, I. and Horsfall, F. L. *Proc. Soc. Exp. Biol. Med.* **74**, 108 (1950).
Tamm, I. and Horsfall, F. J. *J. Exp. Med.* **95**, 71 (1952).
Tiselius, A. *Biochem. J.* **31**, 1464 (1937).
Tiselius, A. and Kabat, E. A. *J. Exp. Med.* **69**, 119 (1939).
Trosier, Polonovski, Jayle and Brissaud, *Bull. Acad. Med.* **123**, 239 (1940).
Uzman, L. L., Bering, E. A. and Morris, C. E. *J. Clin. Invest.* **38**, 1756 (1959).
Uzman, L. L. and Rumley, M. K. *Proc. Soc. Exp. Biol. Med.* **93**, 497 (1956).
Verschure, J. C. M. *Clin. Chim. Acta* **4**, 38 (1959).
Viergiver, E. and Pommerenke, W. *Am. J. Obstet. Gynecol.* **54**, 459 (1947).
Warfringe, L. E. *Acta Med. Scand.* **153**, 49 (1955).
Warren, L. *J. Clin. Invest.* **38**, 755 (1959).
Weimer, H. E., Mehl, J. W. and Winzler, R. J. *J. Biol. Chem.* **185**, 561 (1950).
Weimer, H. E., Redlich-Moshin, J., Salkin, D. and Boak, R. A. *Proc. Soc. Exp. Med. Biol.* **87**, 102 (1954).
Weimer, H. E. and Winzler, R. J. *J. Biol. Chem.* **90**, 458 (1955).
Werner, I. *Acta Soc. Med. Upsal.* **58**, 1 (1953).
Werner, I. and Odin, L. *Acta Soc. Med. Upsal.* **57**, 230 (1952).
Wescoe, W. C., Hunt, C. C., Riker, W. F. and Litt, I. C. *Amer. J. Physiol.* **149**, 549 (1947).
West, R. and Clarke, D. H. *J. Clin. Invest.* **17**, 173 (1938).
White, J. C., Elmes, P. C. and Whitley, W. *Nature* **183**, 1810 (1959).
Winzler, R. J., Devor, A. W., Mehl, J. W. and Smyth, I. M. *J. Clin. Invest.* **27**, 609 (1948).
Yamashina, I. *Acta Chem. Scand.* **10**, 1666 (1956).
Zipkin, I., Adamik, E. R. and Saroff, H. A. *Proc. Soc. Exp. Biol. Med.* **95**, 69 (1957).

Chapter 9

LIPOCARBOHYDRATES

Introduction

INCREASING interest in the last decade in a group of human disorders of the lipidosis group has focused attention on a series of lipocarbohydrates of which the most notable are the gangliosides and cerebrosides. Starting from sphingomyelin which contains a fatty acid, sphingosine [CH_3 . $(CH_2)_{12}$. $CH = CH$. $CH(OH)$. $CH(NH_2)$. CH_2OH], phosphate and choline [$HOCH_2$ $CH_2N(CH_3)_3{}^+$. OH^-] the metabolic chain appears to lead first to cerebrosides, which contain a fatty acid, sphingosine and a hexose, and thereafter to the gangliosides which contain a fatty acid, sphingosine, hexoses, hexosamine and neuraminic acid. It is probable that in the different types of lipidoses, different enzymes may be lacking or malfunctioning, so causing the chain reaction to be interrupted at different stages and intermediate products to accumulate. The determination of the precise structure of these lipocarbohydrates therefore becomes of the utmost importance. It is generally considered that the myelin sheath in brain contains cerebrosides together with sphingomyelin, cholesterol, proteolipid and plasmalogens, while the axis cell and nerve cell contains ganglioside together with lecithin, cephalin and a trace of cholesterol (Cumings, 1959).

Cerebrosides—Cerasine

Isolation of cerasine (Rosenheim 1913, 1914).

Macerated brain was successively extracted with acetone and petroleum ether. Treatment of the dried residue with pyridine at 45–50° gives an extract which, on concentration and addition of acetone (3 vol), yields crude cerebrosides. After further purification by Soxhlet extraction with ether and removal of phosphorus containing impurities, fractional crystallization from acetone affords first phrenosine (at 37°) and later cerasine (at 0°). Further purification of both these cerebrosides can be accomplished by solution in chloroform and re-precipitation with acetic acid followed by recrystallization from acetone containing 50% pyridine (for phrenosine) and a large amount of 90% acetone containing 2% pyridine (for cerasine).

Structural determination

Hydrolysis of cerasine in methanol containing 10% sulphuric acid yields mainly the methyl ester of lignoceric acid (tetracosanic acid),

181

$CH_3(CH_2)_{22}COOH$, methyl sphingosine and methyl galactoside. On cooling in a refrigerator the methyl ester of lignoceric acid precipitates and can be washed with ice-cold methanol (Klenk, 1926b, 1927). The galactose has been shown to have the D-configuration (Brown and Morris, 1890) and to be present in the pyranose form (Pryde and Humphreys, 1924, 1926). The structure assigned to cerasine (Fig. 9·1) awaits rigid chemical proof since some of it is based on analogy with other galactose containing cerebrosides.

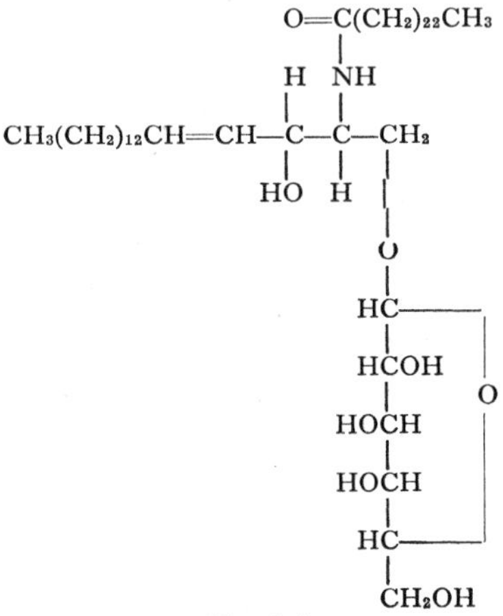

$$O{=}C(CH_2)_{22}CH_3$$

$$\begin{array}{c} H \quad NH \\ | \quad | \\ CH_3(CH_2)_{12}CH{=}CH-C-C-CH_2 \\ | \quad | \\ HO \quad H \end{array}$$

$$\begin{array}{c} O \\ | \\ HC\underline{\quad\quad} \\ | \\ HCOH \quad\quad O \\ | \\ HOCH \\ | \\ HOCH \\ | \\ HC\underline{\quad\quad} \\ | \\ CH_2OH \end{array}$$

Fig. 9.1

Phrenosine

A simplified procedure for the isolation of phrenosine from beef spinal cord lipids has been described by Radin, Brown and Lavin (1956).

A commercial concentrate was extracted with ether and hot 95% alcohol and then processed chromatographically with Florisil to remove phospholipids. After treatment with mixed ion exchange resins a cerebroside fraction was obtained assaying at 88% purity. For crystallization of phrenosine, the cerebroside fraction (1 g) was dissolved in boiling methanol (50 ml). Celite (2 g) was added and the suspension reheated to boiling point. Barium hydroxide octahydrate (0·77 g) in boiling methanol (40 ml) was added and the whole filtered rapidly. The precipitate was treated with 0·1N–HCl to regenerate the cerebroside and recrystallized by dissolving in warm methanol–chloroform (1:1) and cooling slowly. The monohydrate of phrenosine was obtained (C, 68·4%; H, 11·0%; galactose, 20·7%).

Phrenosine has been isolated from human cerebral tissue (Chatagnon and Chatagnon, 1955).

Structural determination

Treatment with methanol containing 10% sulphuric acid yields the methyl ester of cerebronic acid (α-hydroxylignoceric acid), methyl sphingosine and methyl galactoside. Partial acid hydrolysis yields *inter alia* psychosine. Hydrolysis with barium hydroxide likewise yields this sugar-sphingosine complex (Klenk, 1926a). Psychosine is non-reducing indicating that the galactose is bound glycosidically. The amino-group in the sphingosine is free since psychosine reacts with nitrous acid. Klenk and Härle (1928) methylated dihydropsychosine and among the acid hydrolysis products detected a monomethoxydihydrosphingosine confirming that a true glycosidic linkage was present. Deuel (1951) has suggested the formula in Fig. 9.2 for phrenosine.

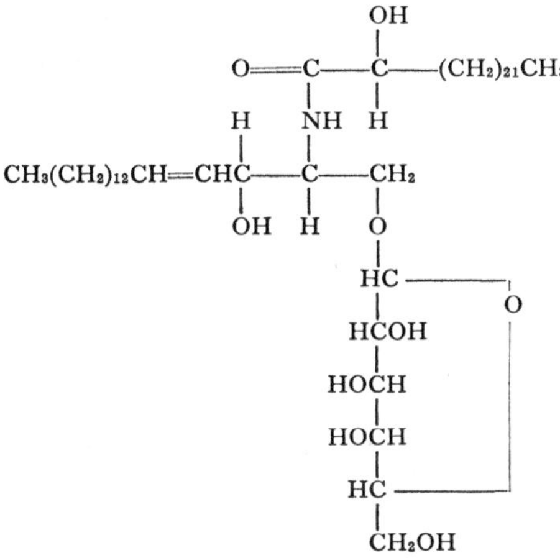

$$
\begin{array}{l}
\overset{\displaystyle OH}{|} \\[2pt]
O\!=\!\!=\!C\!-\!\!-\!C\!-\!\!-(CH_2)_{21}CH_3 \\[2pt]
\underset{\displaystyle H}{|}\ \ \underset{\displaystyle NH}{|}\ \ \underset{\displaystyle H}{|} \\[2pt]
CH_3(CH_2)_{12}CH\!=\!CH\overset{}{C}\!-\!\!-\!\overset{}{C}\!-\!\!-CH_2 \\[2pt]
\underset{\displaystyle OH}{|}\ \ \underset{\displaystyle H}{|}\ \ \underset{\displaystyle O}{|}
\end{array}
$$

HC ——
| ⌐ O
HCOH
|
HOCH
|
HOCH
|
HC ——┘
|
CH₂OH

Fig. 9.2

Further support for this structure comes from the isolation of cerebronyl-N-sphingosine after treatment with acetic acid–10% sulphuric acid. This ceramide on further hydrolysis yields equimolar quantities of cerebronic acid and sphingosine. Since it is neutral in its reactions the two components are joined via a —NH—CO— bond resulting from the amino group of the sphingosine and carboxyl group of the fatty acid (Klenk, 1926a).

Nakayama (1950) has produced evidence that the galactose residue in phrenosine is attached to the terminal carbon atom of sphingosine. This has been confirmed by Carter and Greenwood (1952) in the following manner. When triacetylsphingosine and 3-O-methyl sphingosine are reduced with a platinum catalyst they undergo hydrogenolysis of the allylic carbon–oxygen bond in the 3-position yielding acetic acid or methanol respectively and a derivative of sphingosine. Hence by analogy hydrogenolysis of acetylated cerebrosides substituted at C-3 by galactose should yield free galactose and sphingosine derivatives whereas cerebrosides substituted by galactose at the terminal carbon atom would yield acetic acid and galactosidosphingosine. Catalytic reduction of hexacetylphrenosine yielded acetic acid, but no reducing sugar confirming that galactose is attached to the terminal carbon atom of sphingosine. The β-configuration has been assigned to the galactosyl residues present in cerebrosides since these can be hydrolysed by β-galactosidase but not by α-galactosidase (Fujino and Negishi, 1956).

Detailed examination of the structure of sphingosine has established that the double bond has the *trans* configuration (Mislow, 1953; Fodor and Kiss, 1952) and that the amino carbon atom has the D-configuration (Carter and Humiston, 1951; Kiss, Fodor and Banfi, 1954). Sphingosine, which has been isolated by hydrolysis of cerebrosides in anhydrous acidic methanol, has the *erythro* configuration (Kiss, Fodor and Banfi, 1954; Carter, Shapiro and Harrison, 1953) at the second and third carbon atoms. Hence sphingosine is D_S-*erythro*-1,3-dihydroxy-2-amino-4-*trans*-octadecene. However, the actual configuration (*erythro* or *threo*) of the sphingosine in the cerebroside still remained a problem. Thus from aqueous methanolic hydrolysates of cerebrosides, Seydel (1941) obtained two different bases which were subsequently shown to be *threo*- and *erythro*-sphingosine (Grob and Jenny, 1952). The reason for these differing products under various hydrolysis conditions appears to be that with simple N-acyl derivatives of 1:2-amino alcohols acid hydrolysis results in an N → O shift of the acyl group and that this shift can occur either with retention or with inversion of configuration of the hydroxyl carbon atom (Welsh, 1949). Carter and Fujino (1956) prepared, as a model substance, phrenosine from spinal cord using a modification of the procedure of Klenk and Leupold (1944). The best procedure to elucidate the stereochemistry of the second and third carbon atoms in sphingosine was found to be as follows: Alkaline hydrolysis of phrenosine yielded psychosine (galactosidosphingosine) in good yield. Catalytic reduction of psychosine yielded dihydropsychosine which could be hydrolysed with 1·6N-ethanolic hydrochloric acid (prepared by adding conc. HCl to ethanol) without inversion of the third carbon. A high yield of *erythro*dihydrosphingosine was obtained—none of the *threo* isomer could be detected in the hydrolysate. Hence sphingosine, as it exists in the phrenosine molecule, has the *erythro* configuration.

Nervone

This cerebroside has been isolated by Klenk (1925) from human brains.

The dried tissue was extracted with petroleum ether, the extract concentrated and the precipitated protagon removed. Five volumes of alcohol were added to the pet. ether filtrate, the precipitate discarded and the pet. ether removed by evaporation *in vacuo*. Addition of a hot saturated alcoholic ammoniacal lead acetate solution and cooling gave a lead precipitate which was decomposed by passage of hydrogen sulphide into a hot alcoholic solution. After removal of lead sulphide the crude nervone separated on cooling to 0° overnight. After further purification, involving washing with acidified acetone and precipitation from a methanol solution with cadmium acetate, the nervone was finally obtained pure by fractional crystallization from chloroform–methanol (1:2). It had m.p. 180°, $[\alpha]_D^{16} = -4\cdot33°$ in pyridine.

The components of nervone have been identified as nervonic acid, sphingosine and galactose and hence its formula is as shown in Fig. 9.3.

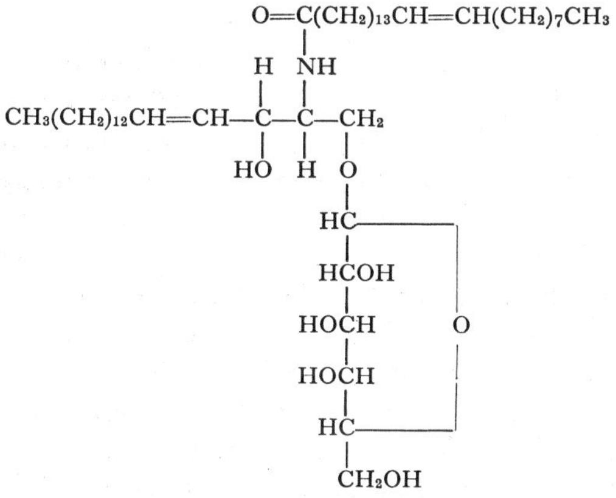

$$O{=}C(CH_2)_{13}CH{=}CH(CH_2)_7CH_3$$

$$CH_3(CH_2)_{12}CH{=}CH{-}\underset{\underset{HO}{|}}{\overset{\overset{H}{|}}{C}}{-}\underset{\underset{H}{|}}{\overset{\overset{NH}{|}}{C}}{-}\underset{\underset{O}{|}}{\overset{}{C}}H_2$$

HC————
|
HCOH |
|
HOCH   O
|
HOCH |
|
HC————
|
CH$_2$OH

Fig. 9.3

Oxynervone

This is another galactocerebroside in which the components are galactose, sphingosine and α-hydroxynervonic acid ($CH_3(CH_2)_7CH{=}CH$. $(CH_2)_{12}$. CHOH . COOH) (Klenk, 1928).

Normal Human Brain Cerebrosides

A comprehensive study of the cerebroside content of normal young developing brains has been made by Cumings, Goodwin, Woodward and Curzon (1957–8). Little difference was noted in the cerebroside content of the cortex and white matter until the infant was a few months old. Thereafter a much larger quantity of cerebrosides was encountered in the cerebral white matter. Some of the results (in g/100 g fresh tissue) are quoted in Table 9.I.

This pattern agrees with earlier studies by Johnson, McNabb and Rossiter (1948) and Brante (1949). The rate of increase of cerebroside in the white matter runs parallel to the degree of myelination shown histologically.

Table 9.I. *Cerebroside content of normal brain*

Age	Full term	1 day	7 days	2 months	3 months	10 months	3 years	7 years
White matter	0·6	0·5	0·32	1·1	1·15	2·5	3·13	5·15
Cerebral cortex	0·5	0·6	0·37	0·9	0·48	0·48	1·03	0·67

Gaucher's Disease

This disease is regarded as a disturbance in the metabolism of the reticuloendothelial tissue. The RES cells of the liver, spleen, lymph nodes, bone marrow and other organs become infiltrated with cerebrosides. Generally the nervous tissue is involved only in the acute infantile form. Many workers have isolated the cerebrosides stored in the spleen. In most cases a glucocerebroside is found (Klenk and Rennkamp, 1940, 1942; Danielson, Hall and Everett, 1942), but in rare instances a galacto-cerebroside is encountered (Lieb and Günther, 1941). The normal galactocerebrosides predominate in the brain (Klenk and Rennkamp, 1940).

Rosenberg and Chargaff (1958) have carried out an extensive study of a crystalline cerebroside isolated from the spleen of a patient with Gaucher's disease. This cerebroside had m.p. 183–185°; $[\alpha]_D^{23} - 3·9°$ in chloroform–methanol (1:1 vol/vol). Its infrared spectra differed somewhat from phrenosine. Analysis showed C, 70·6; H, 11·6 and N, 1·72. Acid hydrolysis of the cerebroside and enzyme assay with glucose oxidase established that the only sugar present was D-glucose. Infrared spectra suggested the β-glucosyl configuration. The iodine value of the glucocerebroside was 29 (calculated for behenylglucocerebroside, 31). Examination of the methyl esters obtained after methanolysis (10% H_2SO_4 in anhydrous methanol) suggested that the fatty acid component was mainly behenic rather than lignoceric acid. The presence of sphingosine was established and hence the cerebroside was considered to be a behenylglucocerebroside.

Further elucidation of the structure of cerebrosides stored in the spleen during Gaucher's disease has been achieved by Marinetti, Ford and Stotz (1960). It was demonstrated that (i) the glucose was attached to the primary hydroxyl group of sphingosine (ii) the sphingosine moiety had the *trans* configuration and (iii) that in this case the major cerebrosides were lignoceryl, behenyl and palmityl derivatives, the stearyl and arachidyl derivatives were minor components. These fatty acid components were determined by gas chromatography and further characterized by paper chromatography. It should be recalled that Rosenberg and Chargaff (1958) in postulating a behenyl derivative in their cerebroside assumed this on the basis of elementary analysis and on the yield of mixed fatty acid esters.

Cerebroside Sulphate

Blix (1933) first noted the existence of a cerebroside sulphate in beef brain and reported that it contained cerebronic acid, sphingosine, galactose and sulphate.

Isolation. The acetone dried beef brain was extracted with 95% ethanol at 37° for 3 days (Thannhauser, Fellig and Schmidt, 1955), filtered and the precipitate washed with more ethanol and with ether. The dry solid was further Soxhlet extracted for 3 days with ether. The residue was refluxed with 90% acetone for 24 hr and the extract concentrated. The residue was dissolved in pyridine at 60° and cooled to 0° overnight. The precipitate was filtered off. Repetition of this crystallization procedure with one-half and one-fourth of the original volume of pyridine eliminated the remaining cerebrosides. The final precipitate was washed further with ether, dissolved in warm pyridine and chromatographed on alumina (Alcoa F-20). The cerebroside sulphate was mainly absorbed on the alumina. It was freed from the remaining cerebroside by Soxhlet extraction with chloroform–methanol (2:1) and finally recovered by extraction with boiling 90% acetone. The concentrated extract was recrystallized from 5 volumes of hot chloroform–methanol (2:1).

Structure

The cerebroside sulphate ($C_{48}H_{92}O_{12}NS$) had C, 62·22; H, 10·86 and S, 3·25%. It was methylated using methyl iodide/silver oxide in chloroform–methanol (3:1) to yield a methyl ether $C_{53}H_{102}O_{12}NS$ having C, 61·2; H, 10·09 and OCH₃, 15·33%. This was treated with 8% methanolic hydrogen chloride at 100° for 6 hr and then cooled. The methyl esters of the fatty acids were removed and the residue made alkaline to precipitate the sphingosine. Further fractionation of the residue yielded mainly 2:3:4-tri-O-methyl D-galactose. Hence the sulphate group in cerebroside sulphate was on C_6 of the galactose moiety and the structure of cerebroside sulphate was as shown in Fig. 9·4.

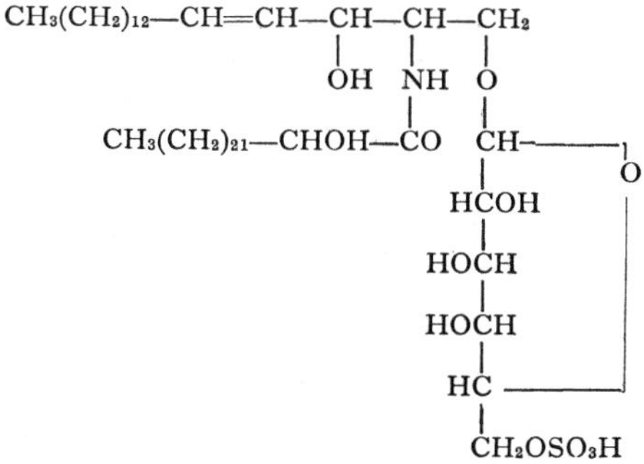

$$CH_3(CH_2)_{12}-CH{=}CH-CH-CH-CH_2$$

$$\begin{array}{ccc} & | & | & | \\ & OH & NH & O \end{array}$$

$$CH_3(CH_2)_{21}-CHOH-CO \quad CH-$$

$$HCOH$$

$$HOCH$$

$$HOCH$$

$$HC$$

$$CH_2OSO_3H$$

Fig. 9.4

Confirmation of the presence of cerebronic acid was obtained (Thann-hauser, Fellig and Schmidt, 1955). No anticoagulant activity was exhibited by cerebroside sulphate.

Metachromatic Leucodystrophy

Late infantile metachromatic leucodystrophy has been classified as a generalized lipidosis because of the accumulation of lipid metachromatic substances in various organs (Austin, 1958; Hagberg, Sourander, Sven-nerholm and Voss, 1959; Jatzkewitz, 1958). These were identified as sulphatides, the sulphuric acid esters of cerebrosides. The accumulation of sulphatides in the brain gives rise to disorder of myelin formation with accompanying mental and neurological disturbances. Increased excretions of sulphatides in the urine and bile together with cholecystopathia and metachromatic granular bodies in the urinary sediment are other clinical manifestations (Hagberg and Svennerholm, 1960). The concentration of total proteins in the cerebrospinal fluid was markedly increased but the relative distribution remains normal.

To detect the sulphatides in the urinary sediment the latter was ex-tracted with chloroform–methanol (2:1 vol/vol). After dialysis the lipid extract was chromatographed on paper using a tetrahydrofuran-di*iso*-butylketone-water 45:5:5 (vol/vol) mixture as the irrigating solvent. The sulphatides were detected with cresyl violet and Rhodamine B. The same chromatographic technique could be applied to brain lipid extracts (Hag-berg and Svennerholm, 1960).

Norman, Urich and Tingey (1960) have confirmed the accumulation of sulphatides in two cases and reported sulphatide contents (g/100 g dry tissue) of 3·68 and 3·62 respectively in the kidney compared with 1·42 in a normal adult kidney. In the white matter the figures were 9·57 and 9·90 respectively compared with normal figures of 2·07–3·74. Neutral cerebroside was considerably reduced from normal.

It is interesting to note that Jatzkewitz (1958) in his characterization of the storage substance in this type of lipidosis actually encountered two compounds. One was a cerebroside sulphate containing fatty acids, sphingosine, galactose and sulphate, the other contained phosphate as well as these constituents. The two components had different R_F values on paper chromatograms.

Human Dihydrocerebroside

Okuhara and Yasuda (1960) have detected a new dihydrocerebroside in human brain which has an iodine number of zero. The ether extract of acetone-dried minced brain was extensively fractionated to yield 3·5 g of fine white crystals (m.p. 196–8°; $[\alpha]_D^{23} + 10°$ in pyridine) from 90 kg of human brain. Calc. for $C_{48}H_{95}O_9N$: C, 69·44; H, 11·53; N, 1·68%. Found: C, 69·11; H, 11·35; N, 1·66%. When examined in the usual way the components of the glycolipid were characterized as hydroxylignoceric acid, galactose and dihydrosphingosine. This is the first time dihydrosphingosine has been isolated from human brain although it has been previously found in other tissues.

Cytosides

Intermediate between the cerebrosides and gangliosides there exists a family of substances containing two monosaccharide residues. Rapport, Graf and Alonzo (1959) have coined the term 'cytoside' for this class of compounds composed of ceramide (fatty acid amide of sphingosine) linked to two monosaccharides. A compound of this type was reported to occur in ox spleen (Klenk and Rennkamp, 1942). Rapport, Graf, Skipski and Alonzo (1959) isolated cytolipin H from human epidermoid carcinoma (H. Ep. 3) grown in conditioned rats. This was a water-soluble substance containing equimolar proportions of fatty acid, sphingosine, glucose and galactose. Cytolipin H is a hapten, i.e. it reacts with antibodies provoked by repeated injection into rabbits of cell fractions or homogenates of foreign tissue. Rapport, Graf and Alonzo (1960) have compared human cytolipin H with preparations of similar composition isolated from ox spleen. The essential steps in isolation were preparation of the crude lipid extract, removal of water soluble substances, fractionation on silicic acid, fractionation on Florisil and recrystallization from pyridine-acetone. Only 50 mg of pure ox spleen cytoside was obtained from 10 kg of tissue. Chemical analysis of human tumor cytolipid ($[\alpha]_D - 10·8°$) revealed 36·8% hexose (of which 49·7% was glucose and the rest galactose), an iodine number of 32·0 and N, 1·38%. Ox spleen cytolipid ($[\alpha]_D - 7·3°$) contained 34·0% hexose (of which 48·9% was glucose and the rest galactose), an iodine number of 22·6 and N, 1·36%. More than one double bond per mole of cytoside is indicated by the iodine number of human cytolipin H. The ox spleen cytoside is more saturated and the lipid base may in part be dihydrosphingosine. Both ox spleen cytoside and human tumour cytoside were serologically identical in the complement fixation test with specific antibody. The differences are therefore probably in the fatty acid residues rather than in the carbohydrate portion.

Gangliosides and Related Mucolipids: Introduction

Much confusion exists in the literature as to what is meant by the term ganglioside. Landsteiner and Levene (1925, 1926) first described a water-soluble glycolipid fraction resembling the cerebrosides but exhibiting a purple colour when heated with Bial's reagent. Compounds resembling this material were later reported in spleen (Walz, 1927), normal brain (Blix, 1938), and in the brain of cases of Niemann–Pick disease (Klenk, 1935) and Tay–Sachs disease (Klenk, 1939–40). Confusion arose because the material present in these cases of lipidoses was termed ganglioside (Klenk, 1942) and this same name was used to describe the material present in normal brain. Another entity obtained from ox brain was called strandin (Folch, Arsove and Meath, 1951; Folch, Meath and Bogoch, 1956). In the ensuing discussion the author's own terms have been used to describe the glycolipides—it is obvious however, that many of these are synonomous.

Isolation

A typical fractionation of the brain lipids can be accomplished as shown in the flow sheet (Fig. 9.5) and is based mainly on the work of Folch, Ascoli, Lees, Meath and Le Baron (1951) and Radin, Brown and Lavin (1956).

It will be seen that in the dialysis-partition process the gangliosides, together with possibly strandin, strandin peptide and brain diphosphoinositide partition into the water phase. Such a partition is generally an

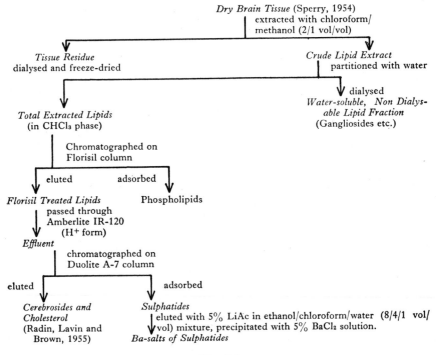

Fig. 9.5

essential step in any isolation of gangliosides. No significant amounts of cholesterol, phosphatides or cerebrosides partition into the water phase (Radin, Martin and Brown, 1957).

Ox Brain Ganglioside

An electrophoretically homogeneous ganglioside has been isolated by Bogoch (1958) from ox cerebral hemispheres. These were freed from meninges and blood vessels and thereafter the hemispheres were extracted with hot methanol. After precipitation in the cold and partition between the two phases formed by chloroform–methanol (2:1, vol/vol) and water (12·2% by volume) crude ganglioside was recovered from the upper phase by solvent removal and dialysis. The yield at this stage was 2 g/kg of fresh cerebral hemispheres. After repeated treatment in chloroform–methanol (2:1 vol/vol) and water (6·6% by volume) the ash content was reduced by repeated acidification and dialysis in the cold. The pure ganglioside contained N, 2·9%; hexose 24% (as galactose); neuraminic acid, 30·3%; free amine N, 0·5% and was free of phospholipids (P, 0·07%). The final yield of the pure material was 1 g/kg.

Structure

The structure of ox brain ganglioside shown in Fig. 9.6 is based on the evidence provided by a stepwise hydrolysis of brain ganglioside (Bogoch, 1958).

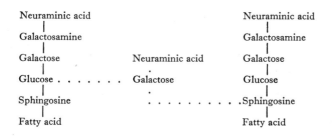

Fig. 9.6

Autohydrolysis of the ganglioside at 100° for 18 min followed by dialysis yielded dialysable material (20·8%) consisting mainly (88·0%) of neuraminic acid. Since the dialysate contained 2·5% of bound galactosamine only liberated after further hydrolysis, Bogoch (1958) concluded that the neuraminic acid was bound through its reducing group to an N-acetyl galactosamine residue. Further hydrolysis (0·09N-HCl at 100° for 50 min) of the non-dialysable autohydrolysate residue liberated a further

14

18·5% of the neuraminic acid, 24·2% of the galactosamine and 15% of the hexose present originally in the ganglioside. Galactose was the only hexose detected. The second non-dialysable residue was then treated drastically with 6N-HCl at 100° for 5 min. The dialysate of this hydrolysate contained the balance of the recoverable neuraminic acid, galactosamine and galactose. Glucose was also present. The non-dialysable residue contained the sphingosine and fatty acid present in the original ganglioside and some 8% of its hexose. It was partitioned between chloroform–methanol (2:1 vol/vol) and water. The fraction recovered from the upper phase contained sphingosine attached to glucose. The order in which the constituents of the ganglioside were released was thus neuraminic acid, galactosamine, galactose, glucose, sphingosine and fatty acids. Further partial hydrolyses yielded a glucocerebroside ($[\alpha]_D^{20} - 2 \cdot 08°$) containing C, 67·13; H, 10·95; N, 1·86 and hexose, 21·8% agreeing well with that calculated for $C_{42}H_{81}O_8N$, H_2O. C, 67·65; H, 11·14; N, 1·88 and hexose, 22·0%. This glucocerebroside was not identical with phrenosine, kerasine or nervone and was believed to be a glucostearocerebroside.

Bogoch (1960) repeatedly injected bovine brain ganglioside (0·5 mg) into rabbits intraveneously and found that it gave rise to specific antibodies. From quantitative precipitin tests between ganglioside and anti-serum it was found that the peak of the precipitation curve was quite sharp. About 50 per cent of the added ganglioside precipitated in the zone of antibody excess. With increasing amounts of ganglioside the precipitates in the zone of antigen-excess contained decreasing amounts of antibody and increasing amounts of ganglioside. With such antisera using the fluorescent antibody technique (Coons and Kaplan, 1950) it was possible to demonstrate the nerve cell body localization of brain ganglioside in bovine brain. Such a method should be applicable to the histological localization of any normal or abnormal brain constituent to which antisera can be prepared.

Biological activity

Ox brain ganglioside is an inhibitor of the haemagglutination reaction of influenza virus (Bogoch, 1957) and will also inhibit in low concentrations the neurotoxic effect in mouse brain of influenza PR 8 and NWS viruses (Bogoch and Bogoch, 1959). In concentrations as low as 0·06 μg/cm³ the brain ganglioside caused a definite increase in the amplitude of contraction (12·30%) of the heart of a clam (*Venus mercenaria*). At doses greater than 0·4 μg/c.c. an increase in amplitude of contraction was accompanied by an increase in rate as well. These and other effects at higher concentrations prompted Bogoch and Bogoch (1959) to suggest the possibility that brain ganglioside might play a part in transmission phenomena in the central nervous system.

Ox Brain Mucolipide

Rosenberg, Howe and Chargaff (1956) distinguished two kinds of complex glycolipids in ox brain. One of these he has termed brain mucolipide and the other is ganglioside. While the former exhibited a strong inhibiting action on the agglutination of chicken erythrocytes by influenza virus (PR 8) the ganglioside preparation was completely inactive. To isolate the mucolipid, portions of freshly obtained grey matter were treated with 10 parts (vol/wt) of chloroform–methanol (2:1 vol/vol) in a high speed mincer for 2 min. After dialysis against distilled water for 3 days the aqueous phase inside the dialysis sack was concentrated *in vacuo* at 30°, repeatedly dialysed, centrifuged and finally freeze-dried (yield 0·3% of starting material).

The mucolipide contained N, 3·9%; P, 0·7%; galactose, 23%; galactosamine, 4·5% and 20% of a compound (probably neuraminic acid) giving a direct Ehrlich reaction, i.e. a colour reaction with *p*-dimethylaminobenzaldehyde without previous treatment with alkali. Other components of the mucolipid included a fatty-acid fraction and a number of amino acids constituting a polypeptide moiety. After incubation with influenza virus 24·5% of the 'direct chromogen' was split off in a dialysable form. *Vibrio cholerae* neuraminidase also removed 39% of the 'direct chromogen' from the mucolipid. The power of the mucolipid to inhibit virus haemagglutination was abolished by treatment with crystalline trypsin. The mucolipid was soluble in water, chloroform–methanol, moist benzene and methanol.

In a further report on ox brain mucolipide, Rosenberg and Chargaff (1956) obtained this material sedimenting with a single boundary in the ultracentrifuge ($S_{23°}$,w = 13s; $D_{4°}$, w = 3·8 . 10^{-7} cm^2/sec^{-1}) and migrating with single sharp ascending and descending boundaries in a Tiselius apparatus ($\mu_{pH\ 5\cdot1}$ = 9·0 . 10^{-5} cm^2/volt^{-1}/sec^{-1}; $\mu_{pH\ 8\cdot6}$ = 11.10^{-5} cm^2/volt^{-1}/sec^{-1}). The further purification was effected by dissociation with calcium chloride in chloroform-methanol followed by repeated partition between chloroform/water with the aid of methanol. The pure material had $[\alpha]_D^{25}$ = −18° and exhibited ampholytic behaviour. Evidence was presented which strongly supported the author's contention that the glycolipid existed in chemical combination with a polypeptide present to the extent of 5%. Mild hydrolysis of the mucolipide yielded crystalline *N*-acetylneuraminic acid (d.p. 183–185°). Sphingosine was also established as a constituent of the mucolipide.

Rosenberg and Chargaff (1958) state that the ox brain mucolipide has a molecular weight of 180,000. The amino acids composing the peptide moiety were mainly glutamic acid, glycine, serine, and alanine together with smaller amounts of threonine, aspartic acid, phenylalanine, lysine, arginine, histidine, valine, cystine and proline (?). The composition of the pure mucolipide expressed as μ moles per mg mucolipide was fatty acid,

0·56; sphingosine, 0·55; hexose (galactose:glucose, 8:1), 1·3; *N*-acetyl-galactosamine, 0·20; sialic acid, 0·84; amino acid, 0·32. A considerable proportion of the fatty acids was *n*-tetracosanoic (lignoceric) acid.

In recent studies on the action of *Vibrio cholerae* sialidase (neuraminidase) on ox brain mucolipide, Rosenberg, Binnie and Chargaff (1960) report that the optimum pH for enzyme action is 6·6–6·9. Under varying conditions only 66–72% of the neuraminic acid present in the mucolipide was released.

Guinea-Pig Gangliosides

The subcellular distribution of gangliosides in guinea-pig cerebral cortex has been studied by Wolfe (1960). The subcellular fractions were prepared by differential centrifuging of 0·32M-sucrose homogenates and by subfractionating further in sucrose density gradients by the method of Whittaker (1959). It was found that all the gangliosides occurred in the particulate fractions if the microsomal fraction was separated at 10,000,000 g min. Up to 20% of the total gangliosides appeared in the supernatant fraction when the microsomes were separated at 3,000,000 g min.

Cattle Brain Strandin and Strandin Peptide

Folch, Arsove and Meath (1951) reported the presence in brain tissue of a substance of high molecular weight (< 250,000) which on drying from aqueous solution formed strands—hence the name strandin. It was extracted with chloroform–methanol (2:1) and was particularly abundant in grey matter. The constituents of strandin peptide included fatty acids, sphingosine, carbohydrate (20–21%) but apparently less than 1·5% neuraminic acid. Its nitrogen content was 2·6% and it was relatively free from phosphorus (< 0·2%) and sulphur (< 0·2%). When isolated from brain by the partition-dialysis method amino acids were also present. The claim that strandin was free from neuraminic acid was shown to be unfounded (Rosenberg, Howe and Chargaff, 1956; Rosenberg and Chargaff, 1956; Chatagnon and Chatagnon, 1954) and was later retracted (Folch, Meath and Bogoch, 1956). Strandin peptide is therefore probably mainly Chargaff's ox brain mucolipide (Rosenberg and Chargaff, 1958) and strandin itself is identical with Bogoch's ganglioside.

Extraction of strandin (Folch-pi and Lees, 1959). Homogenized grey matter or whole brain was extracted with five volumes of methanol at 60°. The hot filtrate was cooled to 4° overnight to precipitate the crude strandin. Purification was effected by extraction of the precipitate with chloroform–methanol–water and exhaustive dialysis. These last procedures had to be repeated three times with extracts from grey matter and up to five times with whole brain.

The strandin prepared by this method was essentially free of amino-acids (α-amino acid N, after hydrolysis; < 0·02%) and contains only small amounts of phosphatides (P, $<0.1\%$) and sulphatides (S, $<0.05\%$). It contained N, 2.9%; neutral sugars, 24%; galactosamine, 10.2%; sialic acid, $30-31\%$; and about 30% fatty acid(s) and sphingosine. Stepwise hydrolysis similar to that effected by Bogoch (1958) revealed that (1) sialic acid was attached through its reducing group (2) the ceramide moiety (fatty acid-sphingosine) was combined mainly, if not exclusively, with glucose and (3) glucose, galactose and galactosamine are combined with each other. Strandin peptide was isolated by Folch-pi and Lees (1959) from the first upper phase in the chloroform–methanol–water procedure and could be enriched by solution in four times its weight of water and dilution 50-fold with 9:1 methanol:chloroform vol/vol. The resulting clear solution deposits a precipitate strandin peptide on cooling to $-10°$ overnight. Such material contained as much as 18% combined amino acids. It had 5.5% N, $<0.02\%$ P and S and $<0.05\%$ α-amino acid N. While it was readily soluble in water it was only sparingly soluble in organic solvents. The amino acids present in decreasing concentration were glutamic acid, aspartic acid, glycine, alanine, serine, lysine, leucine, arginine, threonine, valine, phenylalanine, γ-aminobutyric acid and traces of methionine.

Meltzer (1958) has applied a technique involving distribution between three immiscible phases in a further study of strandin. At least 15 components were demonstrated in one preparation of strandin! The further application of this powerful technique is awaited with interest.

Beef Spleen Ganglioside

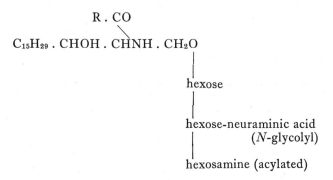

Fig. 9.7

The elementary composition of beef spleen ganglioside has been given (Klenk, 1959) as C, 59.3; H, 9.2; N, 2.07%. As shown in Fig. 9.7 the neuraminic acid is present ($>20\%$) as its N-glycolyl derivative. The fatty acids are mainly lignoceric acid and nervonic acid. The approximate molar ratio of fatty acid, neuraminic acid and hexose (including hexos-amine) was 1:1:3.

Ganglioside and Glycolipid from Horse Erythrocytes

Various workers (Yamakawa and Suzuki, 1952; Yamakawa, 1956; Klenk, 1959) have shown that in horse erythrocytes there exists both a ganglioside-like lipid and almost the same amount of neuraminic acid-free glycolipid. The ganglioside contains N-glycolylneuraminic acid (Klenk and Uhlenbruck, 1957, 1958), and its other constituents include nervonic acid, galactose and glucose (Klenk and Wolter, 1952). The glycolipid has a much higher sugar content than cerebrosides corresponding to a disac-charide (possibly lactose) content. Slightly more galactose than glucose was present. A lignoceryl-sphingosine-dihexoside structure in which hexosamine was absent was postulated (Klenk and Wolter, 1952). Elemen-tary analyses quoted for the ganglioside were C, 60·37; H, 9·11; N, 2·10% and for the other glycolipid C, 66·53; H, 10·34; N, 1·33%.

Normal Human Ganglioside and Mucolipid

Cumings, Goodwin, Woodward and Curzon (1957–8) have carried out detailed analyses of normal brains covering a range from those obtained at

Table 9.II

10 weeks foetus	38 week foetus	Full term	2 months
109	223	217–319	328
4 months	10 months	2 years	3 years
347	355	377	396
5 years	6 years	7 years	12 years
413	351	552	223

autopsy from the foetus, prematurely born infants, from infants dying at or just before birth and from children of up to 12 years of age. In each case cerebral cortex and cerebral white matter were carefully separated. Values for neuraminic acid found in the cerebral cortex, reflecting mainly ganglioside contents, are shown in Table 9.II as mg/100 g dry tissue.

Normal human brain mucolipid has been isolated by Rosenberg and Chargaff (1959).

The fresh tissue was extracted in the cold with chloroform–methanol followed by dialysis of the filtered extract against water (partition dialysis). The resulting aqueous upper phase was concentrated, redialysed and freeze-dried. After further purification by dissociation with calcium chloride and successive re-partition between chloroform and water with the aid of methanol, the mucolipid was submitted to counter current distribution between the two phases formed on mixing carbon tetrachloride, methanol and water (1·5:1·5:0·5).

Normal human mucolipid contained 21% sialic acid, 33% hexose (glucose:galactose, 1:8), 4·4% N-acetylgalactosamine and numerous amino acids. When treated with $V.$ $cholerae$ neuraminidase 51% of the sialic acid present in the mucolipid was rendered dialysable. The muco-lipid was active in haemagglutination inhibition.

Svennerholm (1956) using an improved method for the purification of gangliosides (Svennerholm, 1954) from human brains has shown the existence of more than one type of ganglioside.

The methanol–chloroform (2:1 vol/vol) extract of acetone-dried human grey matter was concentrated in $vacuo$. The extracted lipids were chromatographed on a cellulose column which was successively eluted with chloroform:ethanol: water (16:4:1), chloroform–methanol–water (5:15:1) and finally methanol:water (9:1). Two ganglioside fractions were obtained, one having a sialic acid:hexos-amine ratio of 3:1 and the other of 12:1.

Purification of the first fraction was effected by dialysis and obtained as crystalline birefringent rods from ethanol:water. Analysis showed that it was the potassium salt of ganglioside having N, 2·97%; hexose (as galac-tose) 24·6%, chondrosamine, 11·6%; sialic acid, 24·1%. No phosphorus was present. These data conformed to a formula of fatty acid-sphingosine-hexose-hexose-chondrosamine-sialic acid.

Further evidence for the structure of two brain gangliosides has been presented by Klenk and Gielen (1960). Both of these were examined by partial acid hydrolysis and identification of the split off products. Further-more, after methylation (86% of theoretical), the methylated gangliosides were hydrolysed and the methyl sugars identified. This enabled Klenk and Gielen (1960) to postulate the structures (Fig. 9.8) on pp. 198-9 which are still subject to verification.

Tay–Sach's Disease

Klenk (1939) showed that the brain mucolipid which accumulated in the ganglion cells of human subjects having Tay–Sach's disease was ganglioside. In a series of cases studied about ten to twenty times the amount of gangliosides found in normal brains was encountered (Klenk, 1940; Klenk, 1939; Klenk, 1942). Such an accumulation of gangliosides can also be detected by histochemical methods (Diezel, 1954). Quantita-tive determination is generally based on the colour reactions exhibited by the neuraminic acid constituent and can be applied to 5–50 mg of dry tissue (Klenk and Langerbeins, 1941). Only the grey matter appears to contain the stored gangliosides. It is important to note that pieces of brain obtained from a case of infantile amaurotic idiocy which had been kept in formaldehyde for a long time were unsatisfactory for assay. Klenk, Vater and Bartsch (1956–7) found that the ganglioside content decreased and glycolipides with a rather high content of amino sugars, but free of neuraminic acid, were formed.

The limitations of Klenk and Langerbein's (1941) method for the estimation of ganglioside can be largely overcome by the use of the Svennerholm (1957) method which reduces the loss of ganglioside to a minimum.

Ganglioside I $(C_{67}H_{121}N_3O_{26})$

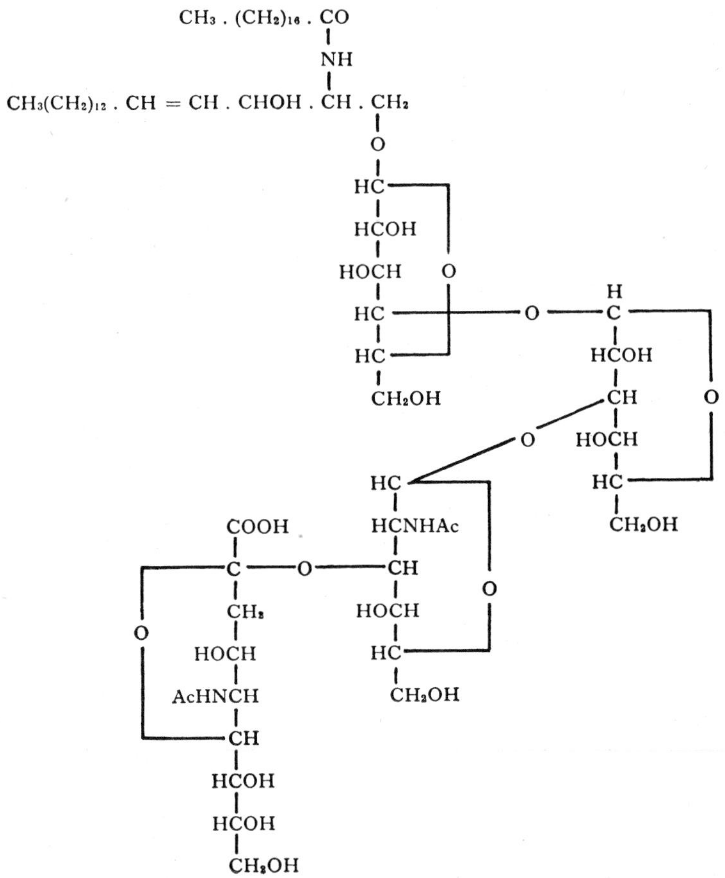

```
        CH3 . (CH2)16 . CO
                   |
                   NH
                   |
CH3(CH2)12 . CH = CH . CHOH . CH . CH2
                                    |
                                    O
                                    |
                         HC ──────┐
                          |        │
                         HCOH      │
                          |        │
                         HOCH    O │                  H
                          |        │                  |
                         HC ──────┴─── O ──── C ─────┐
                          |                   |      │
                         HC ──────┐          HCOH    │
                          |       │           |      │
                         CH2OH    │          CH      O
                                  │         ╱ |      │
                               O ╱   HOCH   │
                         HC ◢─────┘     |    │
                          |            HC ──┘
          COOH           HCNHAc        |
            |             |           CH2OH
        ──C ──── O ──── CH
        │ |             |
        │ CH2           HOCH
        │ |             |      O
     O  │ HOCH          HC────┘
        │ |             |
        │ AcHNCH        CH2OH
        └──CH
            |
          HCOH
            |
          HCOH
            |
          CH2OH
```

Ganglioside II ($C_{65}H_{118}N_2O_{26}$)

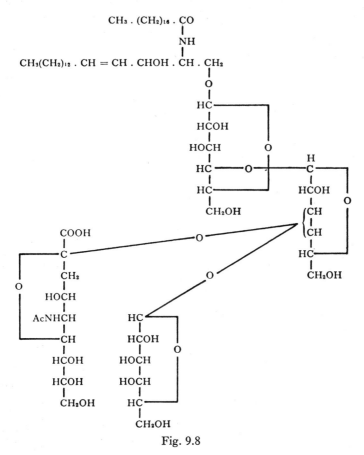

Fig. 9.8

Extraction of ganglioside. Rosenberg and Chargaff (1959) extracted the finely divided whole brain of a case of Tay-Sach's disease with several changes of cold acetone and thereafter dried and pulverized the residual tissue. Repeated extracts of this residue with boiling anhydrous methanol (wt/vol 1:3) were cooled and the resulting 'protagon' precipitate reprecipitated from chloroform-methanol (2:1 vol/vol) and twice again from methanol.

The ganglioside so obtained was electrophoretically homogeneous and was homogeneous in the ultracentrifuge. It contained 24% sialic acid, 32% hexose (glucose:galactose 1:7), 8% N-acetylgalactosamine and only traces of amino acids. It was very resistant to V. *cholerae* neuraminidase; less than 10% of the sialic acid being split off. Following up an observation of Feyrter (1939) that the nerve cells in Tay–Sach's disease were strongly metachromatic, Rosenberg and Chargaff (1959) investigated the *in vitro* reaction of ganglioside. Whereas both the Tay–Sach's ganglioside and beef brain ganglioside were strongly metachromatic, only a slight metachromatic effect was exhibited by normal brain mucolipid.

In an elegant investigation of a series of representative cases of cerebral lipidoses Tingey (1958–9) found a considerable increase in neuraminic acid both in the cortex and in the white matter with cases of Tay–Sach's disease. Large amounts of hexosamine were also found in all fractions. No increase in neuramine acid was found in cases of the Batten type of amaurotic family idiocy either in the classical juvenile or in the precocious (late infantile) form. No increase in neuraminic acid or hexosamine could be demonstrated in cases of gargoylism in conflict with the views of Brante (1957) and Klenk (1955).

Human Blood Lipocarbohydrates

Klenk and Lauenstein (1951) have prepared a lipocarbohydrate from human blood cells which resembles spleen ganglioside in composition. It contained fatty acids (mainly lignoceric acid) 29%, sphingosine 20%, and 40-41% carbohydrate consisting of glucose, galactose and chondrosamine.

Beef Brain Phosphoinositide

Isolation

The cephalin fraction of beef brain is a mixture of the different phosphatides phosphatidyl serine, phosphatidyl ethanolamine and a phosphoinositide (Folch, 1949).

The cephalin was dissolved in chloroform (1 g in 8 c.c.) and ethanol (11·8 c.c.) added. After centrifugation the supernatant solution, which contains most of the phosphatidyl serine and phosphatidyl ethanolamine, was discarded (Folch, 1949). On treatment of the viscous bottom layer with more ethanol the phosphoinositide can be recovered (5 g/kg of initial tissue). Further fractionation with chloroform–methanol was required to purify the phosphoinositide.

Structure

Folch (1949) showed that phosphoinositide contained as constituents fatty acids, glycerol and an inositol phosphate in equimolar proportions. An inositol metadiphosphate was isolated from among the products of short time acid hydrolysis of phosphoinositide. A reinvestigation of the structure of beef brain phosphoinositide was made by Grado and Ballou (1960) because of the susceptibility of *myo*inositol phosphate esters to acid catalysed migration. Their preparation contained P, 6·5%; *myo*inositol, 12% and had a phosphorus to *myo*inositol molar ratio of 3:1. Base hydrolysis of the phosphoinositide gave a mixture containing one major *myo*inositol monophosphate $[\alpha]_D - 1\cdot3°$, two *myo*inositol diphosphates $[\alpha]_D - 15\cdot2°$ and $+3\cdot4°$ and two *myo*inositol triphosphates $[\alpha]_D - 15\cdot5°$ and $-27\cdot4°$ in the following molar percentages (5:10:8:10:31). Periodate oxidation of the triphosphate mixture, reduction of the resulting dialdehyde and dephosphorylation gave L-iditol. Hence the *myo*inositol triphosphate mixture must have the structure shown in Fig. 9·9b. The structure of the *myo*inositol monophosphate was also established (Fig. 9·9a).

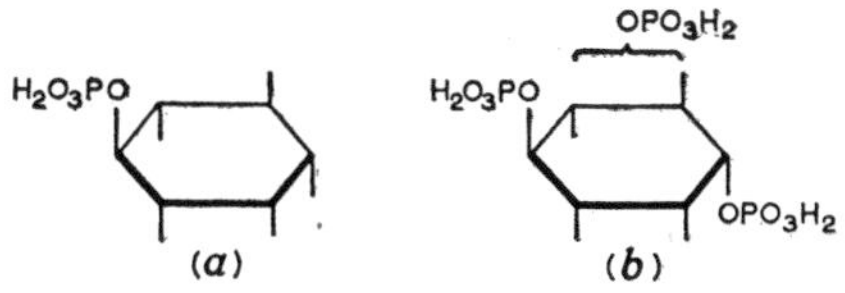

Fig. 9.9 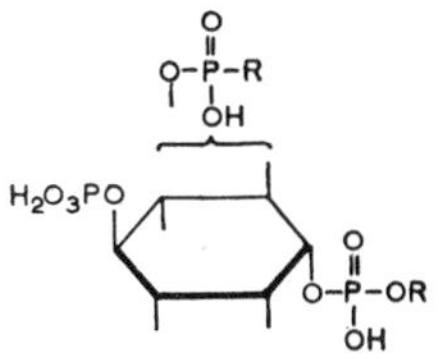   Fig. 9.10

Grado and Ballou (1960) suggested that all the *myo*inositol phosphates obtained on base hydrolysis could come from one triphosphoinositide of the formula shown in Fig. 9.10.

Horse Liver Phosphoinositide

Various methods have been described for the isolation of a monophosphoinositide from dog and horse liver (McKibbin, 1956). The fractions from horse liver contained inositol, phosphorus, glycerol and fatty acid in a simple molecular ratio of 1:1:1:2 respectively. It resembled a similar inositol glycerol phosphatidic acid isolated by Faure and Morelec-Coulon (1954) from beef heart except that the iodine numbers of the fatty acid constituents were 110 from beef heart and 44–56 from horse liver.

REFERENCES

Austin, J. H. *Proc. Soc. Exp. Biol. Med.* **100**, 361 (1959).
Blix, A. *Z. physiol. Chem.* **219**, 82 (1933).
Blix, G. *Skand. Arch. Physiol.* **80**, 46 (1938).
Bogoch, S. *Virology* **4**, 458 (1957).
Bogoch, S. *Biochem. J.* **68**, 319 (1958).
Bogoch, S. *Nature* **185**, 392 (1960).
Bogoch, S. and Bogoch, E. S. *Nature* **183**, 53 (1959).
Brante, G. *Acta physiol. scand.* **18**, supp. 63 (1949).
Brante, G. *Cerebral Lipidoses* Ed. Cumings. Oxford Univ. Press (1957).
Brown, H. T. and Morris, G. H. *J. Chem. Soc.* **57**, 57 (1890).

Carter, H. E. and Fujino, Y. *J. Biol. Chem.* **221,** 879 (1956).

Carter, H. E. and Greenwood, F. L. *J. Biol. Chem.* **199,** 283 (1952).

Carter, H. E. and Humiston, C. G. *J. Biol. Chem.* **191,** 727 (1951).

Carter, H. E., Shapiro, D. and Harrison, J. B. *J. Amer. Chem. Soc.* **75,** 1007 (1953).

Chatagnon, C. and Chatagnon, P. *Bull. soc. chim. biol.* **36,** 373 (1954).

Chatagnon, C. and Chatagnon, P. *Bull. soc. chim. biol.* **37,** 1305 (1955).

Coons, A. H. and Kaplan, M. H. *J. Exp. Med.* **91,** 1 (1950).

Cumings, J. N. *Biochemical Aspects of Neurological Disorders,* Blackwell Scientific Publications, Oxford (1959).

Cumings, J. N., Goodwin, H., Woodward, E. M. and Curzon, G. *J. Neurochem.* **2,** 289 (1957–8).

Danielson, I. S., Hall, C. H. and Everett, M. R. *Proc. Soc. Exp. Biol. Med.* **49,** 569 (1942).

Deuel, H. J. *The Lipids* Vol. 1, Interscience, N.Y. (1951).

Diezel, P. B. *Deut. Z. Nervenheilk.* **171,** 344 (1954).

Faure, M. and Morelec-Coulon, M. J. *Comp. rend.* **238,** 411 (1954).

Feyrler, F. *Virch. Arch. Path. Anat.* **304,** 480 (1939).

Fodor, G. and Kiss, J. *Nature* **171,** 651 (1952).

Folch, J. *J. Biol. Chem.* **177,** 497, 505 (1949).

Folch, J., Arsove, S. and Meath, J. A. *J. Biol. Chem.* **191,** 819 (1951).

Folch, J., Ascoli, I., Lees, M., Meath, J. A. and Le Baron, F. N. *J. Biol. Chem.* **191,** 833 (1951).

Folch-pi, J. and Lees, M. *Amer. J. Dis. Child* **97,** 730 (1959).

Folch, J., Meath, J. A. and Bogoch, S. *Fed. Proc.* **15,** 254 (1956).

Fujino, Y. and Negishi, T. *Bull. Agr. Chem. Soc. Japan* **20,** 183 (1956).

Grado, C. and Ballou, C. E. *J. Biol. Chem.* **235,** PC 23 (1960).

Grob, C. A. and Jenny, E. F. *Helv. chim. Acta* **35,** 2106 (1952).

Hagberg, B. and Svennerholm, L. *Acta Paediat.* **49,** 690 (1960).

Hagberg, B. and Sourander, P., Svennerholm, L. and Voss, H. *Acta Paediat.* (Upps) **48,** 200 (1959).

Jatzkewitz, H. *Z. physiol. chem.* **311,** 279 (1958).

Johnson, A. C., McNabb, A. R. and Rossiter, R. J. *Biochem. J.* **43,** 573 (1948).

Kiss, J., Fodor, G. and Banfi, O. *Helv. chim. Acta* **37,** 1471 (1954).

Klenk, E. *Z. physiol. Chem.* **145,** 244 (1925).

Klenk, E. *Z. physiol. Chem.* **153,** 74 (1926a).

Klenk, E. *Z. physiol. Chem.* **157,** 283 (1926b); **166,** 268 (1927).

Klenk, E. *Z. physiol. Chem.* **174,** 214 (1928).

Klenk, E. *Z. physiol. Chem.* **235,** 24 (1935).

Klenk, E. *Z. physiol. Chem.* **262,** 128 (1939–40).

Klenk, E. *Ber.* **75,** 1632 (1942); *Z. physiol. chem.* **273,** 76 (1942).

Klenk, E. *Biochem. Developing Nervous System* Edit. Waelsch. H., New York (1955).

Klenk, E. *Amer. J. Dis. Child.* **97,** 711 (1959).

Klenk, E. and Gielen, W. *Z. physiol. Chem.* **319,** 283 (1960).

Klenk, E. and Härle, R. *Z. physiol. chem.* **178,** 221 (1928).

Klenk, E. and Langerbeins, H. *Z. physiol. chem.* **270,** 185 (1941).

Klenk, E. and Lauenstein, K. *Z. physiol. chem.* **288,** 220 (1951); 291, 249 (1952).

Klenk, E. and Lauenstein, K. *Z. physiol. chem.* **295,** 164 (1953).

Klenk, E. and Leupold, F. *Z. physiol. chem.* **281,** 208 (1944).

Klenk, E. and Rennkamp, F. *Z. physiol. chem.* **267,** 128 (1940); **272,** 280 (1942); **273,** 253 (1942).

Klenk, E. and Uhlenbruck, G. *Z. physiol. chem.* **307,** 266 (1957); **311,** 227 (1958).

Klenk, E., Vater, W. and Bartsch, G. *J. Neurochemistry* **1,** 203 (1957).

Klenk, E. and Wolter, H. *Z. physiol. chem.* **291**, 259 (1952).
Landsteiner, K. and Levene, P. A. *J. Immunol.* **10**, 731 (1925).
Landsteiner, K. and Levene, P. A. *Proc. Soc. Exp. Biol. Med.* **23**, 343 (1926).
Lieb, H. and Günther, V. *Z. physiol. chem.* **271**, 211 (1941).
Marinetti, G. V., Ford, T. and Stotz, E. *J. Lipid Research* **1**, 203 (1960).
McKibbin, J. M. *J. Biol. Chem.* **220**, 537 (1956).
Meltzer, H. L. *J. Biol. Chem.* **233**, 1327 (1958).
Mislow, K. *J. Amer. Chem. Soc.* **74**, 5155 (1953).
Nakayama, T. *J. Biochem.* (*Japan*) **37**, 309 (1950).
Norman, R. M., Urich, H. and Tingey, H. *Brain* **83**, 369 (1960).
Okuhara, E. and Yashuda, M. *J. Neurochem.* **6**, 112 (1960).
Pryde, J. and Humphreys, R. W. *Biochem. J.* **18**, 661 (1924); **20**, 825 (1926).
Radin, N. S., Brown, J. R. and Lavin, F. B. *J. Biol. Chem.* **219**, 977 (1956).
Radin, N. S., Lavin, F. B. and Brown, J. R. *J. Biol. Chem.* **217**, 789 (1955).
Radin, N. S., Martin, F. B. and Brown, J. R. *J. Biol. Chem.* **224**, 499 (1957).
Rapport, M. M., Graf, L. and Alonzo, N. F. *Fed. Proc.* **18**, 307 (1959).
Rapport, M. M., Graf, L. and Alonzo, N. F. *J. Lipid Research* **1**, 301 (1960).
Rapport, M. M., Graf, L., Skipski, V. P. and Alonzo, N. F. *Cancer* **12**, 438 (1959).
Rosenberg, A., Binnie, B. and Chargaff, E. *J. Amer. Chem. Soc.* **82**, 4113 (1960).
Rosenberg, A. and Chargaff, E. *Biochim. Biophys. Acta* **21**, 588 (1956).
Rosenberg, A. and Chargaff, E. *J. Biol. Chem.* **232**, 1031; **233**, 1323 (1958).
Rosenberg, A. and Chargaff, E. *Amer. J. Dis. Child.* **97**, 739 (1959).
Rosenberg, A., Howe, C. and Chargaff, E. *Nature* **177**, 234 (1956).
Rosenheim, O. *Biochem. J.* **7**, 604 (1913); **8**, 110 (1914).
Seydel, P. V. *Zur Kenntnis des Sphingosine,* Zürich (1941).
Sperry, M. *J. Biol. Chem.* **209**, 377 (1954).
Svennerholm, L. *Acta Chem. Scand.* **8**, 1108 (1954).
Svennerholm, L. *Nature* **177**, 524 (1956).
Svennerholm, L. *Upsala Läkfören Förh.* **62**, 1 (1957).
Thannhauser, S. J., Fellig, J. and Schmidt, G. *J. Biol. Chem.* **215**, 211 (1955).
Tingey, A. *J. Neurochemistry* **3**, 230 (1958–59).
Walz, E. *Z. physiol. chem.* **166**, 210 (1927).
Welsh, L. H. *J. Amer. Chem. Soc.* **71**, 3500 (1949).
Whittaker, V. P. *Biochem. J.* **72**, 694 (1959).
Wolfe, L. S. *Biochem. J.* **77**, 9P (1960).
Yamakawa, T. *J. Biochem. Tokyo* **43**, 867 (1956).
Yamakawa, T. and Suzuki, S. *J. Biochem. Tokyo* **39**, 175 (1952).

SUBJECT INDEX